I0010714

Working Smarter with Microsoft Outlook

Supercharge your office and personal productivity with expert Outlook tips and techniques

Staci Warne

BIRMINGHAM—MUMBAI

Working Smarter with Microsoft Outlook

Copyright © 2022 Packt Publishing

All rights reserved. No part of this book may be reproduced, stored in a retrieval system, or transmitted in any form or by any means, without the prior written permission of the publisher, except in the case of brief quotations embedded in critical articles or reviews.

Every effort has been made in the preparation of this book to ensure the accuracy of the information presented. However, the information contained in this book is sold without warranty, either express or implied. Neither the author, nor Packt Publishing or its dealers and distributors, will be held liable for any damages caused or alleged to have been caused directly or indirectly by this book.

Packt Publishing has endeavored to provide trademark information about all of the companies and products mentioned in this book by the appropriate use of capitals. However, Packt Publishing cannot guarantee the accuracy of this information.

Group Product Manager: Alok Dhuri
Publishing Product Manager: Alok Dhuri
Senior Editor: Ruvika Rao
Content Development Editor: Urvi Shah
Technical Editor: Maran Fernandes
Copy Editor: Safis Editing
Language Support Editor: Safis Editing
Project Coordinator: Deeksha Thakkar
Proofreader: Safis Editing
Indexer: Tejal Daruwale Soni
Production Designer: Prashant Ghare
Marketing Coordinator: Deepak Kumar and Rayyan Khan
Business Development Executive: Puneet Kaur

First published: July 2022
Production reference: 1150722

Published by Packt Publishing Ltd.
Livery Place
35 Livery Street
Birmingham
B3 2PB, UK.

978-1-80056-070-3
www.packt.com

To my children, Alicia and Matt, for being my greatest teachers. The two of you have taught me more about life, relationships, and unconditional love than I could ever teach you. May you always follow your dreams, and when life gives you a rainy day, I hope you will choose to jump in the puddles and then take the time to watch for the rainbows that will magically appear after the rain.

– Staci Warne

Contributors

About the author

Staci Warne is a **Microsoft Certified Trainer** (**MCT**) with over 25 years of experience in training technology skills to individuals at all skill levels. She obtained her MCT certification in 2008, became a Microsoft Partner in 2015, and obtained her Project Management Professional certification in 2022. Staci holds an array of other certifications, including **Microsoft Certified Professional** (**MCP**), Microsoft Office Master Instructor, Ic3 Internet and Core instructor, Google GAIC, and Google Ads. She has been a financial analyst and lead technology trainer for the Federal Reserve Bank, and the lead trainer at CompUSA. While providing quality training to thousands of professionals in all industries, her biggest joy in the classroom comes from seeing students have those "Aha!" moments learning about a new tool.

I want to thank the people who have been close to me and supported me, especially my husband Jeff, and children, Alicia and Matt. The writing of this book has taken precious time away from me being with you, and I am looking forward to scheduling more time with you now that it has been completed.

I would also like to thank the incredible team at Packt and the talented reviewers that have helped bring this project to completion. You have all displayed true professionalism, along with a collaborative working effort throughout the various stages of this process. I would especially like to acknowledge Alok Dhuri (group and publishing manager); your working ethic is impeccable and your organizational skills have saved me several times. I appreciate the patience and leadership that you provided to me; you are a true ninja! Thank you, Ruvika Rao (senior editor), for showing me how this process works; you held my hand from the beginning and stepped in to explain and take over the process as needed. I appreciate you helping me whenever needed, without me asking or even knowing what I needed. Thank you, Urvi Shah (content development editor), for the countless edits you suggested to me. I have no words to describe what your humor and friendship have meant to me. You have made me a better writer and given me so many suggestions to improve and clarify the writings in this book. I don't know how you kept all the topics you are working on together and didn't skip a beat when editing and working with me. Thank you, Deeksha Thakkar (project coordinator), for making sure everything was running smoothly across all time zones and encouraging me to set realistic deadlines; you graciously rescheduled them as I failed to meet them. You were always right there to push for a new deadline with no judgment, and I am truly grateful. I would like to give a final thank you to the reviewers, Leza Bissell Wood and Mark Hopwood, for their time, patience, and support; to the rest of the Packt staff, Tejal Daruwale Soni (indexer) and Prashant Ghare (production designer); and to Safis Editing (copy and language support editor), among others, that have worked hard throughout this process to make this book a reality.

About the reviewers

Leza Bissell Wood is a **Microsoft Certified Trainer (MCT)**, **Modern Classroom Certified Trainer (MCCT)**, **Microsoft Office Specialist (MOS) Expert**, and adult learning specialist. She is an accomplished professional capable of understanding business needs and addressing those needs using training solutions that include proven adult learning techniques.

Leza's area of software expertise is in the Microsoft Office Suite of products: Excel, Access, Word, PowerPoint, Outlook, OneNote, Publisher, Power BI, and more.

Leza has a Bachelor of Science degree in business, management, and economics with a concentration in training and development from SUNY Empire State College.

Mark Hopwood has worked in the software industry for over 30 years in many different roles, including engineering, testing, support, and project management. Over 15 years of that was working for Microsoft in the Outlook team, and the remainder has been in multiple other divisions at Microsoft, including Windows, SharePoint, and other Microsoft Office products. In each role, Mark's top priority is to always bring a customer focus and passion to delight the user.

Table of Contents

3

Managing Email Accounts

4

Organizing Your Outlook Environment

5
Outlook Mail Merge

Part 3: Beyond Email – Calendars, Contacts, Notes, and More

6
Managing the Calendar

7

Contacts in Outlook

8

Outlook Notes

9

Tasks and To-Dos

Part 4: How to: Share, Search, and Archive in Outlook

10

Save Time Searching

11

Sharing Mail, Calendars, and Contacts

12

Archiving and Backup

Part 5: Outlook Collaboration and Integratio

13
Collaboration and Integration within Outlook

Part 6: Powerful Ways to Automate Outlook

14
Nine Useful Rules

15

Programming with Macros

16

Managing Your Day System

Assessments

Preface

Millions of users across the globe spend their working hours using Microsoft Outlook to manage tasks, schedules, emails, and more. Post-pandemic, many organizations have started adopting remote working, and the need to stay productive in workspace collaboration has been increasing. *Working Smarter with Microsoft Outlook* takes you through smart techniques, tips, and productivity hacks that will help you become an expert Outlook user. This book brings together everything you need to know about automating your daily repetitive tasks. You'll gain the skills necessary for working with calendars, contacts, notes, and tasks, and using them to collaborate with Microsoft SharePoint, OneNote, and many other services. You'll learn how to use powerful tools such as Quick Steps, customized rules, and Mail Merge with Power Automate for added functionality. Later, the book covers how to use Outlook to share information between Microsoft Exchange and cloud services. In the concluding chapters, you'll get an introduction to Outlook programming by creating macros and seeing how you can integrate them within Outlook. By the end of this book, you'll be able to use Microsoft Outlook and its features and capabilities efficiently to enhance your workspace collaboration and time management.

Who this book is for?

This book is for Microsoft Outlook users and business professionals who work with it daily and are interested in learning tips and tricks to explore its full potential.

What does this book cover?

Chapter 1, Getting Started with Outlook, will get you up to speed with the many options that are available to you inside of Outlook. First, we will learn how to manage Outlook's many options and customize the working day for your schedule. You will learn how to use drag and drop to have an email converted into an instant calendar event, task, or contact. We will also discuss other topics that allow you to customize your screen with the Quick Access Toolbar and set multiple time zones.

Chapter 2, Sending and Receiving Emails, shows you how to take control of your emails by creating rules and Quick Steps, effectively using categories, creating multiple signatures, displaying up to three time zones, and mastering setting up multiple email accounts.

Chapter 3, Managing Email Accounts, covers email accounts. Using one email address only works if you only get a few emails a day, but if you get several emails a day, you will find it useful to have multiple accounts. Learn how to start creating a second email by knowing what to look for in an Email provider, how to set up a new domain for a website email, and how to set up and configure an account in outlook. You'll be surprised how easy it really is!

Chapter 4, Organizing Your Outlook Environment, is all about automation. Take back control of your email by implementing the tools that are provided to you within Outlook, including taking instant action on your email with Quick Steps, setting up rules so that you don't even have to react to an email, and creating categories to color-code your emails, calendar items, contacts, and tasks. If you are feeling email overload, this chapter is for you! The more you can automate in your Outlook environment, the easier your life will be when handling loads of emails every day.

Chapter 5, Outlook Mail Merge, looks at timesaving tips and tricks in Outlook. If you send out bulk emails to several people at once, you will need to use the Mail Merge feature inside of Outlook – no more entering names into the **BCC** field so that your recipients don't know who else the message went to. After learning how to create a Mail Merge, we will use Power Automate to perform a Mail Merge with a custom attachment, which will be stored in an Excel document.

Chapter 6, Managing the Calendars, teaches you several fun simple ways to get more out of your Outlook calendars. Manage and control multiple calendars or display colorful events with a click of a button. Get specific with time by letting the Outlook calendar chart your day as you prioritize your appointments and print the events you need. If you have been using Outlook for several years, you will probably say, "I didn't know about these tools."

Chapter 7, Contacts in Outlook, will help you get the most out of your Outlook contacts. Learn where your contacts are stored and how they can be accessed. You will learn the different ways to add contacts to Outlook as well as how to create contact groups. As your contact list starts to grow, you will learn how to create groups and use categories, which will help you to organize your contacts for your viewing pleasure.

Chapter 8, Outlook Notes, explores notes, which are the electronic equivalent of paper sticky notes. Use the notes as you would a sticky note but without the paper. You can leave the note open on the screen or save it to your desktop as a quick note for later use. You will learn how to customize notes to find and organize them when needed. Besides the **Notes** object, learn how to add a quick note to any email message, which will appear as a note section at the top of your email.

Chapter 9, Tasks and To-Dos, covers how to stay organized by building a to-do list when creating tasks in Outlook. Learn how the tasks are stored in Outlook and the default folders that are created. You will learn several tips on how to turn it into a powerful task manager. You will learn how to enhance your productivity by using an Outlook task list as your to-do list.

Chapter 10, Save Time Searching, teaches you how to navigate the search capabilities in Outlook You will learn the difference between instant search and advanced search and when to use them based on your needs. We will then discover Indexing and how that relates to Outlook as well as give you some great Search syntax for Outlook to save you time with your advanced searches.

Chapter 11, Sharing Mail, Calendars, and Contacts, delves into object-sharing. There are a couple of different ways to share your objects in Outlook, such as the calendar and email. Sharing involves giving permission to another user to access a folder in your Office 365 account. In this chapter, you will learn the steps necessary to give or receive that permission, and then you will be able to share other objects as well, such as calendars and tasks.

Chapter 12, Archiving and Backup, teaches you the difference between archiving and backup and which steps you need to take to ensure that your data is backed up. We will also talk about the locations in which you will consider backing your data up. We will discuss the `Drafts` folder and maintaining items in your inbox and other folders for backup. You will learn what a `.pst` file is and how to restore these folders.

Chapter 13, Collaboration & Integration within Outlook, provides a brief introduction introduction to cloud computing and using it to collaborate in integrate with other applications while within Outlook. We will also discuss other options for collaborating by using your Smartphones and tablets. We will discuss integrating other Add-ins and RSS feeds.

Chapter 14, Nine Useful Rules, covers useful rules that can be applied to your email. Steps will be given for setting up the rule and how to manage them as well.

Chapter 15, Programming with Macros, explores how to set up and run nine useful Rules within Outlook. Rules are all about saving you time and these nine rules will do just that. Learn how to delay sending emails and set up Automatic replies for specific texts and redirecting emails to another person automatically and simply purging emails with a certain word in the subject line. Implementing just a couple of these rules could possibly save you time.

Chapter 16, *Managing Your Day System*, introduces you to a complete time management system that you can implement to organize and control your inbox. You will learn how to create useful folders and how to navigate easily to them. You will learn how to declutter and clean out your inbox and not be controlled by what is in it.

To get the most out of this book

Software/hardware covered in the book	Operating system requirements
Microsoft 365 account	Windows, macOS, or Linux
Microsoft Outlook account	

Download the color images

We also provide a PDF file that has color images of the screenshots and diagrams used in this book. You can download it here:

`https://packt.link/dZQUM`

Conventions used

There are a number of text conventions used throughout this book.

`Code in text`: Indicates code words in text, database table names, folder names, filenames, file extensions, pathnames, dummy URLs, user input, and Twitter handles. Here is an example: "Once this password is assigned to use the saved `.pst` file, you will need to know the password that was assigned and enter it to use the `.pst` file."

Bold: Indicates a new term, an important word, or words that you see onscreen. For instance, words in menus or dialog boxes appear in **bold**. Here is an example:

"To customize your own view of the **Calendar** (be sure you have selected the **Calendar** button), click on **View** | **Change View** | **Manage Views…**. You can use the **Manage All Views** dialog box to copy the current view setting of a view and use it to apply that view on an existing view from the list, or copy it to create a **New…** view."

> **Tips or Important Notes**
> Appear like this.

Get in touch

Feedback from our readers is always welcome.

General feedback: If you have questions about any aspect of this book, email us at customercare@packtpub.com and mention the book title in the subject of your message.

Errata: Although we have taken every care to ensure the accuracy of our content, mistakes do happen. If you have found a mistake in this book, we would be grateful if you would report this to us. Please visit www.packtpub.com/support/errata and fill in the form.

Piracy: If you come across any illegal copies of our works in any form on the internet, we would be grateful if you would provide us with the location address or website name. Please contact us at copyright@packt.com with a link to the material.

If you are interested in becoming an author: If there is a topic that you have expertise in and you are interested in either writing or contributing to a book, please visit authors.packtpub.com.

Share Your Thoughts

Once you've read *Working Smarter with Microsoft Outlook*, we'd love to hear your thoughts! Scan the QR code below to go straight to the Amazon review page for this book and share your feedback.

https://packt.link/r/1-800-56070-2

Your review is important to us and the tech community and will help us make sure we're delivering excellent quality content.

Part 1: Introduction to Outlook

You already know the basics of email. This section will cover what you don't know about Outlook email and after implementing these new skills, you will be on your way to working smarter and improving your time management. You can utilize the power of Outlook by following these tips and tricks to help you write better emails but also customize Outlook to work better for you.

This section contains the following chapter:

- *Chapter 1, Getting Started with Outlook*

1
Getting Started with Outlook

Outlook is the main productivity application for office workers today. It has become the main hub for office communication. Over the past few years, there has been an increase in popularity in the use of messengers, social media, and chat applications, yet emails continue to grow and have increased year on year. Email is predicted to grow for several years to come.

In this chapter, we're going to cover the following main topics:

- Managing Outlook
- Drag and drop techniques
- Customizing as per tailored needs

By customizing your Outlook environment, you will create a customized feel for your display that will streamline how you work with Outlook. You will find many tips and tricks in this chapter that can potentially save you a great amount of time, which will ultimately help you regain control of your inbox.

Manage Outlook

Do you feel at times that Outlook is managing you? If you answered *yes*, then it's time to take back control and start managing your Outlook environment. It is estimated that over 316.5 billion emails will have been sent and received in 2021. With this many emails passing through our inboxes, it is time to take control of your email. By using the techniques used in this book, you will be well on your way to having an organized, efficient time management system.

Let's start by looking at the **Options** menu in the **File** tab. These options allow you to control and customize Outlook for the way you want to work. Once you click on **File**, you are in the backstage view. Microsoft's definition of this view is that *"it is everything that you do to a file that you don't do in the file."*

Figure 1.1 – Outlook tabs

Info

First, let's look at the **Info** tab located on the left side of the screen and represented below the left-facing arrow in the following figure (clicking on the arrow will display the Outlook tabs). Use the drop-down arrow by the Microsoft Exchange box at the top of this screen to specify which account you want the information to appear for, and you can select the account you desire from this list if you have various accounts set up. In this example, my account is a Microsoft Exchange account, which is the name for this account in the following figure. You can have a different name here than Microsoft Exchange if you are not using Exchange. Accounts will be discussed in detail in *Chapter 3, Managing Email Accounts*.

To set up a new email account that you have already created from Gmail or another account, click on **+Add Account,** and you will be prompted to add a new email account to the Outlook environment. If you are working in your Microsoft 365 account, you can type in the email address of the email that you would like to track in Outlook, such as your Gmail account.

Because Microsoft Exchange synchronizes email with Outlook, everything will process automatically, and answer the prompts as requested. Once you complete this, you will see a dialog box, indicating that the account was set up successfully. If you have errors or have been given specific instructions for the setup, click on **Advanced Options**, and you will be able to customize the installation.

You can add up to 10 email accounts in Outlook with this method, and if you need more than 10 accounts, that will be discussed in *Chapter 3, Managing Email Accounts*.

Once you have completed the installation, your email account will be added to the navigation pane on the left side of the screen. An email will also be sent to this email account, testing the settings for your account.

Settings in Info

The other settings that you see on this **Info** tab will be discussed throughout this book, and the following table provides a reference for what these buttons are used for and also the chapters that will discuss them in more detail.

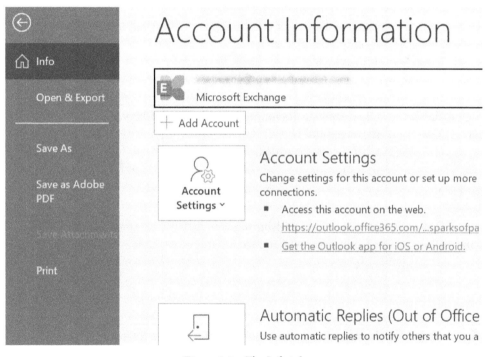

Figure 1.2 – The Info tab

Items	Description	Where is this covered in the book?
Account Settings	Change settings for this account or set up more connections.	*Chapter 3*
Automatic Replies	Notify others that you are out of the office, on vacation, or not available to respond to email messages.	*Chapter 2*
Tools	Manage the size of your mailbox by emptying deleted items and archiving.	*Chapter 12*
Manage Rules & Alerts	Organize your incoming email messages and receive updates when items are added, changed, or removed.	*Chapter 4*
Manage COM Add-ins	Manage COM add-ins that are affecting your experience.	*Chapter 13*
Manage Add-ins	Manage and acquire web add-ins for Outlook.	*Chapter 13*

Table 1.1 – Account information on the Info tab

At the bottom of the navigation pane, on the left side of your screen, are a few more menu items that you will find quite important to customizing your experience inside Outlook. Let's look at the **Office Account**.

Office Account

Use this **Office Account** tab to look at information related to your account. You will find this screen self-explanatory, but if you want to set a new office background or theme, this is the screen from which you can access it. On the right side of the screen in the **Product Information** section, you can identify which version of Outlook is on your computer and what you are in now.

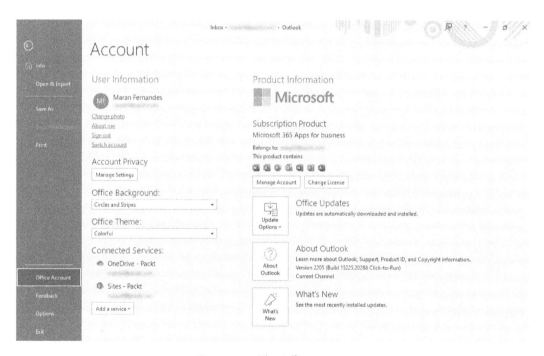

Figure 1.3 – The Office account

Feedback

Microsoft wants to hear from you to help make the application better. You now have an option to give feedback. Use this screen to report what you like and do not like about the application. There is even a button on here to suggest a feature that you would like added to Outlook. This menu is self-explanatory as well, so we will not be covering it in detail in this book.

Feedback

Send a
Smile

I Like Something
It's nice to know when we've made a positive change.

Send a
Frown

I Don't Like Something
If something's not right we'd like to know so we can fix it.

Suggest a
Feature

Suggest a Feature
Do you have an idea for a new feature or an improvement? We look forward to hearing from you.

Figure 1.4 – Feedback

Other options

Several options can be set to affect how Outlook settings will behave. All these settings have a default setting (preset settings from the installation of Outlook). For example, you can control a setting to show three different time zones on your calendar so that you know what time it is in another location when setting up a meeting. The default is to only have the time showing for where you are located in the world. Another example is to set up the *AutoComplete* feature, detailed in *Chapter 2, Sending and Receiving Emails*, so that when you type a couple of letters, the complete name of your corporation will be typed. These settings can save you a lot of time and, in turn, will make you so much more productive.

To view these options in Outlook, click **File | Options**.

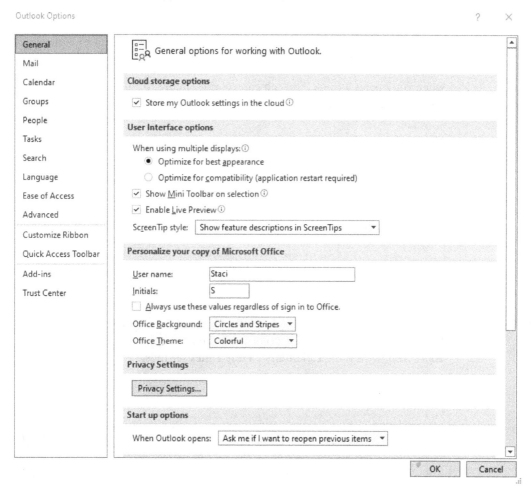

Figure 1.5 – The Options dialog box

There are hundreds of items that you can manipulate in this **Outlook Options** dialog box, and you have a navigation pane on the left to select a category. The following table lists a few of the recommended adjustments you can make:

Advanced	If you have multiple email accounts in Outlook, you can select which account's inbox or folder you would like to have displayed by default when you open Outlook. You can control this feature through **Advanced	Outlook start and exit**. 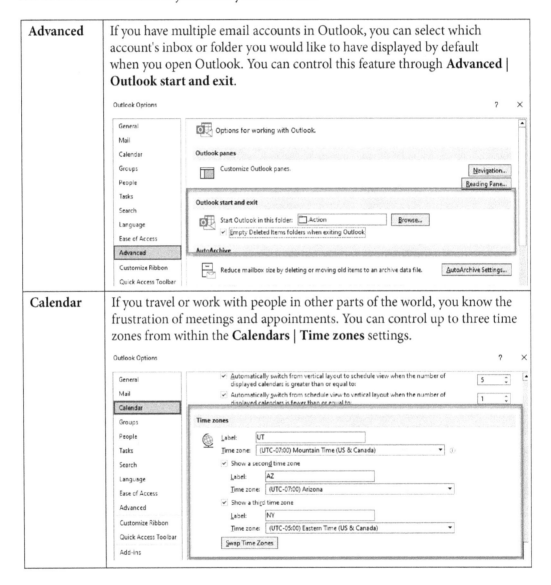
Calendar	If you travel or work with people in other parts of the world, you know the frustration of meetings and appointments. You can control up to three time zones from within the **Calendars	Time zones** settings.

Calendar	The last three sections in the **Calendar** category options dialog box are the **Scheduling assistant**, **Automatic Accept or Decline**, and **Weather** options. In the **Scheduling assistant** group, you are able to choose when and where the calendar details are shown. The **Automatic Accept or Decline** section lets you control automatically what happens when you get a meeting request. 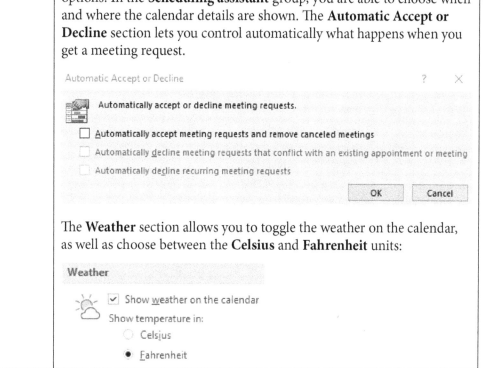 The **Weather** section allows you to toggle the weather on the calendar, as well as choose between the **Celsius** and **Fahrenheit** units:

Mail	You can use the **AutoCorrect** tool on the **Mail** tab to correct typos and misspelled words that you make often or set up a few characters to write out a group of text, such as your company name. Select **Mail	Editor Options	AutoCorrect Options…**:
	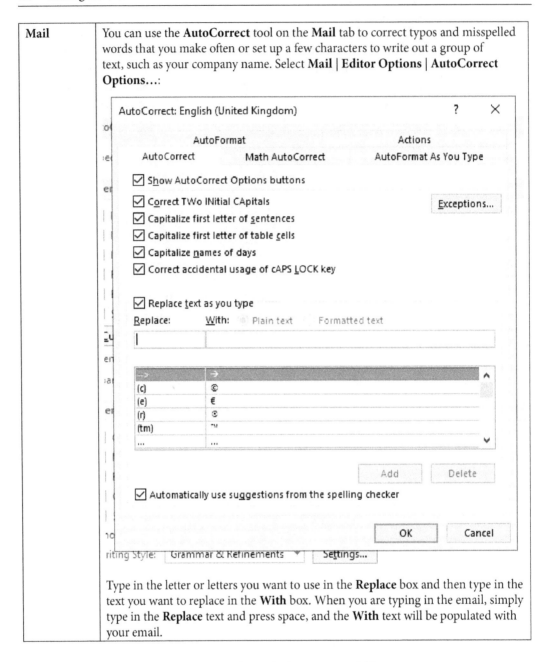
	Type in the letter or letters you want to use in the **Replace** box and then type in the text you want to replace in the **With** box. When you are typing in the email, simply type in the **Replace** text and press space, and the **With** text will be populated with your email.

Table 1.2 – The Outlook options available

This is a very small list, and you are encouraged to spend some time looking over all the possibilities you can adjust. These options are categorized by **Mail**, **Calendar**, **Groups**, **People**, **Tasks**, **Search**, **Language**, **Ease of Access**, and **Advanced**. We will continue to discuss several of these options throughout this book, but we will not cover them all. When you find yourself having troubles or wish you could change the feel or effects inside of Outlook, you will usually find a solution to your troubles in this **Options** dialog box.

Drag and drop techniques

In Outlook, there is a surprisingly simple technique you can use called **drag and drop**. This allows you to drag and drop one object to another object, and at times, doing this will create another item. This technique will help you be more productive, as you will not have to recreate the email content in the item you are creating by dragging the email.

To drag and drop, first move the mouse pointer to the item that you want to drag. Press and hold down the button on the mouse to "grab" the item. Drag the item to the desired location on your computer by moving the mouse pointer to the item. Release the mouse click once you are at the location where you want to drop the item.

Drag and drop to the calendar

As shown in the following example, you can click on an email message and keep the mouse button pressed down while dragging it to the calendar object in the navigation pane. This will create a new calendar item, with the email contents included in the notes section of the calendar event. The steps are as follows:

1. Click on the item you want to copy to a calendar item:

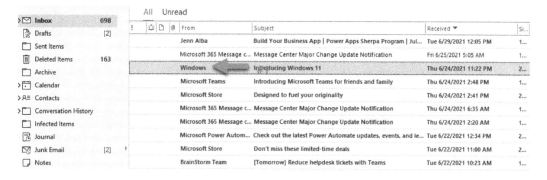

Figure 1.6 – The item to copy

2. Click and hold the mouse down while you move it to the calendar object:

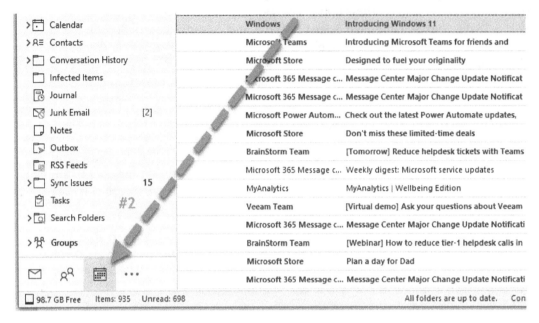

Figure 1.7 – Moving to a Calendar object

3. Drag and drop the item onto the calendar or another object. Fill in the required text for the event and be sure to click **Save & Close**:

Figure 1.8 – Creating the Calendar item

Drag and drop to a to-do Item

To drag and drop an email to the to-do list on the right side of the screen within the TO-DO BAR (turn this on through the **View** menu), first select the email to drag and drop. Drag your mouse to the to-do list, and a thin line will position between the tasks. If you want to move this to the top of the list, just keep the mouse button pressed and relocate that line where you want the task to drop:

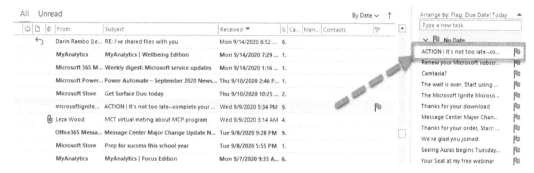

Figure 1.9 – Positioning an item

Note

If you don't have the to-do bar open, you can drag the item to the `tasks` object at the bottom of the navigation bar as well. This technique will open a new task dialog box to create a new task item.

Drag and drop to people/contacts

If you drag and drop an email to a `People` object, Outlook will create a new contact from the email. The email address will become the new contact's name and the email address will be created, and a copy of the email message will be copied to the **Notes** section of the contact, as seen here:

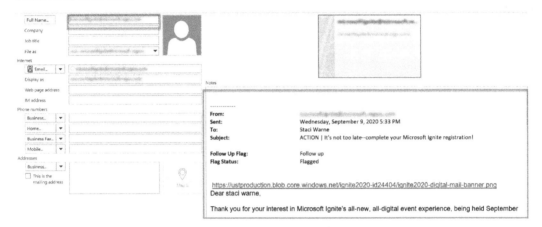

Figure 1.10 – A new contact

Drag and drop other uses

The preceding steps will work to drag and drop an email item to any of the buttons at the bottom of the navigation pane in Outlook, including the following:

- People (Contacts)
- Calendar
- Notes
- Tasks
- Folders
- Shortcuts
- Other applications such as PowerPoint and Word
- Desktop or other folders on the system
- Outlook folders

You can also go in a reverse direction to drag and drop other objects in your system from their folders to an email window. This will automatically open a blank email and attach the object to the email. This can save a lot of time spent clicking on the drop-down arrow by attaching an item and then navigating through your file path. If the folder is open, just select the item (or items) and click and drag them wherever you want them.

> **Note**
> You cannot attach a folder to the email, but you can open the folder and select the files inside the folder to attach.

To access objects not showing on the navigation bar, let's follow these steps:

1. Click the three dots to access more items:

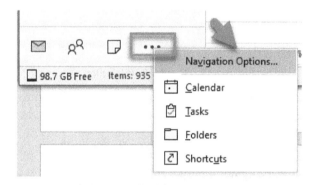

Figure 1.11 – Accessing more items

2. Select **Navigation Options…**:

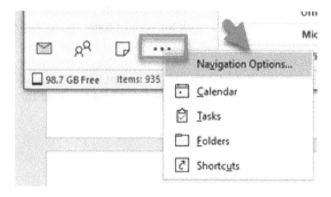

Figure 1.12 – Navigation Options

3. From the **Navigation Options** dialog box, move the object you need to view to the top of the list in the **Display in this order** box:

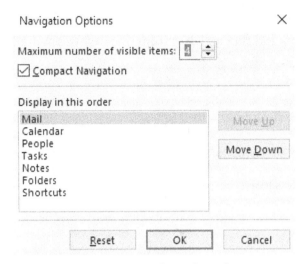

Figure 1.13 – Display in this order

Don't be afraid to experiment; try to drag and drop several objects. You will probably find some other ways to use drag and drop other than what you have seen in this book. It's an amazing feature.

Customizing views as per tailored needs

Outlook provides a seamless and secure management system that will enable you to stay organized and connected in your personal and business life. You have the options to integrate it with other applications or use it as a standalone program. Whichever way you choose, you can customize the views to work for you. In these sections, we will discuss a few of the more advanced techniques that you can use and several you didn't realize were even an option. We will start with the Quick Access Toolbar to customize your frequently used buttons, and then we will discuss setting up different views for your inbox by using multiple views, such as **Outlook Today**, **Options**, and **Show Focused Inbox**, all of which are available to you within Outlook.

The Quick Access Toolbar

Have you ever heard the phrase, *"You don't know what you don't know"?* That could apply to the Quick Access Toolbar. Even though you may have used Outlook for decades, you may have never noticed the toolbar in the top-left corner. This is the Quick Access Toolbar and is a customizable toolbar that displays your most frequently used. By default, this is what you will see on the Quick Access Toolbar:

Figure 1.14 – Quick Access Toolbar

The out-of-the-box default buttons on this toolbar are as follows:

- The **Send/Receive All Folders** button.

- **Undo**.

- The drop-down arrow to add a suggested button or an option to go to **More Commands**, which opens a dialog box to customize the Quick Access Toolbar. This also gives you the option to show this toolbar above or below the ribbon.

Follow these steps to customize this toolbar to fit your needs:

1. Click the drop-down arrow at the right of the Quick Access Toolbar or click **File | Options | Quick Access Toolbar**:

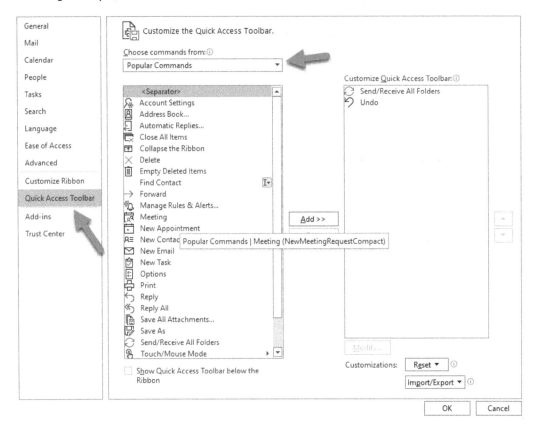

Figure 1.15 – Customizing the Quick Access Toolbar

2. Click the dropdown by **Popular Commands** and select **All Commands**. This will give you access to all of the possible commands that are available to add to this toolbar. The buttons I would recommend that help me are as follows:

    A. **Categories**

    B. **Print**

    C. **Mail**

    D. **New Appointment**

    E. **My Computer**

3. Select a command on the left, and then click **Add >>** in the center between the **Choose commands from** box and the **Customize Quick Access Toolbar** box. The selected command will show in the list of commands to be shown on the toolbar.

4. Click **OK**, and the buttons will now be on the toolbar, as shown here:

Figure 1.16 – The customized Quick Access Toolbar

You can also select a command and then use the up and down arrow to select the order of the buttons that appear on the toolbar. Top down button as shown:

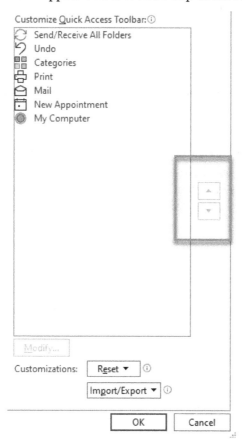

Figure 1.17 – The buttons for moving a selected item up and down

5. Right-click on any of the buttons on the ribbon (any ribbon) to see a drop-down menu that will have the (if available) **Add to Quick Access Toolbar** option. This is a quick way to add the buttons instead of the preceding steps. In this example, I right-clicked on the **Delete** button:

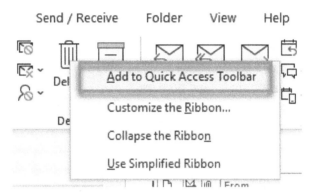

Figure 1.18 – The right-click menu of the Delete button

Outlook Today

Use the **Outlook Today** view to get a convenient, quick interactive view of your day. To access the Outlook Today View, click on the account name box located in the navigation pane. At the top right of this view, you will see the **Customize Outlook Today** link. This view allows you to customize the following items:

- Startup
- Messages
- Calendar
- Tasks
- Styles

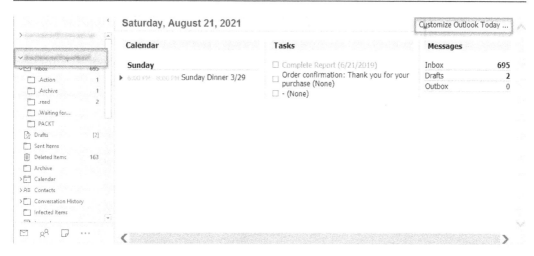

Figure 1.19 – Customize Outlook Today

Show Focused/Other view

The **Show Focused Inbox** button allows you to separate your email into two tabs, **Focused** and **Other**. Your most important emails will be in the **Focused** tab, and all the others will appear in the **Other** tab. You will have to watch this at first to determine how Outlook is assigning your emails to these folders.

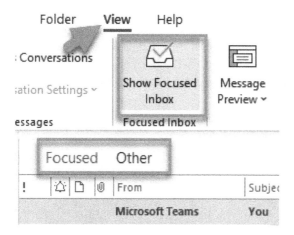

Figure 1.20 – The Show Focused Inbox button

It's not perfect by any means, but it does a pretty good job determining where to put each email. To turn on this feature, click on **View** | **Show Focused Inbox**. If you identify emails appearing in the wrong folder, you can right-click on the email and select **Move to Other** or **Move to Focused**, depending on the location of the email. Over time, Exchange will begin to see your pattern and adjust emails between these folders accordingly.

> **Note**
>
> The **Focused** inbox is only available for Office 365, Exchange, and `outlook.com`.
>
> If you do not see this button on your version of Outlook, then this feature is most likely not available to you. New features are usually rolled out to members of Microsoft's insiders first, and then others are rolled out via updates to your Office programs. To check for any updates, select **File** | **Office Account** | **Update Options** | **Update Now**.

The Layout section

The **Layout** section of the **View** tab has commands available for you to customize the screen for how you choose to be productive. You can see the section in the following figure that represents the layout options for your screen. The **Use Tighter Spacing** command is used to reduce the amount of space between your messages to show more messages on your screen. The **Folder Pane** command has controls for how the navigation pane on the left side of the screen is viewed or not viewed. The **Reading Pane** command lets you control whether the message of the email is opened to view and where that window will open on the screen. The **To-Do Bar** command is my personal favorite, which allows you to view **Calendar**, **People**, or the **Tasks** list on the right side of your screen:

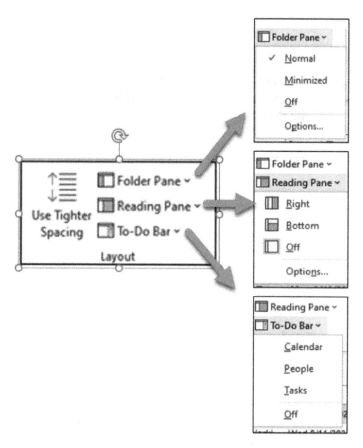

Figure 1.21 – The Layout options

Peek

Peeks was introduced to Outlook with the 2013 version. Peeks works with the To-Do Bar, but it allows you to take a peek at **Calendar**, **People**, or **Tasks**. You can view the Peek when you hover on the **Calendar**, **People**, or **Tasks** button at the bottom of the navigation bar. Once you hover over the button, the specific button's window will show a snapshot view of it. Use the **Dock the Peek** button in the top-right corner to have this view docked on the To-Do Bar.

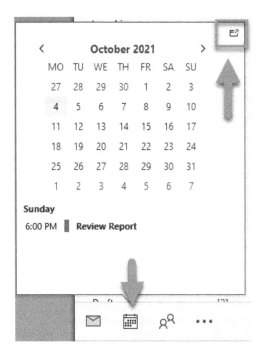

Figure 1.22 – Peek

Advanced View settings

The default view for Outlook is the **Preview** view; however, you can customize the view to your liking and set it up for your own way of working. You can either create, change, or customize a view:

1. Select **View | View Settings**.

2. Select **Other Settings…** in the **Advanced View Settings** box.

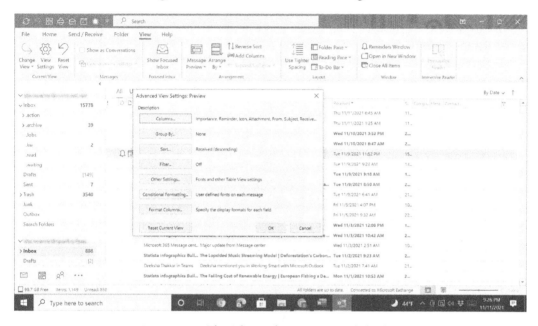

Figure 1.23 – The Advanced View Settings dialog box

Advanced views in Outlook are not the simplest of tasks to set up. The different options for customizing your views with this dialog box will be demonstrated in several topics in this book. Be patient in selecting the view that is right for you. The bottom of the **Advanced View Settings** dialog box has a button to reset the original fields back to the original views.

The Clipboard viewer

Most of you know how to use copy (*Ctrl + C*) and paste (*Ctrl + V*), but few people know that you can open the **Clipboard** viewer to copy multiple items and then paste them in multiple places without having to copy and paste each item separately. The Clipboard viewer is not available to you on the **Home** tab in Outlook as it is in other Microsoft applications. To use the Clipboard Viewer in Outlook, follow these steps:

1. Get the clipboard history at any time by pressing the Windows logo key + *V*.

2. If this is your first time accessing this, you will get the following box. Click the **Turn On** button to start a history of the items you will copy to accumulate in the clipboard.

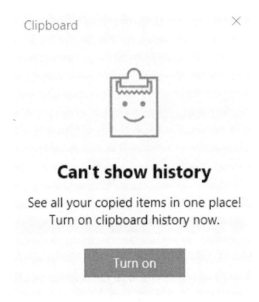

Figure 1.24 – The Turn on history

3. As you copy items to the clipboard, the history will record them, and you will be able to paste and pin frequently used items by choosing an item from the clipboard menu.

After turning on the Clipboard setting, Windows will start keeping a record of the items that you copy so that you can look at the history and place items where you need to, whether that is within Outlook or another application on your computer.

Summary

With Outlook's power comes a lot of options for you to customize your environment. You have seen many techniques in this chapter to start customizing Outlook to your needs. We looked at the **Info** tab in the Backstage view, which holds several tools for setting up more connections, managing rules and alerts. In addition to these tools, we discussed the **Options** dialog box, which allows us to adjust dozens of settings within Outlook.

You need to find a system that works for you and tailor it to your needs. Spend some time exploring your different options and look around, and if you don't like the way something is laid out, there is probably a way to change it. Be creative, pay attention to the way you use Outlook, and be open to making changes along the way. As you spend more time making these adjustments, you will have insight into how you may need to adjust your setting again, and keep evolving with your Outlook environment.

In the next chapter, we will move away from settings for Outlook and concentrate on how you can take control of your email by creating **rules**, **quick steps**, and effectively using **categories**, as well as understanding how to correctly set up one or multiple email accounts.

Questions

1. How do you empty the trash/deleted items and remove a deleted item upon exiting Outlook?

2. How can you change your account name on your email account (not your email ID – just your name)?

3. How do I know which version of Outlook I am using?

4. What is the difference between a **task** and to-do item in Outlook?

5. How do you empty the trash/deleted items and remove the deleted item upon exiting Outlook?

Answers

1. When you delete an email, it is moved to the **deleted items** folder. Once you delete the email, it will be available or recoverable for 14 days. Anything that has been deleted for 14 days can no longer be recovered. To empty the deleted items folder upon exiting Outlook, click on **Tools | Options | Other** and check the box that says **Empty the deleted items folder upon exiting**.

2. The default name on an account when it is set up is the email ID. To change this name, click **File | Info | Account Settings | Account Settings**. From the list of accounts, select the one that you want to change the name of and click on the **Change** button. In the **Account name** field, change the name to one you prefer and click **Next**. You will be shown that your account was successfully updated and then click **Done**.

3. If you are running Outlook 2007, you are running a 32-bit version, but since 2010, you could be running either version. You need to know what version Outlook is running when installing Outlook plugins and add-ons, as some of them are not compatible with the 64-bit version. To check what version your computer is running, select **File | Office Account | About Outlook**, and you will see a line of text indicating 64-bit (as shown in the following figure) or 32-bit:

About Microsoft® Outlook® for Microsoft 365

Microsoft® Outlook® for Microsoft 365 MSO (16.0.14326.20384) 64-bit

Figure 1.25 – 64-bit

There are so many Outlook apps and services that you can use to access Outlook. It's in your best interest to know which version of Outlook you have. To locate your version, select **File | Office Account**. The version will be listed in the **Product Information** folder

4. The **To-Do** list is a collection of items that have been flagged for follow-up in Outlook. This is the list that will appear on the **To-Do** bar if it is displayed. This list also includes the Outlook task, which is a task that has been stored in a **Task** folder. Tasks are created and stored in the **Task** folder, and currently, the **To Do** list doesn't yet support Outlook **Task** fields, such as start and end dates, task status, task completion percentage, multiple priority levels, work hours, colors, or categories that are available in an Outlook task.

5. When you delete an email, it is moved to the deleted items folder. Once you delete the email it will be available or recoverable for 14 days. Anything that has been deleted for 14 days can no longer be recovered. To empty the deleted items folder upon exiting Outlook, click on Tools | Options | Other, check the box that says "Empty the deleted items folder upon exiting".

Part 2: Email Essentials

Take control of your email by creating rules, Quick Steps, and effectively using categories. You can also create multiple signatures, display up to three time zones, and master setting up multiple email accounts. In addition to this, you can use conditional formatting, mail merge, and so much more. In this part, you'll learn how to successfully save time with loads of tips and trips to work smarter while using Outlook and specifically with your email.

This section contains the following chapters:

- *Chapter 2, Sending and Receiving Emails*
- *Chapter 3, Managing Email Accounts*
- *Chapter 4, Organizing Your Outlook Environment*
- *Chapter 5, Outlook Mail Merge*

2
Sending and Receiving Emails

Email has replaced the regular delivery of mail for many businesses and personal communications. No longer do we need stamps, paper, markers, or the time to run to the post office (although some do still utilize these services from time to time). On the whole, most of our communications can be done through email. There are all kinds of guidelines that you can follow to compose the finest emails. As you are composing your emails, there are three basic questions you want to be sure to answer with each of your emails:

1. Is your message understandable?
2. Is the intended message stated clearly?
3. Is the flow of the email easy to follow?

With some simple planning and being aware that the reader must decode the meaning of the communications (because of the lack of nonverbal communication such as facial expressions and body language), you should focus attention on the way you are composing your emails. Using the suggestions presented in this chapter will help to ensure that not only are your intentions written in your emails communicated effectively but you're also composing your emails productively.

In this chapter, we're going to cover the following topics:

- AutoComplete
- Email signatures (HTML)
- Attachments
- Recalling a message
- Voting buttons
- Replies – replying to other emails
- Working offline

For many of the emails that you send, this could be your first point of communication with the receiver. Following these techniques will help ensure that you are perceived correctly.

Sending and receiving email

When you open Outlook, the navigation pane will indicate that the **Mail** view is shown. The **Mail** view with the inbox displayed is the default view that will help you manage and navigate your email messages, unless you have customized your screen for another view to show (which will be covered in *Chapter 16, Managing Your Day System*).

To write and/or send an email, the **Compose** window will be used. Access this window by clicking **Home | New Email**. In this window, you will find the **To** and **Cc** fields. The **Bcc** field can be accessed by clicking on the **To** or **Cc** button, and in the **Select Names** dialog box, enter the email ID of the recipient in the **Bcc** field. If you do not enter a recipient in the **Bcc** field, it will not show in the **Compose** email window. You can also turn on this **Bcc** field by clicking **Options | BCC**.

> **Note**
> If the email address is underlined, that indicates that it is a valid email address. If no underline appears, then double-check the email address, as you will most likely get a delivery error message when you press **Send**. If you are sending to a lot of recipients, I suggest that you click on the **Check Names** button on the ribbon to have the email addresses all verified before sending.

AutoComplete

AutoComplete is word completion feature in Outlook. You may also see this written as the **AutoComplete list**, and the **nickname cache** is another name that it is referred to. The AutoComplete list is automatically populated with these names when you send email messages from Outlook and contains the email or SMTP addresses, legacy `ExchangeDN` entries, and the actual display names for email addresses to previous email recipients. When you begin typing into the **To, Cc**, or **Bcc** field in Outlook, suggestions will appear based on the text that you have entered. These suggestions come from this AutoComplete list, which is continually being updated once created:

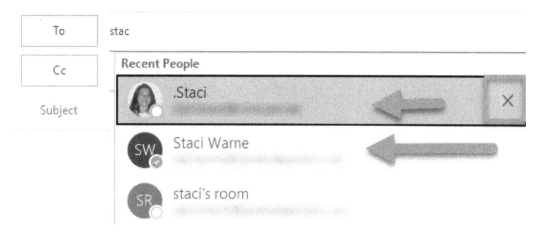

Figure 2.1 – AutoComplete activated for the To recipient

After you reach the limit for entries saved in the AutoComplete list, Outlook uses an internal algorithm to identify names to eliminate them from the list. This is built on **usage weighting**. Because Outlook limits the number of entries you can save, you may discover names surprisingly removed.

The limits that are stored in the AutoComplete list are 1,000 entries for Outlook 2003, 2010, 2013, 2016, 2019, and 2021. The limit for Outlook 2007 is 2,000 entries.

Removing AutoComplete list entries one by one

Removing names from the AutoComplete list is the safest way to remove an entry so that a name will not appear on this list when you begin typing in the letters of the name. Keep in mind that once you remove a name from this list, it will be added back to the list once a new email is created again. The steps to remove an entry are as follows:

1.   Open a new email message.

2.   Enter a few characters of the AutoComplete item you want to eliminate from the list. When the name appears in the list of suggested items, hover the mouse pointer over the desired entry to delete. Once it becomes highlighted, wait for the **X** icon to appear next to the highlighted suggestion and click **X** to remove, or press the *Del* or *Delete* key on the keyboard.

Figure 2.2 – Deleting the AutoComplete list entry

Selecting **X** will prevent the named entry from appearing in the AutoComplete list again but won't remove it from your account. Because of this, the entry will still appear in other areas of Outlook, such as in search boxes.

Using contact addresses for the AutoComplete list

Instead of waiting for the AutoComplete list to populate and save all your email names to cache, you can also populate this list with your contact addresses in Outlook by making a new message. Address the message to all contacts. Make sure that you don't send the email messages. The following shows the steps to do this:

1.   On the **Send/Receive** tab, click on the **Work Offline** button so that the email does not actually get sent to your contacts. **Work Offline** will be discussed later in this chapter.

2.   Create a new message using **Home | New Email**.

3.   Click the **To** button.

4. Select the contact list from the address book where you want to add your contacts. Your options will be as follows:

- A contacts folder

- A global address book

- A contacts folder that resides within a public folder

5. Select the first contact, and using your keyboard or mouse, scroll to view the last contact. Press and hold the *Shift* button on the keyboard while clicking on the last contact to select all contacts, and click **OK**. The dialog box will close.

6. Ensure that you placed Outlook in offline mode using the **Send/Receive** tab so that the email does *not* actually get sent to all your contacts. Now, in offline mode, send the email, and then delete the message from your outbox in the navigation bar on the left of the mail view. Once deleted, you can revert to online mode.

7. Test this by addressing a new message; note that the AutoComplete attribute will appear with your contacts' email addresses.

Enabling or disabling the AutoComplete list

The default setting for AutoComplete is turned on or enabled. Here are the steps to locate this setting:

1. Select **File | Options**.

2. Select the **Mail** tab from the menu on the left.

3. Scroll down to the **Send messages** section.

4. Ensure that the **Use Auto-Complete List to suggest names when typing in the To, Cc, and Bcc lines** box is checked. Uncheck this box to turn off the **AutoComplete** list feature.

By deselecting this box, the AutoComplete drop-down box will not appear when you start typing the first few letters of the recipient's email address.

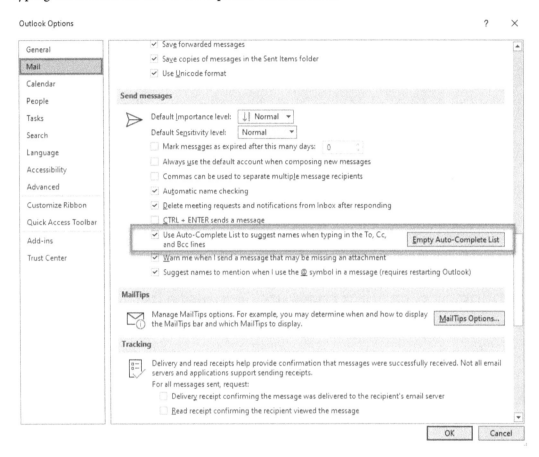

Figure 2.3 – The Outlook options for AutoComplete

Note

For Outlook 2003 and 2007, you will find this setting in the **Advanced Email Options** tab. Check or uncheck the **Suggest names while completing To, Cc, and Bcc fields** option.

☑ Suggest names while completing To, Cc, and Bcc fields

Figure 2.4 – The AutoComplete option for Outlook 2003 and 2007

Clearing all entries from the AutoComplete list

You may decide that there are too many names to delete from your AutoComplete list.

To clear or empty an AutoComplete list, do the following:

1. Go to **File | Options** to open the options dialog box.
2. Click **Mail** in the left navigation menu, and then click the **Empty Auto-Complete List** button in the **Send messages** section.

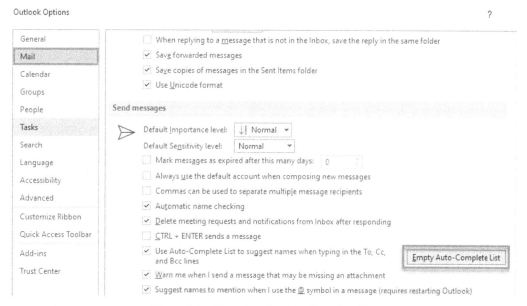

Figure 2.5 – Emptying the AutoComplete list

A dialog box will appear and ask for your confirmation to empty the AutoComplete list. Click the **Yes** button, and then click the **OK** button in the **Outlook Options** dialog box.

3. Now, the AutoComplete cache will be cleared from Outlook.

> **Note**
> Once you start creating new emails, the cache will display again.

HTML email signatures

Outlook signatures appear at the bottom of your email and usually contain your contact information for the recipient to easily get a hold of you. You can enter more information in this box besides text. Some types of data you can include are as follows:

- Text
- Images
- Electronic business card
- Logo
- Handwritten signature

Outlook signatures will be automatically inserted into every outgoing message. Create them if you wish to add them to your emails as needed.

A good Outlook signature is typically an *HTML* signature. Without HTML, an image will usually get distorted on different devices, and with simple text, it will look unprofessional. An *HTML* signature makes your email look professional and makes a great impression on your recipients, which will encourage them to get in contact with you.

Before you can insert the *HTML* signature in Outlook, you first must create the signature. There are tools online to help you do this or a graphic designer can do it for you. Once they give you the file, you will need to save this to your computer in a location from which you will be able to easily access it.

The steps to insert an *HTML* signature into Outlook are as follows:

1. Have your created *HTML* signature saved to your computer in an easily accessible location.
2. In Outlook, select **File** | **Options** | **Mail** and click on **Signatures…**.

3. Click on **New** to add a signature, *give a name*, and click **OK**. Select the email account on the right of the box. Close the signature dialog box and close Outlook.

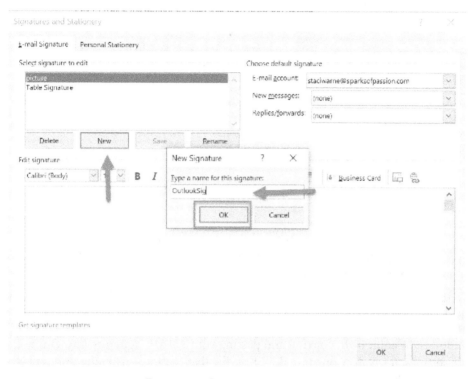

Figure 2.6 – Creating a new signature

4. Hold the *Ctrl* key on the keyboard and click on the **Signatures** button. This will open the File Explorer with the **Signatures** folder open, which is where Outlook saves the signature files on the computer. Select the .htm file that was created in the previous step and delete the file.

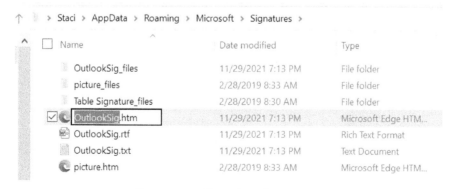

Figure 2.7 – File Explorer | Signatures

5. Now, select the HTML file that you saved on the computer in *step 1* and copy the file. Then, go back to the Outlook signature file location and click **Paste**. Right-click on the file to rename the file as whatever you named it in *step 3*. Change the file extension to `.htm` instead of `.html`. Press *Enter* and confirm the file extension change.

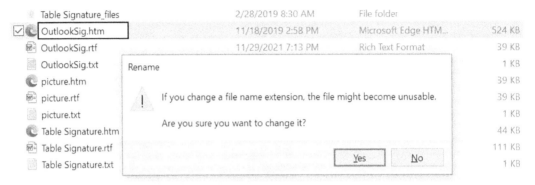

Figure 2.8 – Changing the extension to .htm

6. Switch back to Outlook and click on **Signatures** again. You will see that the new signature has been created; however, you may not be able to view the picture.

7. To test, create a new message, and the *HTML* signature should be inserted within the body of the message.

This method is different from copying and pasting your *HTML* signature into Outlook's signature settings. It involves opening the `.htm` file that Outlook generates and replacing it, which ensures that the correct *HTML* and image paths are being sent. This method ensures that the images are clear. If you install your email signature by copy and pasting, Outlook edits your code, replacing it with its own Microsoft Word-rendered code, and compresses your images, which will reduce their quality.

Attachments

Attaching files, pictures, contacts, emails, and many other items to your Outlook messages is a very easy process. To attach a file, simply click on **Insert | Attach File** on the ribbon. Next, choose the file from one of these locations, prompted by the drop-down menu:

- **Recent Items** – The 12 most recent files worked on will be displayed.
- **Browse This PC...** – Opens File Explorer to navigate to the file.
- **Browse Web Locations** – Including OneDrive, SharePoint sites, and other locations. Select one of the locations and then select your attachment.

If you select a file on your computer, a copy of the file will be attached to the email; however, if you choose a file in the cloud, you can follow the steps that follow to add cloud file attachments in Outlook.

Cloud file attachments in Outlook

The attachment options allow you to control how a file that you attach from OneDrive or SharePoint is attached to your email. The default settings ask you how you want to attach a file to an email every time. To change this default, select **File | Options | General** and select your preference under the **Attachment options** section. Your options are as follows:

1. **Ask me how I want to attach them every time**
2. **Always share them as links**
3. **Always attach them as copies**

> **Note**
>
> If you do not have the attachment options displayed on the **General** tab, you will need to install the KB4011240 update for Outlook 2016, dated November 7, 2017.

Multiple attachments

If you are sending multiple attachments in one email, you can download them to your computer in one step instead of opening each attachment and saving it to your computer. Click on the middle of the attachment, click the drop-down arrow next to the attachment, and click on **Save All Attachments…**. Then, you will be prompted to save all the files to a selected location on your computer.

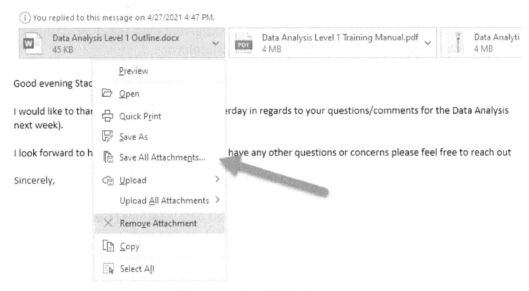

Figure 2.9 – Save All Attachments…

Changing the file association for an email attachment

Many file attachments can be opened by more than one type of program on your computer. One example would be opening a photo with the **Photos** program or with **Paint**. The following steps can be used after you have saved an attachment.

To open the default program with another type of file instead of the file type of the sent attachment, follow these steps:

1. Locate the file to open in the File Explorer on your computer.
2. Right-click on the file and select **Open with…**.
3. Select the application that you want to associate the file with or select the store to find a suitable application.

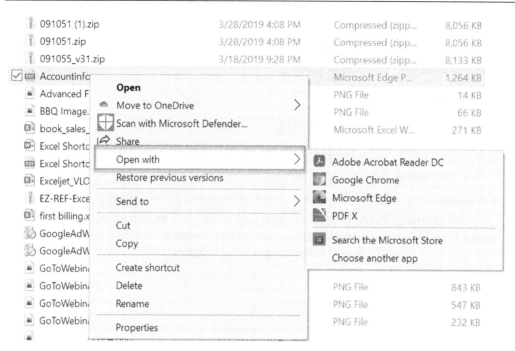

Figure 2.10 – File association

You will need to change the program to open a file with if you do not have the software on your computer. In most cases, you will have an adequate program with which you can view the attachment. However, if that is not possible, you may have to ask the sender to convert the file to a compatible format for you to view.

Voting buttons

By using voting buttons in email messages, you can poll all your recipients and ask questions with a limited set of answers, which is especially useful for large groups. The recipients can use the voting buttons to respond to your email, and by doing this, your results will automatically calculate for you. You can also export the responses to an Excel worksheet.

> **Note**
> A Microsoft Exchange Server account is required to use voting buttons.

Inserting voting buttons

1.   Click **Create**, **Reply to**, or **Forward** from an email you received.

2.   Choose **Options | Use voting buttons**.

3.   Select one of the following:

- **Approve; Reject** – Used for receiving authorization for an action.

- **Yes; No** – Used for a quick poll with yes or no.

- **Yes; No;Maybe** – Used to offer alternative responses to yes or no.

- **Custom** – If you choose this option, you will need to use the **Voting and Tracking options settings** in the **Properties** box, and check the **Use voting buttons** checkbox, as shown in the following screenshot. Delete the default text and replace it with your own, using semicolons between each entry.

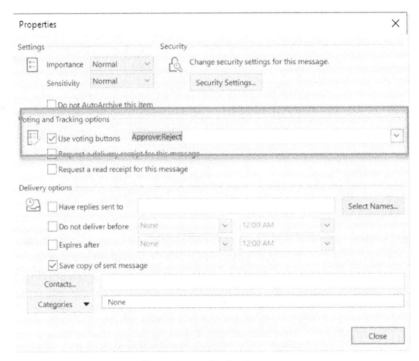

Figure 2.11 – Voting buttons

Occasionally, you may have a recipient of your email not realize that there are voting buttons in the email to click on to place a vote. I would suggest including a reference them in the subject to make them aware of the voting buttons, which may help you receive responses promptly and correctly.

Tracking and printing results

After receiving results from the recipients of a sent email, it is efficient to use the Excel tracking feature to track and print them:

1. In Outlook's **Sent Items** folder, locate and open the email message you sent.
2. Click the **Message** tab | **Tracking**. The **Tracking** button will not be seen until at least one person has voted in the poll from this sent email.
3. The results will appear in the **Results** window with a blue box that shows the tally for the responses. You can then print the window using **File** | **Print**, selecting a printer, and selecting **Print**.
4. Send the results to an Excel workbook by clicking **Message** | **Tracking**. Click and hold *Ctrl*, and then *click and drag* to select the names and responses. Copy the selection, open a blank Excel workbook, and paste the data into Excel at your desired location. You will then need to adjust the column widths and so on in the worksheet to be able to see all the data.

Recalling a sent message

I bet that we have all sent an email in error. This can easily open the potential for some real damage, although it is usually just plain embarrassing. Outlook has tools built-in for these scenarios, and I suggest you practice this tip before suddenly needing it. This is a good technique to pull in a co-worker and practice sending and recalling messages between one another so that if or when the time comes to act, you will be ready to act fast and not have to figure it all out. Once you realize that you sent an email in error, these are the steps to quickly recall that message:

1. Select the **Sent Items** folder.
2. Double-click on or select the message so that it opens in another window.
3. Select **File** | **Info**.
4. Select **Message Resend and Recall** | **Recall This Message**.

5. Select **Delete unread copies and replace with a new message** to replace the sent message with a new message. When you click **Send**, the original email message will be deleted and replaced with the newly edited one if the email has not been read.

6. Select the **Tell me if recall succeeds or fails for each recipient** checkbox. Then, select **OK** to close the dialog box.

> **Note**
>
> If your office account is an **IMAP** or **POP** account, in *Chapter 3, Managing Email Accounts*, a recall won't work. Also, the recipients must be on Exchange or Microsoft 365 and reside within the same organization to be able to recall a sent message.

Handling replies

When a person replies to your emails, that reply by default will go back to the originator of the email message. In Outlook 2016 and later, you have the option to redirect replies to another email address than yours. This is very useful if you are going on vacation and want messages replied to someone other than yourself for that time period.

To have replies directed to someone else, click the **Options** tab | **Direct Replies To**.

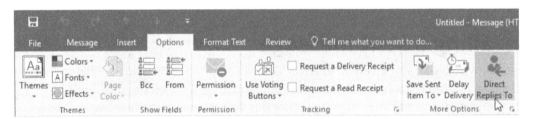

Figure 2.12 – Direct Replies To

Within the **Properties** dialog box, **Delivery options** will have a checkbox by **Have replies sent to**. If the box is not checked, you need to check it.

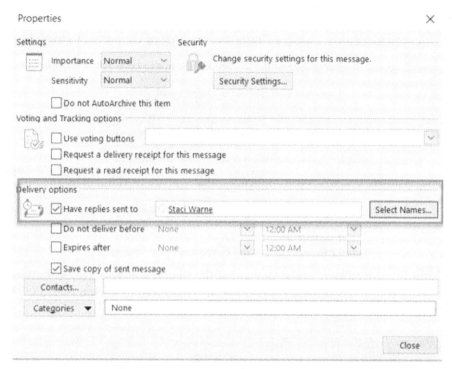

Figure 2.13 – Properties for Delivery options

In the box to the right of this, enter the name of the email ID that you want the replies sent to from now on. You need to remember to change this as needed. If you prefer, or do not know the email address, you can click on the **Select Names…** button and then choose a name from the selections.

> **Note**
> The recipient won't know that you have chosen to redirect replies to another address until they click the **Reply** button and see a different email address shown in the **To** field.

Working offline

The **working online/offline** feature was added to Outlook in the 2010 version and has remained in all later versions. The purpose of this button is to allow users to be able to access their work on Outlook without internet connectivity. In offline mode, you are still able to access loaded emails and compose new emails; however, you can't send or receive new emails. If you send in offline mode, your emails will be scheduled to be sent as soon as an internet connection is available and when you have regained online features.

Is Outlook working?

There are two ways to identify whether Outlook is working or connected to the internet:

The display settings on the status bar will indicate that you are connected to the Exchange server on the status bar.

Figure 2.14 – Outlook is connected to the internet

If the internet is down, you will see an indication that you are working in offline mode.

Figure 2.15 – Outlook is not connected to the internet

Click the Send/Receive tab, and at the far right of the ribbon is a Work Offline button. If the button is not grayed out, it indicates that you are connected to the internet, and the status bar will show that you are connected.

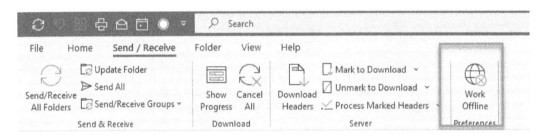

Figure 2.16 – Outlook is connected to the internet

If this button is grayed out, then the internet is not connected, and you will see the Work Offline text on the status bar.

Figure 2.17 – Outlook is not connected to the internet

When Outlook shows that it is disconnected

If your Outlook is indicating that your status is working offline, then it most likely is an issue with your network connectivity. Start the troubleshooting steps by first clicking on the **Work Online** button. This may be the only problem, but if not, you need to begin checking with your internet provider or IT staff to determine whether they have a problem. If not, here are some possible connectivity issues to consider:

- Mail server issues.

- Incorrect account settings.

- An outdated operating system.

- The Outlook Exchange server is down – you can log on to the web account to check.

- Check for any Outlook updates that are needed to be installed.

There are several possible solutions to get you back online. You can connect with Microsoft or your email provider, who will quickly get you up and running. If you do have internet connectivity, you can reach out to Microsoft at `https://support.microsoft.com/`.

Summary

Like it or not, email is here to stay, and it is important to have an efficient workplace. The topics in this chapter will help you to communicate and distribute your content in a professional matter to your clients, coworkers, management, or anybody that you have a need to communicate with. You may feel that your email is overwhelming. It's time to take back control by utilizing the AutoCorrect feature, creating email signatures, and having replies sent to another person, which were all established to save you time.

In the next chapter, we will discuss managing your email accounts and what is necessary for setting up and maintaining those accounts. We will discuss selecting an email provider, selecting domain names, and using multiple email accounts.

Questions

1. How can you have an attachment appear in the body of an email?
2. Why might your Outlook suddenly disconnect?
3. Can you swap one signature for another in an Outlook email message?
4. What is the Outlook web app?
5. What is the maximum size limit for an attachment in Outlook?

Answers

1. Create a new email message (you can also reply to or forward an email) and select **Insert** and the drop-down arrow next to **Link**. Choose a file from the most recently used items, or at the bottom of this list, choose **Insert Link...** and the file to attach, and click **OK**. To attach more than one file, hold *Ctrl* while selecting multiple files. The link for the file or picture, if selected, will appear in the message of your email.

2. This is most likely due to a temporary hiccup in the connectivity to the network/ **Virtual Private Network** (**VPN**). Check to see whether you are still online by looking at the status bar, which will display **Connected to: Microsoft Exchange** or **Working offline**.

Figure 2.18 – Working offline

Outlook will automatically try to reconnect to the server, but if that does not work, you can click on the **Send / Receive** tab | **Work Offline** button. If this button is grayed out, you are offline, and no shading indicates that you are working online.

3. In a new email message window, select the **Message** tab | **Signature** drop-down arrow. Any previously created signatures will appear in this selection. Select the signature that you want to swap the current signature for. You can also select the **signature....** option to create a new signature from this menu button.

4. **Outlook Web App** (**OWA**) allows you to access your email account from a web browser. Outlook on the web does not include all the features found in the Outlook desktop version. It is a slimmed-down version that allows you to access your email while away. You can access the web browser at `outlook.office.com`.

5. Microsoft has a 20 MB limit on attachments that you can send through email. It does not matter whether this is a single file or several files attached to one email. The total size of all attachments cannot exceed 10 MB to 35 MB, depending on your plan. If you need to attach a file that is larger than what your plan allows, you should consider putting the file in a shared location and emailing a link to that location instead. See *Further reading* for the Exchange Online limits.

Further reading

- *Exchange Online limits*:

   `https://docs.microsoft.com/en-us/office365/`
   `servicedescriptions/exchange-online-service-description/`
   `exchange-online-limits?redirectedfrom=MSDN#MessageLimits`

3
Managing Email Accounts

The biggest issue facing today's society is *data security*. This is mainly because our information is available to everyone, and it is important that we select an email host that can provide the security and services that we require.

In this chapter, we will discuss what you need to look for in a host and what Outlook provides for you. Then, we will discuss setting up your domain name, the best practices for selecting it, and how to connect it to your email ID within Outlook.

In this chapter, we are going to discuss the following topics:

- Why have multiple email accounts?
- Selecting an email host
- Email protocols
- Setting up email accounts
- Changing a mail server
- Domain names

Knowing the different email platforms that are available to you and how to set them up in Outlook is an important topic to address, and you will gain that insight in this chapter. You can set up one account or multiple accounts using the automatic and manual settings provided. You can use these techniques on multiple devices as well, such as computers, tablets, and various mobile devices. Understanding these terms will make account installation simpler for you.

Why have multiple email accounts?

Reading email is the first morning activity for many people and has increasingly become an important method of business communication. Email is fast, inexpensive, easily accessible, and has become an efficient and effective way to communicate.

There are several reasons why a person would want to have multiple email accounts. To separate your online presence, I would encourage you to set up several email accounts according to the activities that you encounter in your sending and receiving of emails. Some of these categories can be the following:

- Personal
- Business
- Temporary or "throwaway"
- Social networking
- Journals and newsletters
- Adverts
- Occasional sign-ups at events

This list could go on and on for every individual person. Before you jump in and start creating these various accounts, I would recommend taking inventory of the emails you currently receive and then looking at the current activity that you have in each of your accounts.

The main purpose of creating multiple email accounts is to streamline the various types of communications you have consistently. It can get very overwhelming to keep up with incoming emails and reply to them in a timely manner. Having multiple email accounts can help you to stay ahead of this task or, as I like to refer to it, stay ahead of the game. In *Chapter 16, Managing Your Day System*, I will provide you with some ways to manage your accounts.

Selecting an email host

Email is crucial to businesses in today's fast-paced environment. No matter how much you may want to get away from this, it is here to stay, which makes choosing a *host* very important. The email host that you select will handle the technical details of day-to-day operations, such as allowing you to send emails from your own domain, spam filtering, phishing scams, storing files, or it may provide a whole suite of tools, such as, in the case of Outlook, calendars, contact management, and to-do lists.

> **Note**
>
> A simple way of defining an email *host* would be to say that email hosting is a service where a *hosting provider*, such as *Microsoft*, *Yahoo*, or *Gmail*, rents out email servers to its users to allow them to send and receive emails over networks.

There are three main ways to host your email:

- **Self-hosted**: You must have your own servers, which give you more control and the ability to customize. The disadvantages would be the added cost to build and maintain a server and the challenge of having your emails marked as spam.

- **Shared web hosting**: This is where your data is shared on a dedicated hosting server that shares multiple sites. This is cheaper than the alternatives and is sometimes free. This is also a great way to get your site up and running fast and affordable. The disadvantages would be that your site shares server CPU resources and, depending on spikes from those other sites, your pages might load slowly or not at all.

- **Third-party hosting**: Use this when you need to run your business with more features than your web host provides.

Most businesses are steering away from running in-house email servers due to the lower costs associated with *third-party hosting*. Third-party hosting such as Outlook and Microsoft 365 now can manage the large number of accounts needed in large corporations and schools while still offering the latest security protocols, not to mention the simplicity of connectivity and distribution to end users.

Here are the questions to ask when looking for an email host:

- What is your delivery rate? The delivery rate is the percentage of time that you can expect your emails to get delivered to your intended recipient on time. You want that rate to be 98% or higher. If your provider is working with Microsoft, Google, or Yahoo, your chances of this rate being high are good.

- How is the customer service? This service is a part of your marketing team, so it is critical that you have immediate access to customer support to address any issues right away.

- Do they have a 24/7 service line?

- What is your security policy?

- How is your data secured and what is your backup policy?

Knowing the answers to the previous questions will help you feel confident that if something goes wrong, you can get help quickly from the host provider.

Don't confuse an email *host* with an **email service provider** (**ESP**). As indicated, the email *host* is what allows you to send and receive email across all networks. The *ESP* is a provider that allows users to send email campaigns to a list of email users/subscribers. As email marketing becomes more and more popular, more email service providers are entering the market. To date, Outlook does not provide those services.

Email protocols

A protocol in computer science is a set of procedures and rules for transmitting data between electronic devices, such as computers. Without a set of protocols or rules, the sending and receiving computers would not be able to communicate if they were transmitting data differently.

Protocols that run your emails through the host are typically grouped into three categories, Exchange, IMAP, and POP3. Before you can install a new email account on your computer, you must know which of these three platforms you intend to use. It's also important to understand the differences between these platforms before choosing your desired method. The three protocols that we will discuss here, used for setting up an email account, will be POP3, IMAP/SMTP, and Exchange.

POP3

POP3 is used only for downloading emails from a server. **POP** stands for **Post Office Protocol**, and the number is the version. With POP3, you can choose to either delete the copy of the email on a server or retain it. The default is to delete the copy, which means the downloaded emails will only be on the device that you downloaded them to.

Once emails are downloaded, any changes made on the device, such as marking emails as read/unread and deletions, are not communicated back to a server. This means that each device that has the downloaded copy has its own standalone copy of those emails. This protocol does not work well in collaboration with others. The following figure illustrates the steps used in the retrieval process:

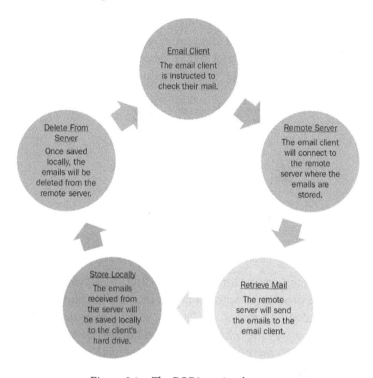

Figure 3.1 – The POP3 retrieval process

The advantages of POP3 are as follows:

- Only an internet connection is required when sending and receiving emails, which means lower bandwidth is needed.
- Some people also choose this method because they believe that since no emails are stored on a server, the data is safe from hackers.

We also have a few disadvantages with POP3:

- It is incompatible with some webmail software.
- If a hardware failure happens on the device of the download, then all the past emails will be lost.

IMAP/SMTPP

IMAP stands for **Internet Access Message Protocol**, and it mainly deals with managing and retrieving email messages from the receiving server. IMAP works together with **SMTP**, which stands for **Simple Mail Transfer Protocol** and is the standard for sending outgoing emails. Together, these two protocols receive the emails with IMAP and send the emails via SMTP.

When manually setting up an IMAP/SMTP account, you will need to provide `imap.domain.com` for the incoming server and `smtp.domain.com` for the outgoing server. The following figure illustrates the IMAP/SMTP relationship with the server:

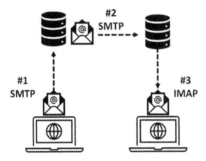

Figure 3.2 – The IMAP/SMTP process

This protocol is used when you are retrieving and sending email from multiple devices, such as a desktop at home or work, a laptop, a tablet, or a mobile phone. With IMAP/SMTP, all changes will be copied between all devices, so if you delete an email from your tablet, it will be deleted across all the other devices. An internet connection is required to access your emails using this method, and because the emails are retained on a server, limited space is required on all your devices.

A disadvantage to this protocol is that because emails are stored on a server, storage limitations can be an issue. Once your inbox is full, emails will get rejected.

Note

One important note is to not mix POP3 and IMAP.

Microsoft Exchange

Exchange is a Microsoft protocol and offers all the same functions as you would get in IMAP. It also has added features to synchronize tasks, contacts, and calendars and view them on multiple devices. If you rely heavily on collaboration among your coworkers and often work remotely, then you will benefit from using Exchange. There are no negative effects of using Exchange instead of IMAP.

The organization that provides you with a work or school email account is generally on a Microsoft Exchange server or on Microsoft 365, which uses the Microsoft Exchange server to provide you with an email account. Google also incorporates Exchange into their Gmail app for Android and with their Google calendars and meeting rooms. Large organizations can benefit from Exchange because it can support an extremely large number of users.

Setting up email accounts in Outlook

Setting up an email account can, at first, seem like an overwhelming event or task. It, however, does not have to be difficult, and Outlook has a wizard to walk you through the process step by step for most setups. If you find yourself switching between different platforms to read your emails, then you will find this to be a very efficient process.

Email account setup – automatic

Let us now understand how to setup the email account.

1. Click on **File | + Add Account** (this will open automatically if you have not set up an account yet):

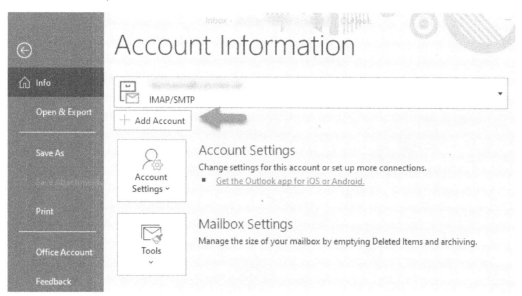

Figure 3.3 – Add Account

2. A box will appear asking for your email address. You can type in the address and Outlook will automatically connect you, using Microsoft Exchange with your Microsoft 365 account. Otherwise, enter your email address and click on **Connect**.

Figure 3.4 – Outlook email setup

The next page will give you options for setting up different types of email. The options are as follows:

A. **Office 365**

B. **Outlook.com**

C. **Exchange**

D. **Google**

E. **POP**

F. **IMAP**

G. **Exchange 2013 or earlier**

If you choose the first option, Office 365, Outlook will take a moment to automatically complete the process of adding the account. This is a big advantage of having a Microsoft 365 account. This will likely take a few moments to process, and you will see a **We're getting things ready** message on the screen. Prior to this, you will also be prompted to enter a password for the account.

Figure 3.5 – Auto setup

3. Once complete, the next page will give you an option to set up Outlook on your mobile phone, too. If you wish to add this to your mobile phone, check the box. Outlook will start the synchronization process, which can take some time.

With this, you will have Outlook email installed on your devices.

Email account setup – manual

There are times when you must manually set up an account because Outlook cannot detect the setting that you need for an automated setup. This would be the case if you are setting up an account outside of the Exchange network.

The steps to complete this manual setup are as follows:

1. Click on **File | New Account**.
2. Enter the email address for the account you want to set up.
3. Click on the drop-down arrow for **Advanced options**.

4. Click on the box to select **Let me set up my account manually**, as shown in the following figure:

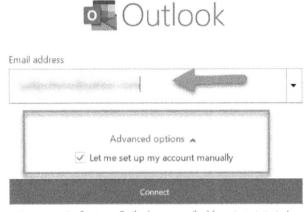

Figure 3.6 – Manual account setup

5. Click **Connect**. Next, select the type of account you are setting up and enter the appropriate settings.

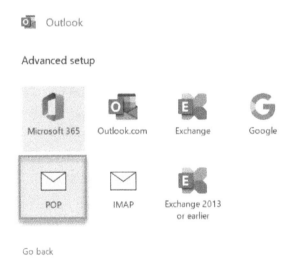

Figure 3.7 – Advanced setup accounts

6. Once you click to select the email type, the **Account Settings** box will show. You will need to locate the settings necessary for the type of account you are setting up. In this example, I am setting up a POP account for a Yahoo email address.

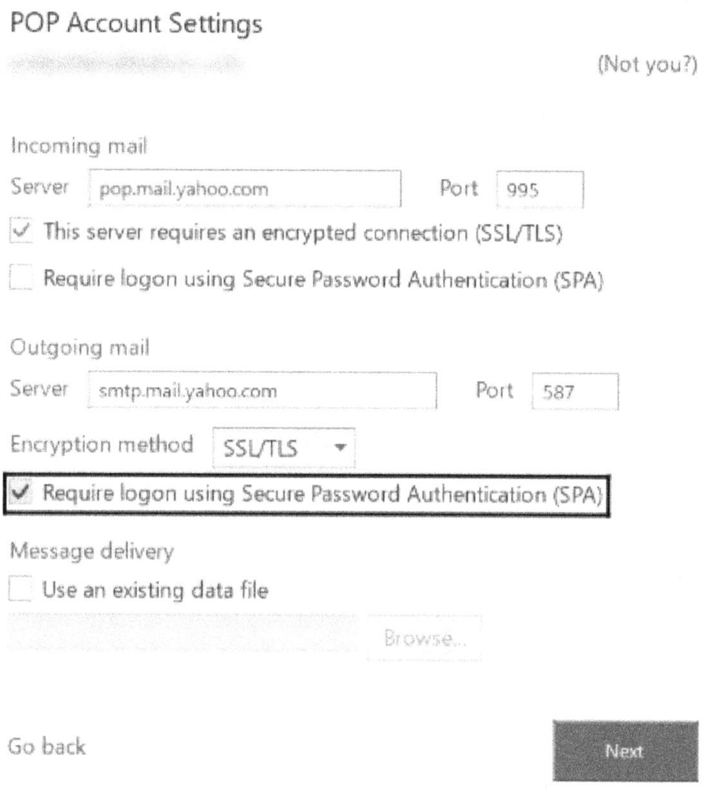

POP Account Settings

(Not you?)

Incoming mail

Server pop.mail.yahoo.com   Port 995

☑ This server requires an encrypted connection (SSL/TLS)

☐ Require logon using Secure Password Authentication (SPA)

Outgoing mail

Server smtp.mail.yahoo.com   Port 587

Encryption method   SSL/TLS   ▼

☑ Require logon using Secure Password Authentication (SPA)

Message delivery

☐ Use an existing data file

Browse...

Go back   Next

Figure 3.8 – POP account settings

7.   Enter a password for the email account you are setting up.

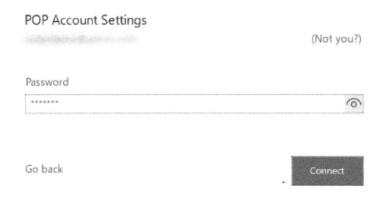

Figure 3.9 – POP Account Settings – Password

8.   Select the **Connect** button. Outlook will display the **We're getting things ready** message and set up the email account for you, providing your settings are given correctly.

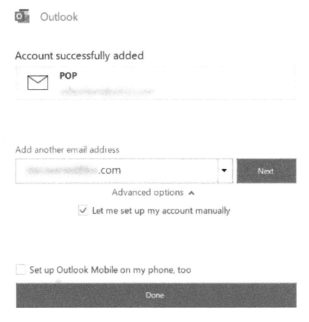

Figure 3.10 – POP account added

9. Once complete, you will get a dialogue box indicating that the account is successfully added, and you can add another account or click the **Set up Outlook Mobile on my phone, too** option.

10. Click **Done** to complete the setup. Close the **Account Settings** box.

Your email account will now be displayed in the navigation bar on the left side of the email window.

Figure 3.11 – Email added to the navigation bar

> **Note**
>
> Some apps, such as Microsoft 365, require a separate, one-time password to sign in. Go to the settings in your email program, such as Yahoo, to generate this password. Once it's generated, you will use that one-time password to sign in through the **Account Settings** password box, not the password to open the Yahoo email.

Deleting an email account from the navigation pane

1. To delete an email account from the navigation pane in the email view, right-click on the name of the email account you want to remove and select **Remove "judipickens@yahoo.com"** (containing your equivalent name).

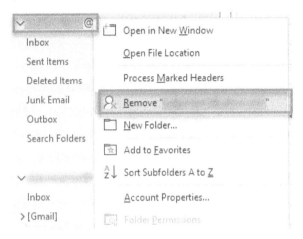

Figure 3.12 – Removing an email account

2. Click **Yes**, noting the warning that the account content will be deleted.

Microsoft Outlook

!   Careful, if you remove this account, its offline cached content will be deleted. Learn how to make a backup of the offline .ost file.

Do you want to continue?   Yes   No

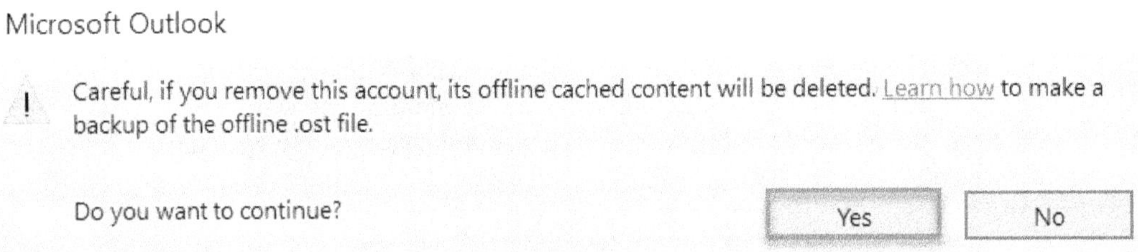

Figure 3.13 – Deleting an account

Modifying email account settings

Changing your email settings is easy inside Outlook; just follow these steps to access these settings:

1. Select **File | Account Information**.

2. Click the drop-down selection to choose the account you want to change.

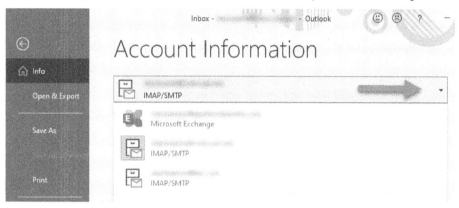

Figure 3.14 – Changing the account dropdown

3. Select **Account Settings**.

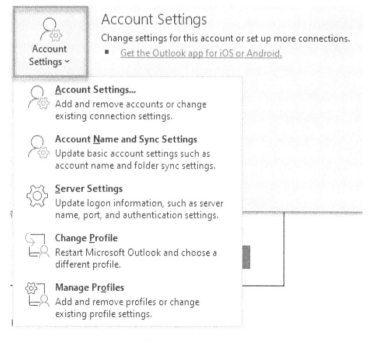

Figure 3.15 – The Account Settings dropdown

4. Select from the list the settings that you want to change:

A. **Account Settings…** – Add or remove accounts and server settings.

B. **Account Name and Sync Settings** – Update the name of the account and synchronize *x* days' worth of emails.

C. **Server Settings** – Change login information, password settings, the server name, the port, and authentication settings.

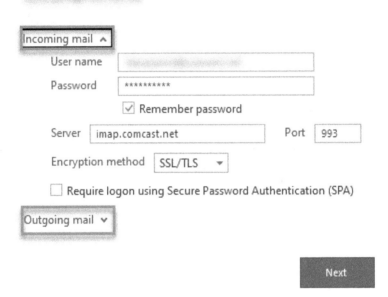

Figure 3.16 – IMAP Account Settings

D. **Change Profile** – Switch to a new profile.

E. **Manage Profiles** – Change, add, and remove profile settings.

5. Once you've made the changes, select **Next | Done**.

Changing a mail server

You have the option to send email from Gmail, Hotmail, Yahoo, or other accounts. You will need to know your provider's POP3, IMAP, and SMTP settings, as defined previously in this chapter. The following is a list of those settings for Microsoft's providers:

*Provider	POP settings	IMAP settings	SMTP settings
Microsoft 365 Outlook Hotmail Live.com	Server: outlook.office365.com Port: 995 Encryption: SSL/TLS	Server: outlook.office365.com Port: 993 Encryption: SSL/TLS	Server: smtp.office365.com Port: 587 Encryption: STARTTLS
MSN	Server: pop-mail.outlook.com Port: 995 Encryption: SSL/TLS	Server: imap-mail.outlook.com Port: 993 Encryption: SSL/TLS	Server: smtp-mail.outlook.com Port: 587 Encryption: STARTTLS

Table 3.1 – Server settings for Microsoft providers

*For providers not listed, you must reference your provider's information on their website or contact them to have them provide this information to you.

Multiple email accounts in Outlook

Have you had an event or meeting occasionally missed because of email overload? Managing several email accounts can be overwhelming. If you learn how to manage your email, this won't happen again.

Once you have added all your desired email accounts to Outlook, you can switch between them through the navigation pane on the left side of the Outlook window. This is a convenient way to scroll down and look at each email account in one location.

Figure 3.17 – The navigation pane to view different accounts

By setting up your individual email accounts and managing them in one location, you won't have to switch back and forth between your multiple accounts. You won't have to worry about forwarding your emails to another account or linking accounts together. You won't have to find an app. With this method, you can easily manage them in one location inside Outlook.

Domain names

What is a domain name? A domain name is like your digital street address. A domain, however, is a web address consisting of a website name and a domain name extension. The name is your choice if it is available and not registered to someone else. The extension is a few letters that identify the type of domain. The domain extension is like your zip code, and it gives a little more information about your website. Extensions used to be somewhat limited, but more and more extensions are now available.

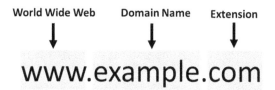

Figure 3.18 – A domain name

Once you have purchased your own custom domain name from a domain name registrar, you can add it to Microsoft 365. You must have a Microsoft 365 subscription, which is not available in the trial version of Outlook. Once connected and verified, you will be able to have the domain accept email through your Microsoft 365 account. You can purchase your domain name through several providers by using `https://www.godaddy.com/`; the procedures to connect your accounts will be simplified through the Microsoft 365 interface.

Anyone can buy a domain name through a domain name registrar. However, you can't buy just any domain – only names that are not registered by another person or business. Domain name registration is typically done on a yearly basis. However, you can prepay for up to 10 years if you want to guarantee that you will have a name for at least 10 years.

With over a billion websites registered to date, it's important to find the right one for your business brand. The following are my recommendations for choosing a domain name:

- Use `.com` whenever possible.
- Keep it short, unique, and brandable.
- Make it easy to spell and pronounce.
- Avoid double letters.
- Use domain generators for ideas.
- Act quickly before it is taken.
- Avoid using hyphens.

The following are some examples of the top extensions:

- `.com` – The most popular, indicating a for-profit business.
- `.net` – A popular alternative to `.com`. Keep in mind that some people will associate this with technology.
- `.org` – Created for a not-for-profit or information-driven business.
- `.co` – This was originally designated as a country code for Columbia but has since become a popular option for global domains. It is now used to designate a company, corporation, or commercial venture.
- `.us` – This is reserved for business operations prominently in the United States.
- `.gov` – Government agencies.
- `.edu` – Educational institutions.
- `.info` – Short for *information*.

Adding a custom domain

Adding a custom domain to your Microsoft 365 account will not only give you email with your domain but also let your users sign into Microsoft 365 services such as Exchange Online, Office 365, SharePoint Online, and Skype, using a personalized email address that matches your domain.

When you initially sign up for your Microsoft 365 subscription, Microsoft assigns your account or tenant with a default domain name. It will be a name that you choose and will look like `name.microsoft.com`. If you are in business, you will most likely use your domain for this name.

To add a custom domain, sign in to your Microsoft 365 account and ensure that you are signed in as the administrator of the account because only they have permission to add a custom domain:

1. You will have the administrator icon, as shown in the following figure, if you are signed in to your administrator account. You may need to click on the all apps option to see an expanded list of the applications, where you will also find the admin icon, as shown here:

Figure 3.19 – The admin icon

2. Once you click on the *admin* icon, the *admin center* will open.

3. Click on **Setup**.

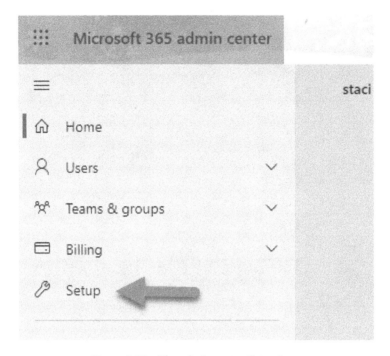

Figure 3.20 – The admin center Setup icon

4. Scroll down to **Sign-in and security**, where you will see a list of tasks that have not been completed yet.

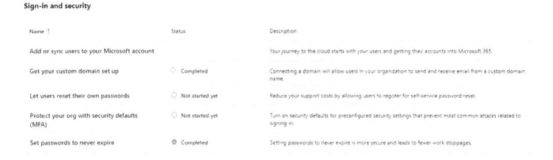

Figure 3.21 – Sign-in and security

5. Click on the **Get your custom domain set up** task. You'll have some information here on what happens when you add a custom domain to your account and specifically on how users sign on with your domain. Click **Get Started**, and the next screen will ask you to enter your domain name. (purchased previously).

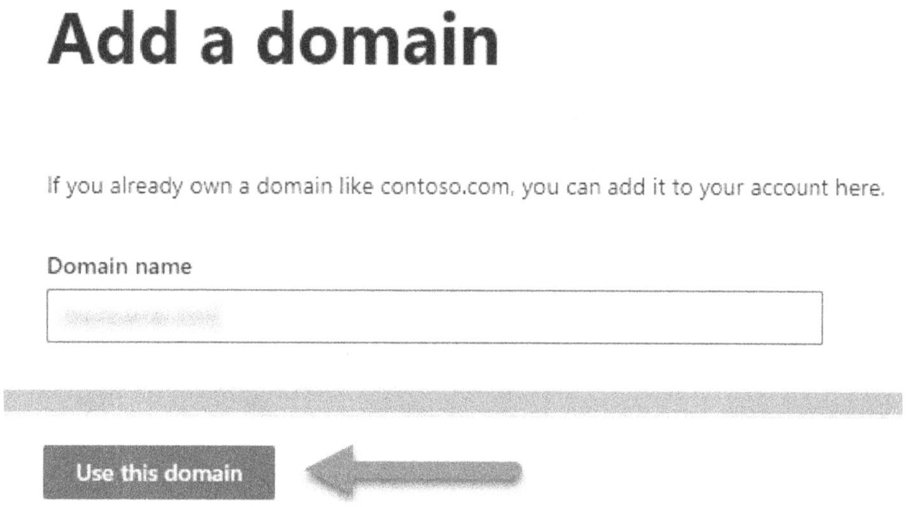

Add a domain

If you already own a domain like contoso.com, you can add it to your account here.

Domain name

[   ]

[Use this domain] ⬅

Figure 3.22 – Add a domain

If you are using a `GoDaddy.com` domain name registrar, the next screen will automatically detect whether you will see the screen asking you to verify your domain with your host/registrar. If you are using *GoDaddy*, simply select that option, and it will prompt you to sign in to your *GoDaddy* account with a username and password. Click the **Connect** button to authorize Microsoft to enable the services. Microsoft can add the DNS records if your domain name was purchased from one of the following registrars:

*   IONOS
*   EuroDNS
*   Cloudflare
*   GoDaddy
*   `WordPress.com`
*   Plesk
*   Media Temple

If you are not using one of these registrars, you can continue by selecting the option you want to use to verify your domain. This step is necessary to ensure that you do own your domain. It is a security measure put in place to secure who is setting the domain up for sending and receiving email.

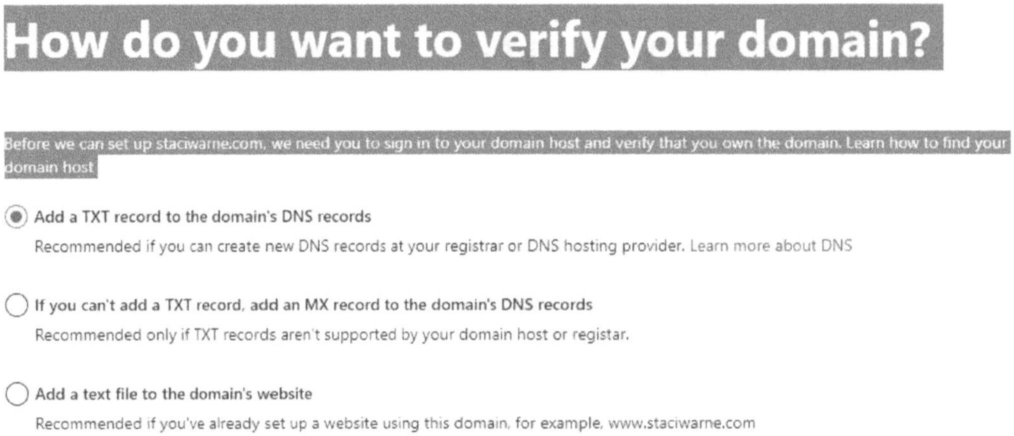

How do you want to verify your domain?

Before we can set up staciwarne.com, we need you to sign in to your domain host and verify that you own the domain. Learn how to find your domain host

◉ Add a TXT record to the domain's DNS records
Recommended if you can create new DNS records at your registrar or DNS hosting provider. Learn more about DNS

◯ If you can't add a TXT record, add an MX record to the domain's DNS records
Recommended only if TXT records aren't supported by your domain host or registar.

◯ Add a text file to the domain's website
Recommended if you've already set up a website using this domain, for example, www.staciwarne.com

Figure 3.23 – Verifying your domain

I am using a third party for this setup, so I am going to select **Add a TXT record to the domain's DNS records**. Click on the **Learn more about DNS record** link to learn more about this option from Microsoft. Once you are done, click on **Continue**.

Figure 3.24 – Verifying the domain

6. Verify with a **TXT** or **MX** record. There is a link in the **Verify you own this domain** box for step-by-step instructions.

7. Now, send the information provided by Microsoft 365 to your third-party host. My host is Nerds by Night, and they will perform these steps for my account. It is not unusual for this provider to complete these steps for you, and you need to provide them with the information that was supplied in the **Verify you own this domain** dialog box.

The information you need to have available is as follows:

- **TXT name**: @

- **TXT value**: **MS=ms######## (a unique ID from the admin center)**

- **TTL**: **3600**

The following figure demonstrates the steps necessary for this to happen:

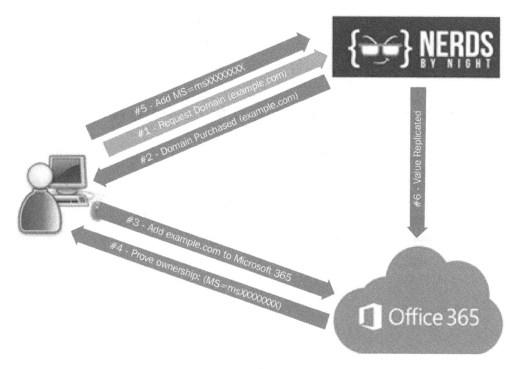

Figure 3.25 – The DNS process

These steps are as follows:

1. The administrator will request and purchase a domain from the domain name registrar.

2. If the name is available, the administrator will purchase the domain from the registrar.

3. The administrator will add the domain to the Microsoft 365 admin portal.

4. Microsoft 365 will provide the administrator with the following values:

    -   The *txt* value, which is used to prove ownership of your domain that you have purchased from a domain provider. Office 365 will give you a txt value that you or your host will need to add as a txt record on your domain/host provider website. Once added, that value will be replicated globally on the internet and your domain will be verified.

    -   The mx value, also called a mail exchange record, which is used to receive emails from external domains. This will allow your host to send your emails to Microsoft 365.

    -   The cname value, which is used by the Autodiscover service. Outlook and *Free/ Busy* are a couple of services that rely on this.

5. The administrator will provide these values to the registrar to be published on your registrar provider's website.

6. The value is replicated by Microsoft 365 and confirms that the domain is owned by the administrator.

Once these steps are complete, you can click on **Verify**, and the records show as complete in Microsoft 365 portal. You can set up a user account for email and begin sending and receiving emails using the new domain email ID.

Figure 3.26 – Domain setup is complete

> **Note**
> Up to 5,000 domains can be added to one subscription of a Microsoft 365 business account. You cannot add a domain that you are already using in another cloud service.

Summary

Many people struggle with keeping their personal and business emails together. Reducing the places where you read messages is a benefit of using Outlook. In this chapter, we discussed the benefits of using multiple email accounts within Outlook. We discussed the difference between Exchange, POP3, and IMAP/STMP accounts. We then discussed the advantages of using a domain with your email account to make your business look more professional. Outlook makes all these tasks easy and helps organize your day and save you time.

In the next chapter, we will discuss how to manage all the emails that you receive throughout the day, and we will teach you different ways to organize your personal environment inside Outlook by setting your option preferences, using color to identify important emails quickly, using flags, categories, and Quick Steps. These are some of the must-know tools for incorporating best practices into your day-to-day routine using Outlook.

Questions

1. What is the difference between Outlook and Exchange?

2. Are Gmail, Outlook, and AOL ESPs?

3. How many email accounts can I have in my Microsoft 365 account?

4. What is Outlook 365?

5. What is an Outlook profile?

Answers

1. Outlook is a software application that can be installed on your computer, tablet, and mobile devices. Its uses are to communicate and synchronize with Exchange. Exchange is the software that provides an integrated system for your email, calendaring, messaging, and tasks. The two applications, Outlook and Exchange, must work together to run Outlook. With Exchange Server, you or your IT support company maintain the server and have full control of the infrastructure, whereas with Office 365, you do not have control of it, and it is maintained by Microsoft in the cloud.

2. The simple answer is no. Despite providing access to your email, they are not email marketers and do not allow you to use email contact lists and send campaigns to subscribers. An example of this type of provider would be Mailchimp or Constant Contact, and there are several others to choose from.

3. In one Outlook account, you can add up to 20 different email accounts. These accounts do not have to be Outlook accounts; they can be Gmail, Yahoo, and various others.

4. Outlook 365 does not exist. It was rebranded as **Microsoft 365** on April 21, 2020, with the same productivity suite of services still being offered, which includes Outlook. The reason for the rebranding was the inclusion of additional software beyond the core Office software such as cloud-based productivity tools and features with artificial intelligence.

5. Profiles in Outlook are created when you set up Outlook. Most people don't realize that you can have multiple profiles and only use one profile. It is convenient to set up separate profiles to help organize your emails – for example, you can have one profile for work and another for home. If you have several people using the same computer, you can set up a separate profile for each user. To set up profiles, go to **Control Panel | Mail | Show Profiles | Add…**.

Further reading

- https://www.microsoft.com/en-us/microsoft-365/exchange/email

- https://support.microsoft.com/en-us/office/overview-of-outlook-e-mail-profiles-9073a8ac-c3d6-421d-b5b9-fcedff7642fc

4
Organizing Your Outlook Environment

There are several tools available inside Outlook to help you get organized. Many refer to this as *taking back control of your email*. If you are feeling email overload, this chapter is for you! You will gain confidence in maintaining your emails by organizing your environment with techniques you will learn in this chapter, such as taking instant action with **Quick Steps** to setting rules.

By using color, you will be able to create and use categories to color code emails, calendar items, contacts, and tasks. The more you can automate in the Outlook environment, the easier your life will be when handling loads of emails every day. This chapter is all about automation!

In this chapter, we're going to cover the following topics:

- Conversations
- Quick Steps
- Categories
- Conditional Formatting

- Flags
- Rules and alerts

Conversations

Conversations view lets you manage sent and received messages by grouping them into conversations. Turning on this view will allow you to take action on all emails in a string of conversations at once. To save space in your **Inbox**, you can also use the **Conversation Clean up** feature, which will remove emails that have identical text (that is included in the subject line of the replies).

Conversation view

To group your emails into conversations, click **View | Messages | Show as Conversations**.

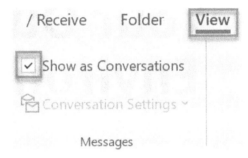

Figure 4.1 – Turning on conversations

A dialog box will open, as shown in *Figure 4.2*, asking whether you want to show messages arranged by conversations in the following places:

- **This folder**: To show conversations in the current folder, which is usually the **Inbox**
- **All mailboxes**: To show conversations in other folders, such as the **Sent Items** folder, as well

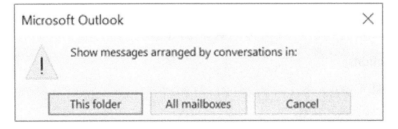

Figure 4.2 – Show messages arranged by…

In the viewing window of your **Inbox**, you will now see items shown as a single item.

1. To view all the messages in a conversation group, click the arrow icon to the left.

Figure 4.3 – Collapsed conversation

2. Click this arrow twice to see the full conversation, including your sent items, as shown in the following figure:

Figure 4.4 – Expanded conversation

When you receive a new message that is part of a conversation, this email moves to the top of the conversation message list. Unread messages will have a bold subject and the count will be displayed next to the subject.

Conversation settings

There are a few conversation settings that you can change. The checkmark toggles on and off each time you select the desired setting.

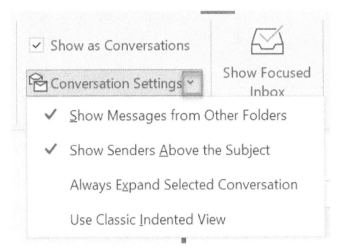

Figure 4.5 – Conversation Settings

Turn on (check) the following:

- **Show Messages from Other Folders**: To display any messages that have been moved to various folders and messages in your **Sent Items** folder.

- **Show Senders Above the Subject**: To show the sender's name above the conversation instead of showing the name in the subject.

- **Always Expand Selected Conversation**: To expand the currently selected conversation automatically when selected.

- **Use Classic Indented View**: To indent the conversation message based on what position it appears within the conversation. Outlook 2016 and later no longer use this view.

Conversation Clean Up

To keep your mailboxes cleaned up, you can run the **Conversation Clean Up** tool. You can choose to clean up a single conversation within all your folders or just from the current folder. You can adjust these settings by clicking on **Home | Clean Up**.

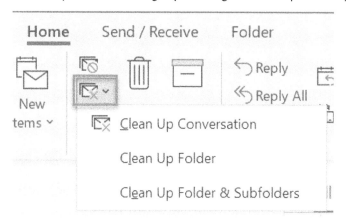

Figure 4.6 – Clean Up

This tool will remove redundant messages within the selected conversation. You will also have the option to select the **Settings** button.

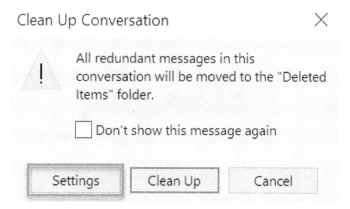

Figure 4.7 – Settings in Clean Up Conversation

By clicking on **Settings** in the **Clean Up Conversations** dialog box, an **Outlook Options** dialog box will open, and you can scroll down to the **Conversation Clean Up** section if needed. A checkmark in the box indicates that the feature is turned on.

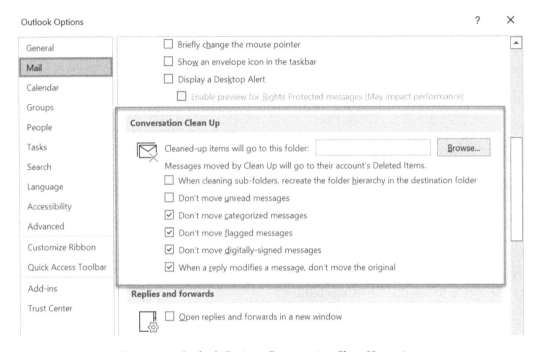

Figure 4.8 – Outlook Options Conversation Clean Up settings

> **Note**
>
> You will have to run **Conversation Cleanup** periodically yourself. It does not run automatically. To remember to do this, you may want to set up a recurring appointment.

Quick Steps

Quick Steps lets you reduce the steps you take to create a group or an item to manage your email. You can reduce several steps down to one click with Quick Steps. To set up and use Quick Steps, click **Home | Quick Steps**.

Figure 4.9 – Quick Steps

3. The first time you use **Quick Steps**, you will be prompted with the **First Time Setup** dialog box. If the quick step had been assigned an action, Outlook would have done that action instead. If you want to change the settings for the button, then you click on the dialog box launcher button at the bottom right of the **Quick Steps** section, then click **Manage Quick Steps**.

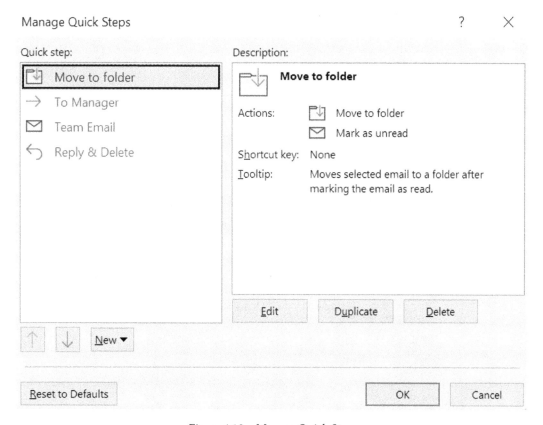

Figure 4.10 – Manage Quick Steps

4. Select the quick step that you want to change and then click **Edit**. The **Edit Quick Step** dialog box will open, and you can select the steps you want to take to have the button selected take on actions to perform when clicked on.

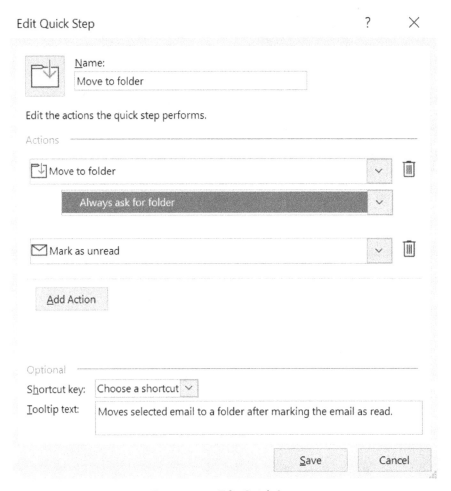

Figure 4.11 – Edit Quick Step

Six quick steps are installed with the initial setup of Outlook. You can also use the additional Quick Steps templates that are available. To use these templates, click the **Inbox** folder in the **Mail Objects** folder navigation pane, or you can press *Ctrl + Shift + I*. Choose one of these six templates and then select your desired action.

- **Move to Folder**: Moves to a specified folder.

- **Flag & Move**: Moves selected message to a specified folder, marks the message as read, and assigns the follow-up flag.

- **New Email To**: Opens a new message window with the **To** field containing the recipient's email ID.

- **Forward To**: Opens a forward message window with the **To** field containing the recipient's email ID.

- **New Meeting**: Opens a **New Meeting** window with the **To** field containing the email ID of the invitees.

- **Custom**: Opens the **Edit Quick Step** window. Create your own quick step as desired.

> **Note**
> Once you set a quick step to an email, you cannot undo the action with *Ctrl + Z* or undo commands.

Categories

All Message, Task, Calendar, Note, and Contact items can be color coded to help keep you organized. You assign a category to an object to apply an assigned color that you can customize for your system.

Applying a category

Let's learn how to apply a category:

1. Select an email message and click **Home | Categorize**.

Figure 4.12 – Categorize

2. Select a color or category to use.

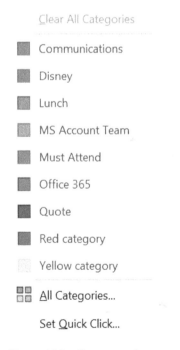

Figure 4.13 – Category colors

3. You can also click on **All Categories…** to customize the list of colors to your liking. Using the buttons on the right side of the **Color Categories** dialog box allows you to create a new category, rename categories, delete categories, change the color, and apply a shortcut key.

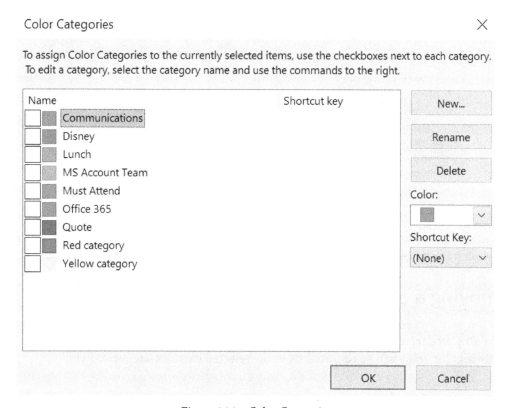

Figure 4.14 – Color Categories

4. Once the category has been assigned to the email, you will be able to view the color in the **Category** field in the inbox.

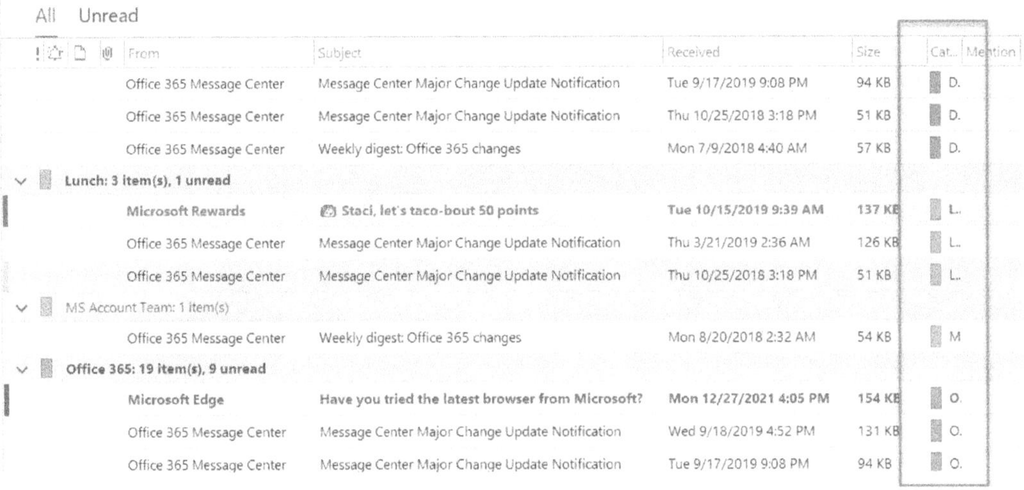

Figure 4.15 – Inbox with Category field

Now we can learn how to remove a category.

Removing a category

Select the item that you want to remove the category from, then select **Home | Categorize | Clear all Categories**, or you can right-click the category and choose **Clear All Categories**. The color will be removed from the selected email's **Categories** field.

Conditional Formatting

Applying different formatting to messages can help you view and read your email messages faster. When you see a specific color or formatting applied, you will know what the message is regarding or possibly who it is coming from. To apply this formatting automatically, you can use **Conditional Formatting**. This tool is also available in other Microsoft applications. But it is used and turned on differently within Outlook. With **Conditional Formatting** in Outlook, create the condition by clicking on **View | View Settings**.

Default Conditional Formatting rules

When you open your **Inbox**, you have probably noticed your email messages are bold if you have not clicked on the message to open it. You may have also noticed that once you click on a message and view it, the bold format goes away, and it appears in normal text. This applied formatting is the effect of a **Conditional Formatting** rule. These are examples of two of the eight preconfigured **Conditional Formatting** rules that are set up by Outlook by default.

To view and apply these rules, first click **View | View Settings**. This will display the **Advanced View Settings** dialog box. Click the **Conditional Formatting…** button.

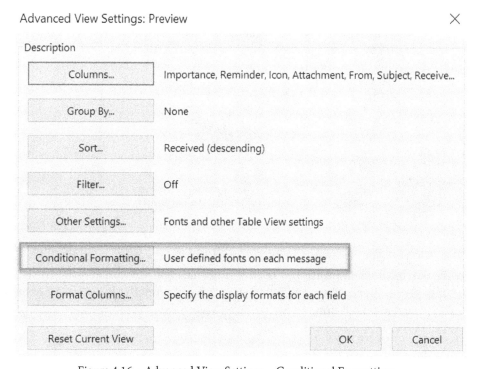

Figure 4.16 – Advanced View Settings – Conditional Formatting…

Selecting the **Conditional Formatting...** button will open the **Conditional Formatting** dialog box. The default rules will be displayed in the **Rules for this view** section. When you click on one of the rules, the properties of the rule will be displayed in the bottom box.

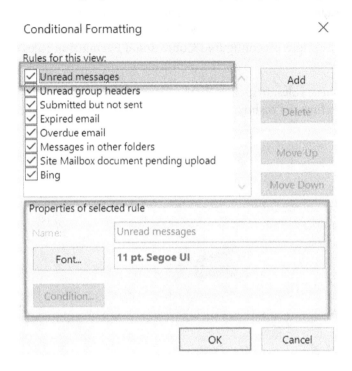

Figure 4.17 – Conditional Formatting rules

These are the seven default **Conditional Formatting** rules that you can apply in the Outlook 2021 version. In previous versions, there were eight, but the **Bing** rule, as shown in *Figure 4.17*, is not a default now.

The seven default rules are as follows:

- Unread messages
- Unread group headers
- Submitted but not sent
- Expired email
- Overdue email

- Messages in other folders

- Site Mailbox document pending upload

Each selected rule will apply the assigned font settings from the rule to any messages that match the specified rule, that is, unread messages will have a bold blue font applied to the message.

To turn off the rule, click in the selection box to the left of the rule's name. It will still be available to you if you wish to enable it later. You can also make changes to the properties or formatting of these rules by clicking on the **Font…** button for the selected rule.

Click the **Add** button to create a new **Conditional Formatting** rule.

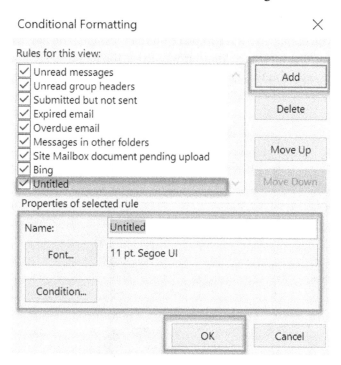

Figure 4.18 – Adding a new rule

Now, you can make changes to the default rule. You can use the following options to make changes:

- **Name**

- **Font…**

- **Condition…**

To create rules beyond **Conditional Formatting**, see the *Rules and alerts* section of this chapter.

Flags

Attach a flag to a message to mark its importance or to set a reminder to follow up or come back to it later.

Steps to set a flag

Let's understand the steps in detail:

1. Select the message you want to attach the flag to. Select **Home | Follow Up**.

2. Choose the type of flag you want to place on the message. The flag will appear in the flag field for that message. Another way to set the flag is to right-click on the flag in the message. You will get a drop-down menu and you can select the flag from this list.

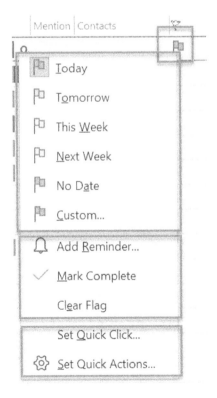

Figure 4.19 – Right-click menu for flag

The right-click menu has the **Add Reminder…**, **Mark Complete**, **Clear Flag**, and **Set Quick Click…** options.

3. When you select **Add Reminder…**, you will get the **Custom** dialog box.

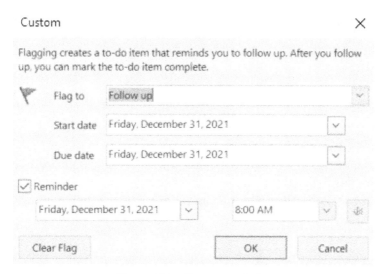

Figure 4.20 – Custom reminder

4. This **Custom** dialog box helps you to set up flags, reminders, and dates and times for reminders. There is also a **Clear Flag** button if you no longer want to have the flag. Click **OK** and at the designated time, Outlook will display a reminder for the email message as set by you.

5. If you find yourself always wanting to apply a specific flag instead of right-clicking on the flag field, you can use **Set Quick Click…**. You can set this from the right-click menu on the flag field.

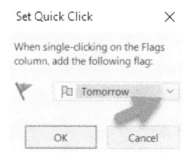

Figure 4.21 – Set Quick Click

6. Click the drop-down selector for the flag and you will see a list of the possible flags.

7. Select the one you want to set as a quick click. When you click on the flag, instead of right-clicking, use a left-click and that flag will be applied to the message. When you click on the flag a second time, it will change the flag to a checkmark, indicating that the message is complete and the flag is no longer applied.

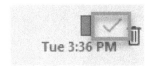

Figure 4.22 – Flag complete

Flags are very useful if you like reminders. They are a great way to remind you that you need to take action on an item. Let's now discuss how to use rules and alerts, which not only are useful for flagging items in your email but also give you the power to stay up to date and organized by automatically managing your mail before those messages arrive in your mail folders.

Rules and alerts

Create rules to move, flag, and respond to email messages automatically. Rules typically process your emails as they arrive in your **Inbox**. Some examples of rules you can create are as follows:

- Move email to a folder

- Play a sound

- Display a new item alert

- Set a flag

- Multiple steps combined

Creating rules

The steps to create a rule to apply to a selected email ID are as follows:

1. Select a message that you would like to base the rule on. (Only select a message if you want the rule to be based on that type of message.)

2. Click **Home** | **Rules** | **Create Rule….** (This is also found on the right-click menu of a message.)

Rules
OneNote
Assign Policy
Unread/ Read
Categorize
Follo Up
Always Move Messages From: Microsoft Store
Create Rule...
Manage Rules & Alerts...

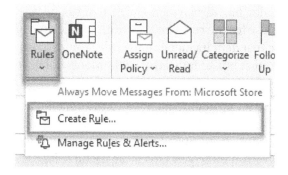

Figure 4.23 – Create Rule…

3. In the **Create Rule** dialog box, check the boxes that you want to include in the rule. Notice that because I right-clicked on the message from Microsoft Edge, that option appears as **From Microsoft Edge**; I clicked the checkbox to select that option to verify that is what I want.

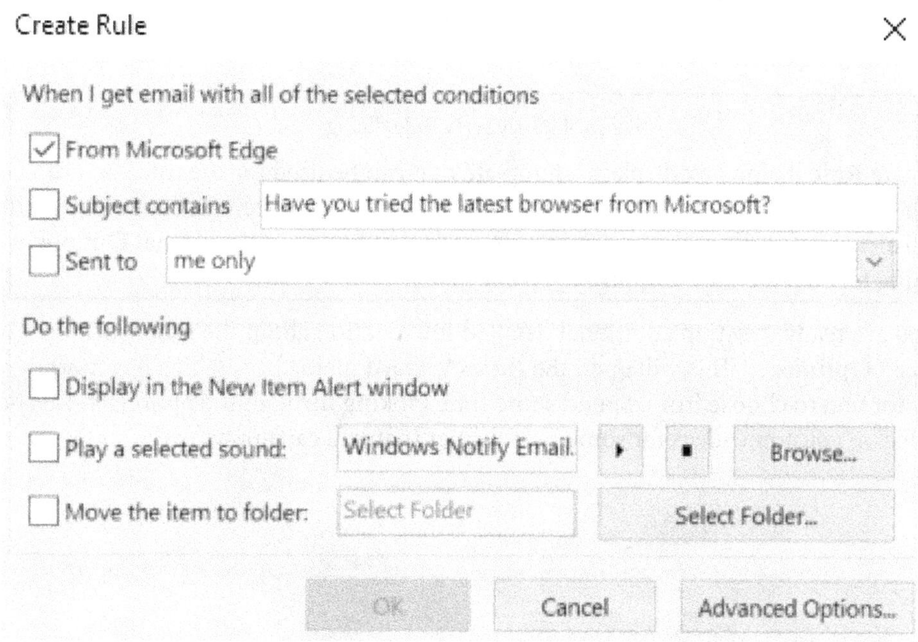

Create Rule
When I get email with all of the selected conditions
From Microsoft Edge
Subject contains
Have you tried the latest browser from Microsoft?
Sent to
me only
Do the following
Display in the New Item Alert window
Play a selected sound:
Windows Notify Email.
Browse...
Move the item to folder:
Select Folder
Select Folder...
OK
Cancel
Advanced Options...

Figure 4.24 – Create Rule

4. The **Create Rule** dialog box displays a template that can be used to prompt you for possible options to use for the rule you are creating. Click the box to the left of the suggestions to have that item included in the rule. You will also need to fill in the information next to that box to indicate what Outlook will be looking for to match the condition you specify.

5. Now you are ready to set up additional detailed information about the rule. Click on **Advanced Options….** This will open the **Rules Wizard** dialog box, which has more options for you to choose from. Spend some time looking through the options in this box as it will give you some ideas for some useful rules that you can apply.

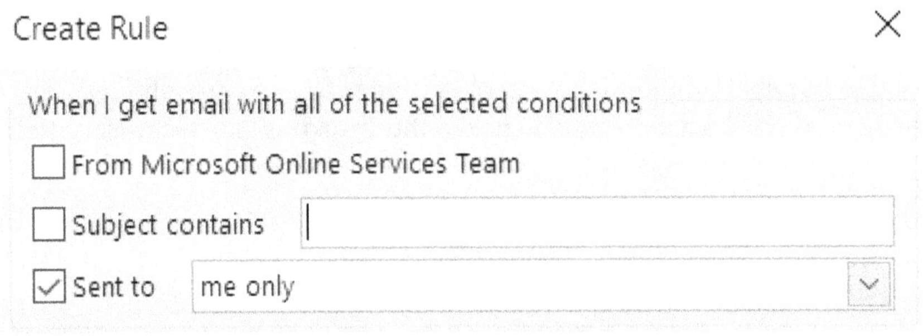

Figure 4.25 – Create Rule dialog

The **Create Rule** dialog box displays a template that can be used for the rule you are creating. Click the box to the left of the suggestions to have that item included in the rule. You will also need to fill in the information next to that box to indicate what Outlook will be looking for to match the condition you specify.

Now you are ready to set up additional detailed information about the rule. Click on **Advanced Options….** This will open the **Rules Wizard** dialog box, which has more options for you to choose from. Spend some time looking through the options in this box as it will give you some ideas for some useful rules that you can apply.

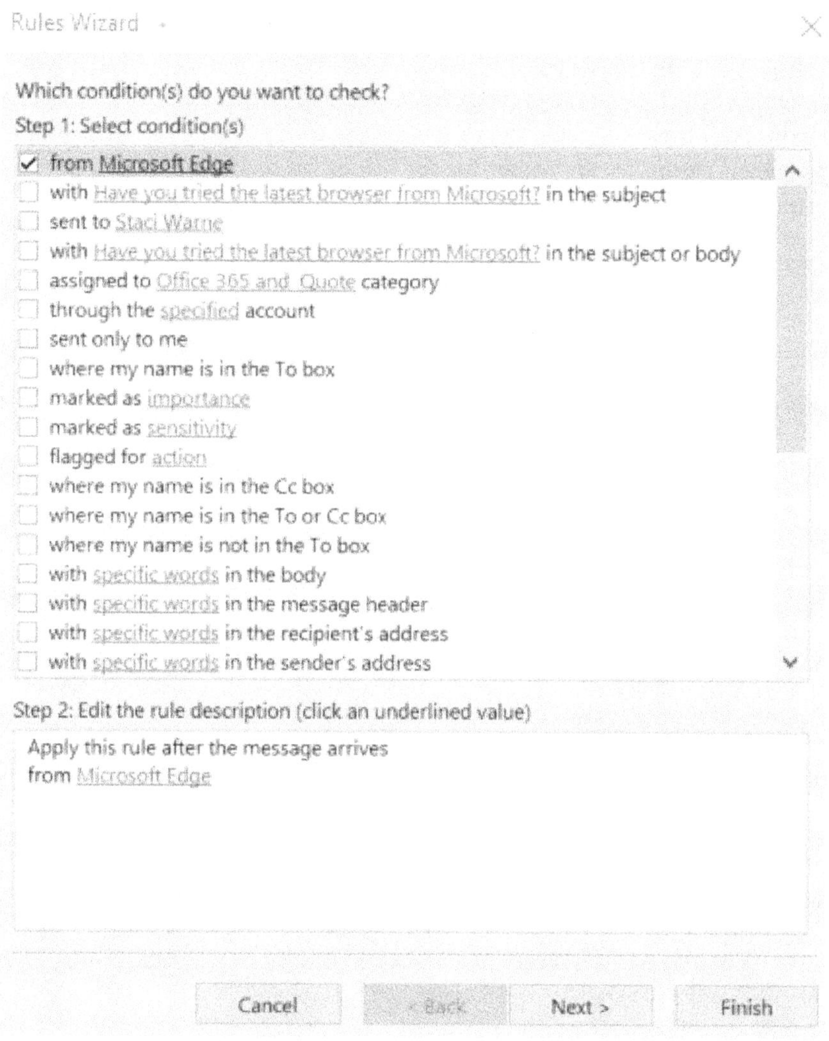

Rules Wizard   ·   ✕

Which condition(s) do you want to check?

Step 1: Select condition(s)

- ✓ from Microsoft Edge   ∧
- ☐ with Have you tried the latest browser from Microsoft? in the subject
- ☐ sent to Staci Warne
- ☐ with Have you tried the latest browser from Microsoft? in the subject or body
- ☐ assigned to Office 365 and Quote category
- ☐ through the specified account
- ☐ sent only to me
- ☐ where my name is in the To box
- ☐ marked as importance
- ☐ marked as sensitivity
- ☐ flagged for action
- ☐ where my name is in the Cc box
- ☐ where my name is in the To or Cc box
- ☐ where my name is not in the To box
- ☐ with specific words in the body
- ☐ with specific words in the message header
- ☐ with specific words in the recipient's address
- ☐ with specific words in the sender's address   ∨

Step 2: Edit the rule description (click an underlined value)

Apply this rule after the message arrives
from Microsoft Edge

Cancel	< Back	Next >	Finish

Figure 4.26 – Advanced Rules Wizard

When you click on the box to select the item to include in the rule in **Step 1**, more information will appear in the **Step 2** box that follows. When you click on the blue hyperlinked items in the box, another **Search Text** box will open where you can enter the specific words or phrases of what the rule is asking for. It is very intuitive, and I have found that just letting the wizard prompt me for responses has helped me to successfully apply these rules.

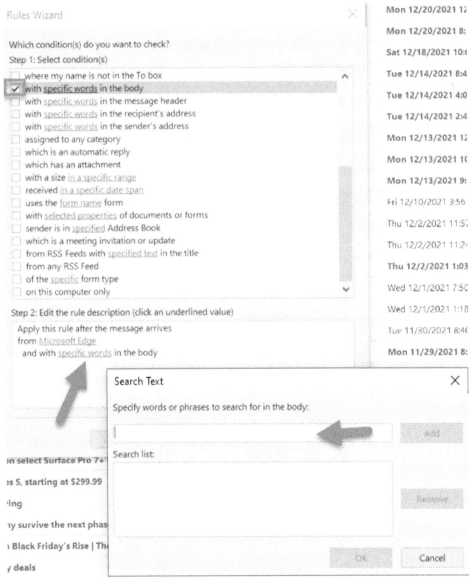

Figure 4.27 – Search Text dialog box

Now, let's understand how we can manage rules.

Managing rules

To maintain your rules, click **Home | Rules | Manage Rules & Alerts**. You may also right-click and then select **Rules | Manage Rules and Alerts**.

The **Rules and Alerts** dialog box will display with the email's **Rules** tab activated. If you don't have an email to begin with, this is another option to create a rule from scratch. From this window, you can do the following:

- Create a new rule.

- Change a rule.

- Delete a rule.

- Copy a rule.

- Move the selected rule.

- Run the rule now.

- Access options to import and export rules from previous versions of Outlook or upgrade.

Rules can be a real time saver; they are extremely important to set up and are especially useful if you want to streamline the emails that come into your **Inbox**.

In *Chapter 14, Nine Useful Rules*, we will go over suggestions for useful rules to use for your business email account.

Summary

This chapter was all about saving you time and automating those tasks that you find yourself doing repeatedly. These chores become a thing of the past when you apply these automation techniques. You can use **Quick Steps** with one click or use rules to process while you're away from Outlook. The formatting and routing of messages can be done with categories and flags to cause messages to stand out so you don't miss an event or deadline again.

In the next chapter, we will discuss a few of Outlook's advanced tips and tricks for sending emails with **Mail Merge** to customize emails for our recipients. We will discuss using color flyers and creating forms and we will save them as templates to use over and over again with ease.

Questions

1. What is the difference between **Quick Steps** and **Quick Parts**?

2. What is the focused inbox feature?

3. Can I set more than one category for an email message?

4. What is the shortcut to go to the next email when you have an email opened?

5. How does flagging a message work with **To-Do List**?

Answers

1. **Quick Parts, New Email | Insert | Quick Parts**, are messages/text that can be inserted into a new email without retyping the text. **Quick Steps** is preformatted actions that are assigned to a button to streamline a task, as was discussed in this chapter.

2. You can turn the focused inbox on or off by going to **View | Show Focused Inbox**. Turning this on will show tabs for **Focused** and **Other** at the top of the **Inbox**. Bulk emails will be pushed to the **Other** folder so that you can use the focused inbox just for important emails. If an email gets through that you don't want in **Focused**, simply right-click on the message and choose **Move to Non-Focused**.

3. There are 25 color tiles available to apply a category to an email message. You can assign the same color to multiple emails.

4. Within an email, to switch to the next email, use *Ctrl + .* (period). To switch back to the previous email, use *Ctrl + ,* (comma).

5. Flagging an email message also adds a task to the **To-Do List** folder. If you delete the message, it also disappears from **To-Do List**. Don't confuse **To-Do List** with a task. A task is an Outlook item that is saved to a task folder. However, **To-Do List** contains all flagged items plus tasks, allowing users to see a list of all items that need to be actioned.

5
Outlook Mail Merge

There are many features of Microsoft 365 that allow you to automate several of your tasks. **Mail Merge** is included in this. If you find yourself writing the same email over and over to different recipients each time, then this is a chapter you won't want to skip. You can save hours upon hours by utilizing the techniques taught in this chapter. Mail Merge is used to send bulk emails, letters, labels, or envelopes to several email accounts and you will be able to personalize the information for each email ID.

We will start by creating a simple mail merge using our contacts information from within Outlook. After that, we will create a more advanced mail merge by first creating an Excel spreadsheet to act as a container to hold our merge information to start our mail merge to send custom invoices to our clients. This will include changing the invoice for each client based on the last name, which we will process through Power Automate.

We will be covering the following topics in this chapter:

- Creating a mail merge in Outlook
- Mail Merge custom attachments, Cc, Bcc, and Subject

Let's begin with examining **Mail Merge**.

Mail Merge

Mail Merge in Outlook allows you to send a message to a large group of people at once without the recipient knowing who else received the message. In many cases, the recipient will not know you sent it to others and will think they were the only one who received the message from you. With Mail Merge, the recipient will only see their own name in the **To** field of the email. It is also possible to personalize other fields within the message or even have attachments personalized as well. Many people try to be discreet in not allowing the recipient to know who the other recipients are by entering the email IDs in the **Bcc** field.

Creating a mail merge in Outlook

There are 10 steps involved in creating a mail merge in Outlook that can be sent via email. These steps are very straightforward and will be described here as we create a mail merge to be sent by email:

1.   The first step is to select **Contacts** in the navigation pane.

2.   Select the contacts that you want to send the email to, or you can select the location of an Excel list or another type of list that contains those names and data. In order to select the **Mail Merge** feature inside of Outlook, you need to select the **Contacts** folder. Another option for this step is to start **Mail Merge** from Microsoft Word.

3.   The next step is to start Mail Merge. Go to **Home | Mail Merge**.

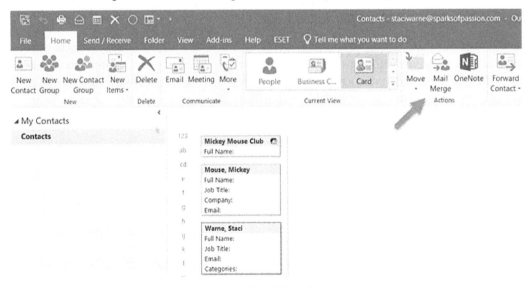

Figure 5.1 – Mail Merge button

4. Next, we must verify that the correct options are selected for **Mail Merge Contacts**.

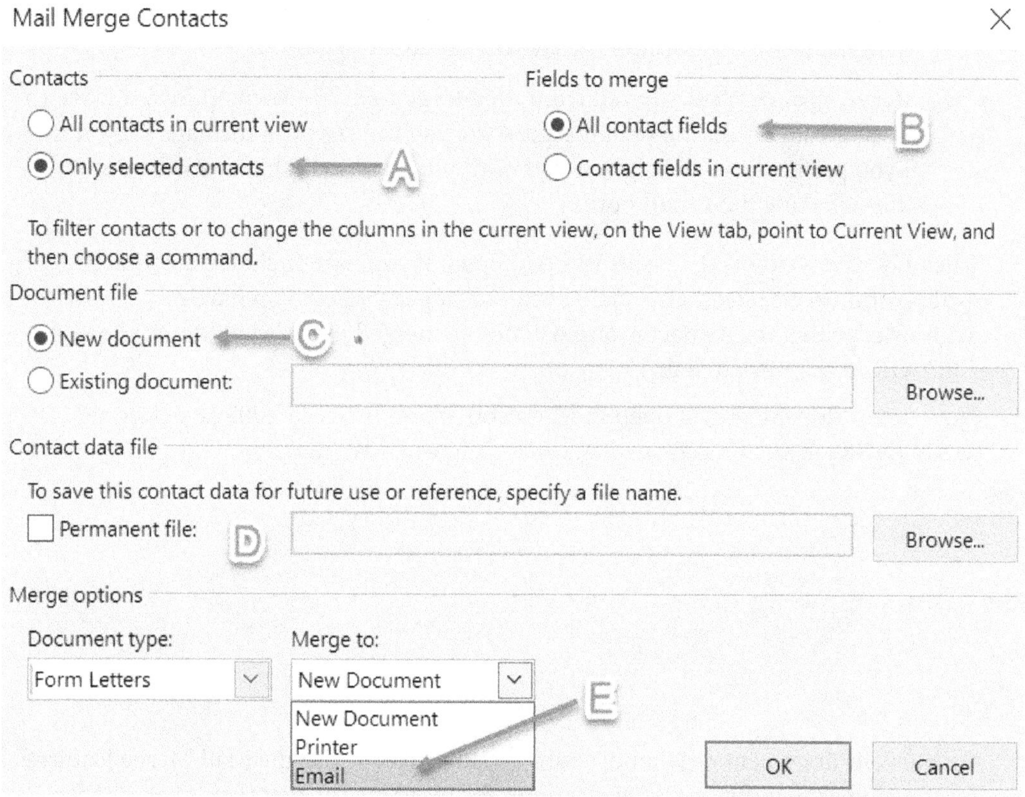

Figure 5.2 – Mail Merge Contacts

The following are the selections that should be made for our mail merge:

- **(A) Contacts**: Select **Only selected contacts** because we selected the contacts at the start of this mail merge.

- **(B) Fields to merge**: Select **All contact fields** to include all of the Outlook fields to use as a possible field in the mail merge. We do not have to use all the fields but they will be available to us if wanted. If you filtered the contacts information, you could choose **Contact fields in current view**.

- **(C) Document file**: Select **New document,** which will start a new document in Microsoft Word. If you have already created a document with the message entered or have a previous email saved in your system, then you should select **Existing document** and you need to specify the location of the file.

- **(D) Contact data file**: No selection is needed in this section for this mail merge. You should use **Permanent file** and enter the location for the file to be saved if you want to save this contact data for future use, or you could click **Browse...** to find a name and location to save the file to.

- **(E) Merge options**: Select **Email** from the **Merge to** drop-down options to have an email created from the mail merge. Also, you can supply a message subject line if you prefer. You will be given that option later as well; this box will appear after selecting the **Email** option.

5. Click **OK** and wait for Microsoft Word to open. If you have included a contact group within your selection, a dialog box will appear, where you have to acknowledge that the contact group will not be merged in the Mail Merge process. Click **OK** to acknowledge this.

6. Now, a new document will open in Microsoft Word. In Word 2007 and later, the **MAILINGS** tab will be activated automatically when Word opens.

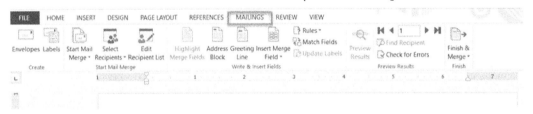

Figure 5.3 – MAILINGS tab in Word

7. Create your document as you normally would in Word. Use the Mail Merge features on the toolbar to insert a special character for inserting the text that is specific for each email (such as a name). If you selected to get this information from another document, such as Excel, the headers from that file will be available to you under the **Insert Merge Field** dropdown.

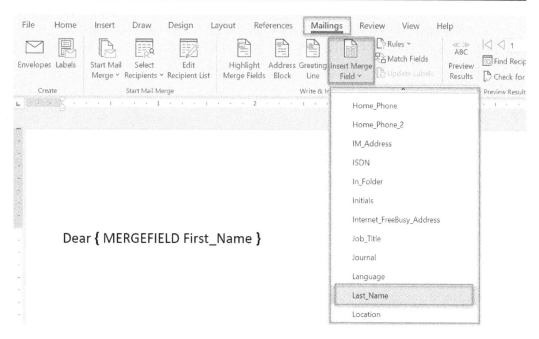

Figure 5.4 – Insert Merge Field in a Word document

8. Upon completion of the email, it is best to preview what it is going to look like when merged on each email. For this, select the **Preview Results** button, then you can use the arrow buttons in the ribbon to browse through all the personalized emails to check that they're correct. Click **Finish & Merge | Send Email Messages….**

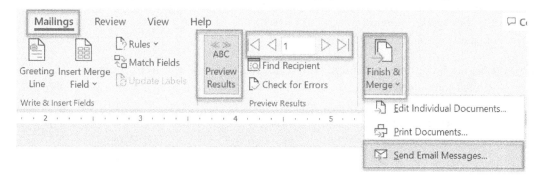

Figure 5.5 – Send Email Messages...

9. In the **Merge to E-mail** dialog box, you can enter text in the **Subject line** field if you did not specify this earlier. You can also change and/or verify that the other settings are correct.

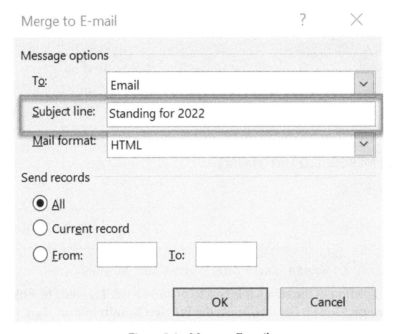

Figure 5.6 – Merge to E-mail

10. Click **OK** to complete the mail merge to send the emails. Be sure you are ready to have the emails delivered or sent, as once you click **OK**, the emails will be generated and sent without warning.

Mail Merge is a technique that sounds more complicated than it is in my opinion. The time efficiency that is saved with this process can enhance your productivity. Many people know that a mail merge can also be created in Word, but few people think of sending the document created as an email through Outlook.

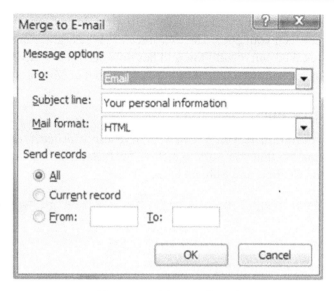

Figure 5.7 – Merge to E-mail

We will now create a mail merge using Power Automate to allow us to send merged attachments along with the mail merge.

> **Note**
>
> Verify with your *ISP* or *mail administrator* that you aren't restricted regarding how many email messages you can send within an hour or in total in a day. You may have this restriction set on your account limits. If you keep your emails to under 100 messages a day, you probably will not run into any issues and there is probably no need to contact your ISP in this case. If there is a limit set, you may want to consider sending out a mail merge in smaller groups over several days or using a *third-party email marketing company*.

Mail Merge custom attachments, Cc, Bcc, and Subject

One disadvantage of the **Mail Merge** process is we cannot send attachments with the emails that we send out automatically. You can download some VBA/macro code to do this, or you can download some paid or free add-ins that will allow this as well. I'm going to teach you how to do this for free using Microsoft Power Automate.

For this example, we want to have a customized *PDF invoice file* as the attachment in the email that goes to each customer. For this example, Phil Barr will have a file called `Invoice_PhilBarr.pdf` as the attachment. If you want, you can also customize the subject line to say `Barr Invoice`. This will be customized for each email as the name changes.

Power Automate is a Microsoft app that can save you a great deal of time in the automation process between your apps. The user interface is easy and fun to use. This application used to be called Microsoft Flow and has now been rebranded as Power Automate, so you may see some documentation referring to it as Microsoft Flow.

Creating a spreadsheet

Before you open Power Automate, you will want to have a spreadsheet created that includes all the information that you want to include for the attachments or dynamic text that you will use in the **Cc**, **Bcc**, and **Subject** lines.

	A	B	C	D	E
1	First Name	Last Name	email	File name	Date
2	Phil	Barr		Invoice_PhilBarr.pdf	1/2/2022
3	Alix	Witt		Invoice_AlixWitt.pdf	3/2/2022
4	Abbey	Inns		Invoice_AbbeyInns.pdf	2/14/2022
5	Chevy	Pool		Invoice_ChevyPool.pdf	1/15/2022
6	Judi	Pickens		Invoice_JudiPickens.pdf	2/22/2022
7					

Figure 5.8 – Excel document for Mail Merge with Power Automate

For the attachments on the Excel spreadsheet, you will include the *filename* of the documents that you want to be merged with the email IDs that will be completed. The actual file needs to be saved in OneDrive in the cloud along with the Excel file to be merged.

You must also select the data in the Excel file and convert it into a table. To do this, click inside the data (assuming you have no blank rows or columns; if you do have these, clean up your data first to remove the blanks), then select **Insert | Table**. The table will now be highlighted, and you can confirm that the **Where is the data for your table?** option has provided the correct cell address. In this example, we will have *cells A1:E6*, written as $A$1:$E$6. Ensure that the box is checked for **My table has headers** and then click **OK**. Once you do this step, it will be formatted as a table. You can adjust the styles as desired.

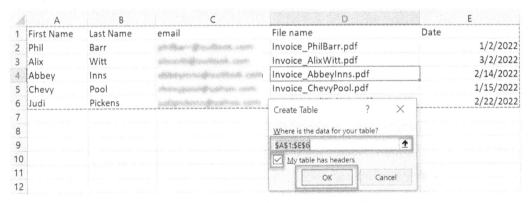

Figure 5.9 – Where is the data for your table?

Assign the table a name by clicking on **Table Design** | the **Table Name** box. I have named my file `TableData`. If you do not see the **Table Design** tab, ensure you have clicked inside the table in Excel. This tab is only viewed when you have clicked on your data in Excel.

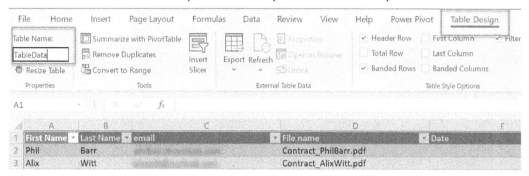

Figure 5.10 – Table Name

Mail Merge with Power Automate

Let's see how to use Mail Merge with Power Automate:

1. Open Microsoft Power Automate, which you will find in the *apps menu* for your `office.com` account. This will also work for the free version of `outlook.com`. I will be demonstrating with screenshots from a Microsoft 365 account. You can access the apps menu from the waffle icon in the top left of your screen. You typically must do this the first time you use a new app. Click on **Power Automate**.

Figure 5.11 – Power Automate icon

You may see some links for what you are trying to complete if you were looking up this topic outside of Power Automate.

2. Click on the **Create** button to start a new flow or process to create.

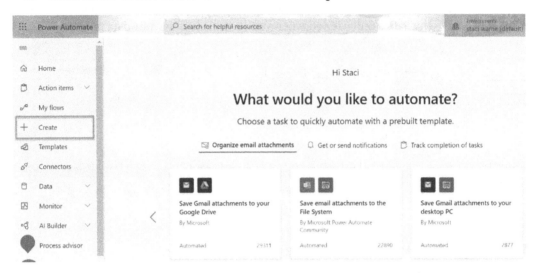

Figure 5.12 – Creating a flow

3. Next, decide what you want to create and what trigger you want to set. Our trigger will be from an Excel file with rows that we will select, so we need to go to the **Start from blank** section and select **Instant cloud flow**.

Figure 5.13 – Instant cloud flow

4. Scroll down the list of options on the right-side menu.

5. Select **For a selected row**, which will trigger a flow for a selected row in an Excel table. Before you click **Create**, give the flow a name in the **Flow name** box; name it `Mail Merge with Attachment`.

6. Now, click **Create**.

Build an instant cloud flow

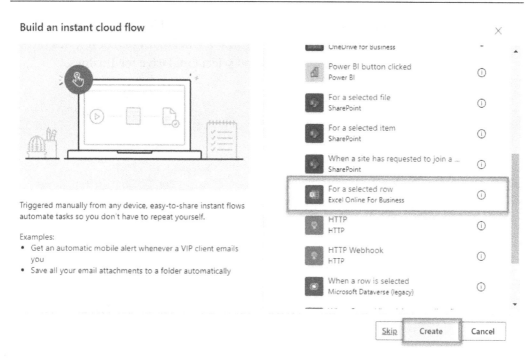

Figure 5.14 – Flow for a selected row in Excel

7. In the **For a selected row** dialog box, enter text for **Location**, **Document Library**, **File**, and **Table** for the Excel file. After filling in the data requested, click the **+ New step** button, as shown in *Figure 5.15*:

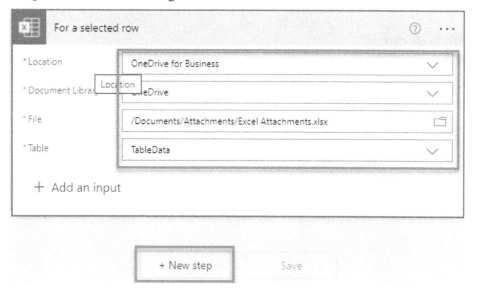

Figure 5.15 – For a selected row

Now, we need to add the ability to look through files in a folder and find the appropriate invoice to attach to each email. This is a OneDrive operation. Click on the **Standard** tab, as shown in *Figure 5.16*, and select **OneDrive for Business**:

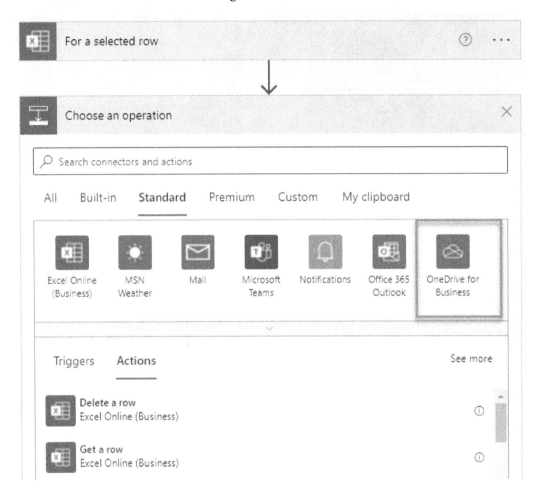

Figure 5.16 – Choosing OneDrive for Business

8. The action that we need is **List files in folder**, which appears in the list of actions for OneDrive for Business.

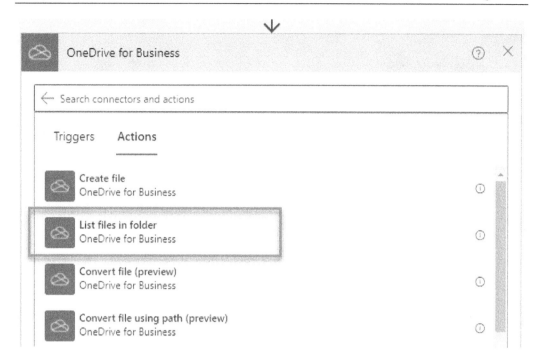

Figure 5.17 – List files in folder action

9. You will now be prompted to sign in to OneDrive and then populate the **List files in folder** box. To do this, click on the folder icon and then select the folder in OneDrive where you have the attachments saved.

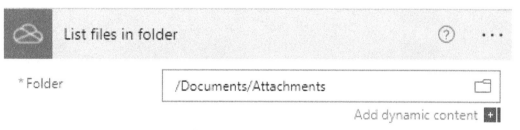

Figure 5.18 – Folder location of files

10. Now, we need to click + **New step** to apply a control that will check the attached file too.

11. Click **Control | Apply to each**.

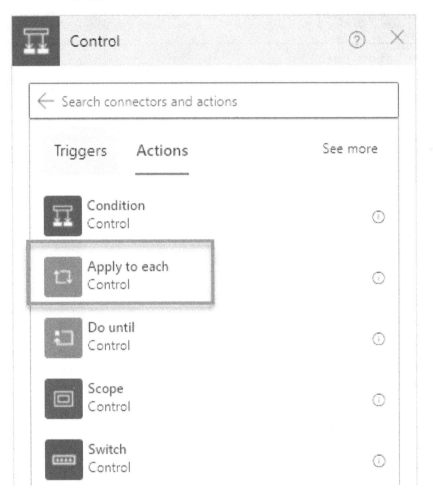

Figure 5.19 – Apply to each

12. In the **Apply to each** dialog box, click on the **Add dynamic content** button and choose **value**. What this is indicating is that for each row in the Excel spreadsheet (**Apply to each** control), complete a loop that will apply an invoice (**value**: list of items) to the email.

Figure 5.20 – value

13. Now, add another condition control by clicking **+ New step | Control | Condition** to cross-check the name with the name you have in the Excel file. This time, we will select the **File_Name** column from the Excel file. If it finds the value in the OneDrive folder that matches the filename in the Excel spreadsheet, the Yes condition will be met; otherwise, the No condition will be met, so we want to choose a dynamic field here. For **File name**, choose **is equal to** and then choose **Display ....**

14. Next, select the **Add an action** button to add a Yes condition. We will not need to set a No condition as we don't want anything to happen if there is not a matching file.

Figure 5.21 – Condition

15. There are two conditions or actions to apply here under the `Yes` condition:

- Retrieve the file content for the attached copy if the filenames match.

- Send the emails. Click **+ Add an action** under the **If yes** condition, then search for `OneDrive for Business` and choose **Get file content**.

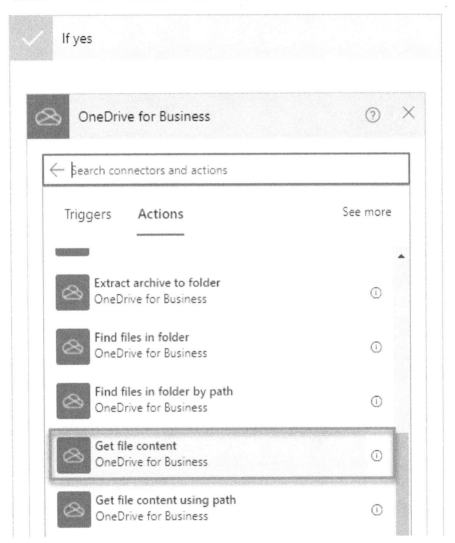

Figure 5.22 – Get file content

16. The unique identifier for this will be **Id**, so click the **Add dynamic content** button and choose **Id**.

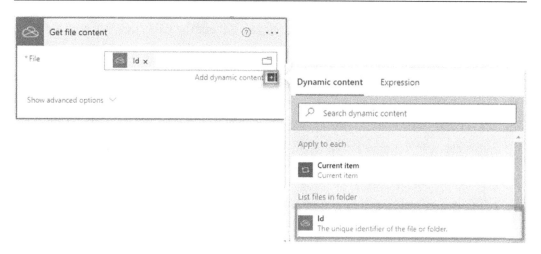

Figure 5.23 – Unique identifier

17. The next condition is for Outlook 365 to send the email. Click **Add an action |
Office 365 Outlook | Send an email (V2)**.

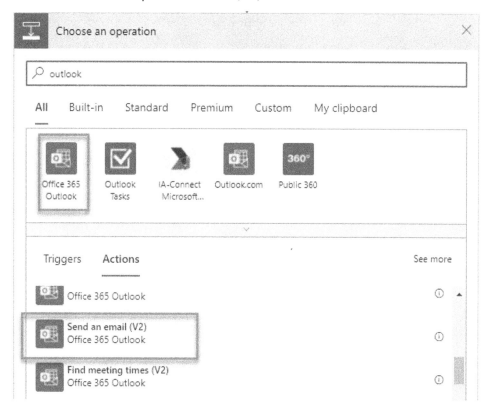

Figure 5.24 – Send an email (V2) action

This dialog box is where you write your email. Fill out the fields that you wish to include and be sure to use dynamic fields where desired. You also need to include spaces where you want a space between the dynamic field and the text you are typing in manually. An example here would be on the **Subject** line: after selecting the **Last Name** dynamic field, add a space and then type Invoice. Next, enter the email in the **Body** field of the message using dynamic controls as desired.

In this example, we have also filled in **Attachment Name** as well as **Attachment Content** for the attachment. This will show us the name of the file as well as the attached file content. We are simply telling Outlook what to attach for each email ID in the spreadsheet. You may also change the **Importance** field to **Normal** as it will email out as *low importance* if you do not change this control.

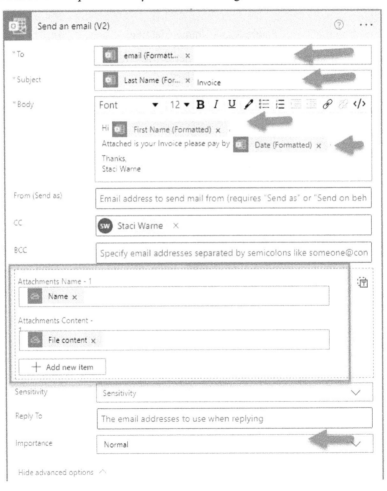

Figure 5.25 – Send an email (V2)

That will complete our flow. There is no need to change the **If no** condition, since we do not want anything to happen if there is not an invoice name to match the filename in Excel. That will be left blank, as shown in the following figure:

Figure 5.26 – If no condition

18. Click **Save** at the bottom of the new flow that is being created.

Figure 5.27 – Saving the flow

Now, let's discuss the Mail Merge flow.

Running the Mail Merge flow

Now you are ready to test or run this flow. Open the Excel file from the OneDrive account and be sure to close the desktop version if it is running so that the two files are not open at the same time:

1. You will need to install **Flow in Excel** if you have not used this feature before. Click on **Insert | Office Add-ins** within the Excel environment, then search for Flow, which is a Microsoft add-on and will be installed quite quickly. Once the installation is complete, click on **Data | Flow** (if added previously), which will appear at the right side or end of the ribbon. Once you click on **Flow**, the **Flow** pane will appear on the right, next to the spreadsheet.

2. With the email selected that you want to process, click on **Flow** and all the flows attached to this spreadsheet will appear in this list. You may be prompted to sign in if you are doing this for the first time. Click on the flow you want to run.

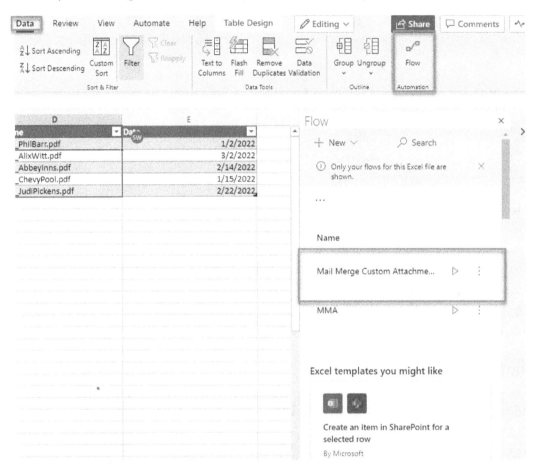

Figure 5.28 – Flow within Excel

3. Click on the run arrow to have the flow process the emails or click on the three vertical dots to open the options menu to access the **Edit, Save As, Turn off** or **Delete** options for the flow. Verify that there are green checkmarks next to the programs, indicating that the application is ready and you are logged in and have permission, then click **Continue**.

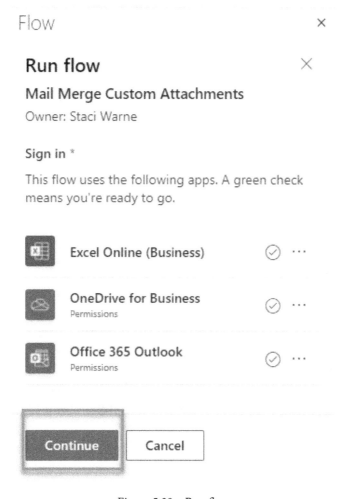

Figure 5.29 – Run flow

4. Click the **Run flow** button to confirm that you are ready to run the flow.

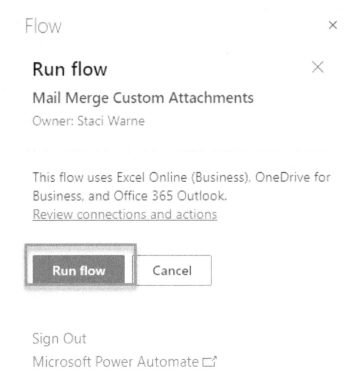

Figure 5.30 – Confirming running the flow

If everything went well and the flow was processed successfully, you will see a dialog box indicating that it was successful.

5. Click the **Done** button to complete the flow. For more information on the flow, you can open it in the original setup in Power Automate, where information about the flow will be displayed.

6. Click on the tab for **My flows** to view a list of the flows available that you have created.

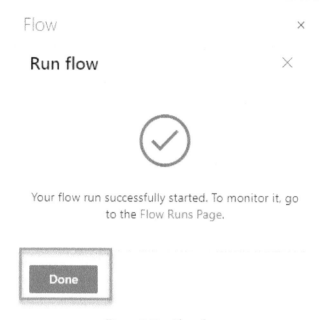

Figure 5.31 – Flow done

I would suggest that you test drive this with your accounts before sending emails out to your customers. This is an easy way to send out customized attachments in emails, as well as customizing the **Subject**, **To**, **Cc**, and **Bcc** fields, which cannot be done otherwise inside Outlook without using code or add-ons.

This is only one of several ways of using Power Automate with Outlook. Seven actions are available inside Power Automate to use with Outlook. They are as follows:

- Launch Outlook.
- Close Outlook.
- Retrieve email messages from Outlook.
- Send an email through Outlook.
- Process email messages in Outlook.
- Save Outlook email messages.
- Respond to Outlook mail message.

I encourage you to look around and get familiar with all these available actions. Outlook is a very powerful tool, and this exercise demonstrated what a great tool it is to utilize with Outlook.

Summary

When you have many personalized emails that you need to send out, but not enough to justify using an email marketing company, **Mail Merge** can be your best productivity tool. You can save hours and hours and headaches by learning how to utilize this technique correctly. Combine this with Power Automate and the sky is the limit in what you can accomplish.

In the next chapter, we will cover the variety of ways that you can manage your calendars using Outlook **Calendar**. The way you use calendars can be different for every individual. You may find yourself not needing every tool available but maybe only one or two. However, I have always been taught that *you don't know what you don't know*. Let's dive into the next chapter and show you the magic behind calendars. That could be in the form of a new view you didn't know you could display or a new way to set up a meeting or color code an event. If you've never used the calendar inside Outlook before, you are in for a big surprise and your productivity is about to soar.

Questions

1. What documents can be created through **Mail Merge**?

2. How do you start **Mail Merge** in Outlook?

3. Can you send emails in Outlook by using the Word **Mail Merge** tool?

4. Can you set up **Mail Merge** to have an email sent on a future date?

5. How many emails can be sent in a day?

Answers

1. Emails, letters, envelopes or labels, and directories.

2. Many people try to find the **Mail Merge** tool on the ribbon in the email object view, but it is not located there. You can find the **Mail Merge** tool in the **Contacts** object view in the actions section.

3. Yes, you can send emails through Outlook by selecting email as the output type for the merge.

4. You can set the date for the **Mail Merge** to a future date using the delayed delivery feature. This, however, will only work if you are using Microsoft Exchange.

5. For Office 365, you can send a maximum of 10,000 emails per day. A single email can be addressed to a maximum of 500 recipients. In `Outlook.com` you can send up to 300 emails per day with a maximum of 100 recipients per message. These limits can be adjusted by your administrator, so it is best to check the limits with that person. To view all of Microsoft Exchange's limits, go to `https://docs.microsoft.com/en-us/office365/servicedescriptions/exchange-online-service-description/exchange-online-limits`.

Part 3:
Beyond Email –
Calendars, Contacts,
Notes, and More

This section looks at everything beyond email. You will master the skills necessary for working with calendars, contacts, notes, and to-do lists, and you'll see how they can all work together. If you're creating an appointment, meeting, or event, adding a new contact and mapping their location, or using an online note or to-do list to save paper, this section has it all. It is up to you to integrate these techniques into your daily routine, but first, you have to know how to go about it. You'll get up to speed by implementing these tricks soon.

This section contains the following chapters:

- *Chapter 6, Managing the Calendar*
- *Chapter 7, Contacts in Outlook*
- *Chapter 8, Outlook Notes*
- *Chapter 9, Tasks and To-Dos*

6
Managing the Calendars

The scheduling power in Outlook comes from the Calendar feature. The Calendar is fully integrated with other objects within Outlook, such as email, contacts, and tasks. This happens seamlessly so you don't see the full functionality that is present.

When you use a desk calendar you simply write where you want your events to appear. It is somewhat the same in Outlook Calendar: you click on a line by a time and start typing what your appointment is. Some of the advantages to using an electronic calendar are that you can do the following:

- Access your calendar from multiple devices, such as a phone, tablet, and computer

- Schedule meetings and appointments from anywhere

- Set up reminders to prevent you from missing important meetings and events

- Schedule time blocks to get work done

- Create recurring items without typing them several times

This list could go on and on. The main advantage of using the Calendar feature is it helps you stay organized so you can accomplish more within your day.

This chapter will help you take advantage of the various tools that you can utilize in Outlook's Calendar feature. We will discuss how you can customize Outlook for your work or home life with the built-in views and set multiple options to tailor Outlook to your workday by changing working times and work days, or simply add time zones for other locations that you interact with consistently. We will cover the following:

- Views and how to customize them
- Calendar options
- Appointments, meetings, and events
- Creating multiple calendars
- Printing calendars

With all these tools available to you through Outlook, you will find if used, they will improve your productivity and help to keep you well-balanced and ready to tackle that next project you take on.

Views

Outlook gives you the choice of using four different views to view your calendar. Open the **Calendar** object first to view your calendar and then click **View | Change View** and you will see the choices available for the Calendar views, which are as follows:

- **Compact** – My version (Microsoft 365 Apps for enterprise) says **Calendar** instead of **Compact**
- **Single** – My version says **List** instead of **Single**
- **Preview**
- **Active** *(New to Outlook 365 for 2021)*

The default view is **Compact**. Unless you have changed this view, that is what you have been or will be using. You have the ability inside of Outlook to change views, modify, copy, and reset them. To change views, click **View** | **Change View** and select the view you want to see.

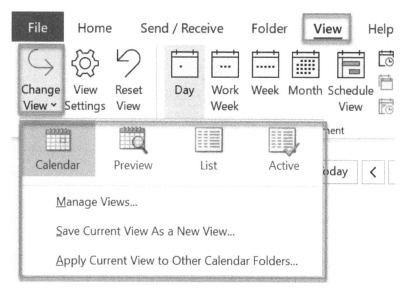

Figure 6.1 – Change View

Occasionally, you may automatically end up in **List** view depending on what Outlook identified as being helpful. This would be the case after you search for an item in your calendar. Follow the previous step to switch back to the **Calendar** view if needed.

Manage Views...

To customize your own view of the Calendar (be sure you have selected the **Calendar** button), click on **View | Change View | Manage Views….** You can use the **Manage All Views** dialogue box to copy the current view setting of a view and use it to apply that view to an existing view from the list or copy it to create a **New…** view.

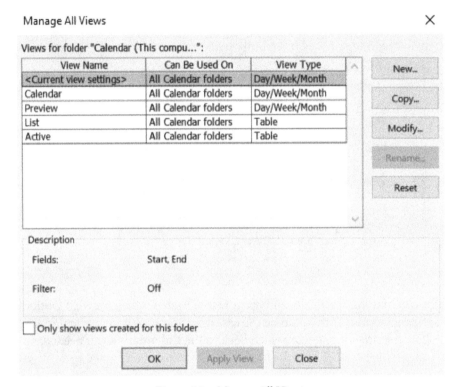

Figure 6.2 – Manage All Views

Note

The **Object** view that you have to show when you click on the **View** tab determines the menu that you get for that current view. You will have a different **View** menu if you have the email, contacts, or calendar view activated.

Customizing your views

Outlook lets you customize your view to fit your working/non-working style. Not everybody works the same hours, lives in the same time zone, or has the same holidays. You may want to turn off the automatic reminders that you get with every new Calendar item or view the weather on the Calendar to help you navigate your activities according to the weather forecast. Using the **Options** dialogue box has these settings for you to adjust. Access this by clicking **File** | **Options** | **Calendar**.

Work time

In the **Work time** section are the items that allow you to control when your workday starts and ends. You can also specify the days of the week that you want to be scheduled as workdays, and you can change the **First day of week** field to begin on other days of the week besides Monday, and **First week of year** as well. This group is useful for having your time set up for you and not the working times that are the defaults within Outlook. If you are working on a different schedule than the default **8:00 AM** to **5:00 PM** or Monday through Friday schedule, this is the place you will want to customize your schedule.

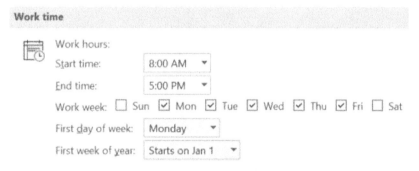

Figure 6.3 – Work Time options

After you customize **Work time** in the **Outlook Options** dialogue box, you will want to look at your calendar by clicking on the **Calendar** button on the navigation pane. Notice the shading by **Work time** that is shown in the timescale on the calendar. You will see darker shading for non-working time and lighter shading for working time.

The following figure, in addition to the working and non-working time, also shows three times zones set up, as discussed later in this chapter in the *Display options* section:

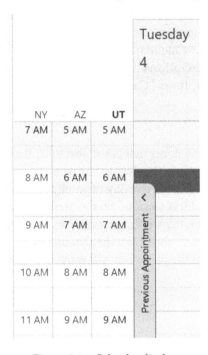

Figure 6.4 – Calendar display

Now, let's move onto the **Calendar options** dialogue box.

Calendar options

This section of the **Outlook Options** box includes options for how you want to control meetings and appointments. You will want to take the time to look at this box. I like to turn off the **Default reminders** setting as I don't want a reminder to pop up for every appointment I set. Unchecking this option means that I need to set that manually when creating my calendar appointments and meeting activities.

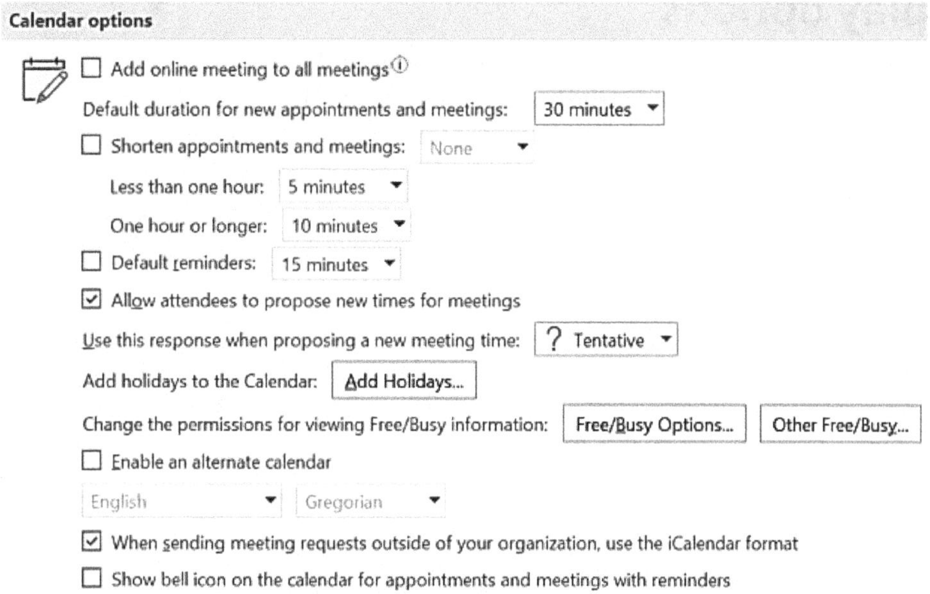

Figure 6.5 – Calendar options

Calendars that are used in Outlook 2016 and later use the Gregorian calendar, which is the most widely used calendar in the world, for the years 2016-2026. If you use a calendar that is not Gregorian, such as the Julian calendar, then holidays that occur during the same period are included.

Should you have problems with holidays, you can use these steps to delete holidays:

Calendar | View | Change View | List.

In the **Arrangement** section, select **Categories**:

1. Scroll to find the **Holidays** category.
2. Select the holidays you want to delete and click **Home | Delete**.
3. Return to the normal calendar view by clicking **View | Change View | Calendar**.

> **Note**
>
> Using the **Add Holidays…** option will enter the holidays in your calendar for that country. Doing this a second time will duplicate the holidays on your calendar.

Display options

In the **Display options** section within the **Calendar** tab, you can specify how you want your calendar to appear in the Calendar display within Outlook. You will find the different groups within this section and a few of the prominent features described after the following figure:

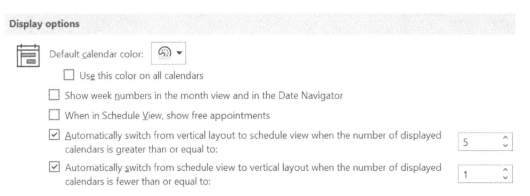

Figure 6.6 – Display options

- **Default calendar color**: Click the drop-down arrow by this button to select the color you would like to work with while in Outlook.

- **Show week numbers in the month view and in the Date Navigator**: This will show the number of the week in the Calendar represented by a number throughout the Calendar, starting at 1 for the first week of the year.

> **Note**
>
> The final two selections for **Display options** are to switch from vertical layout to schedule view according to how many calendars are displayed. Read the selection carefully as these are reversed wording as written for each item.

Time zones

We will configure the time zone that Outlook will use with the options listed in this section. You will also find the options **Show a second time zone** and **Show a third time zone**, which are only available in Outlook 2016 and later. This is useful if you find yourself making phone calls or appointments with people in different time zones frequently.

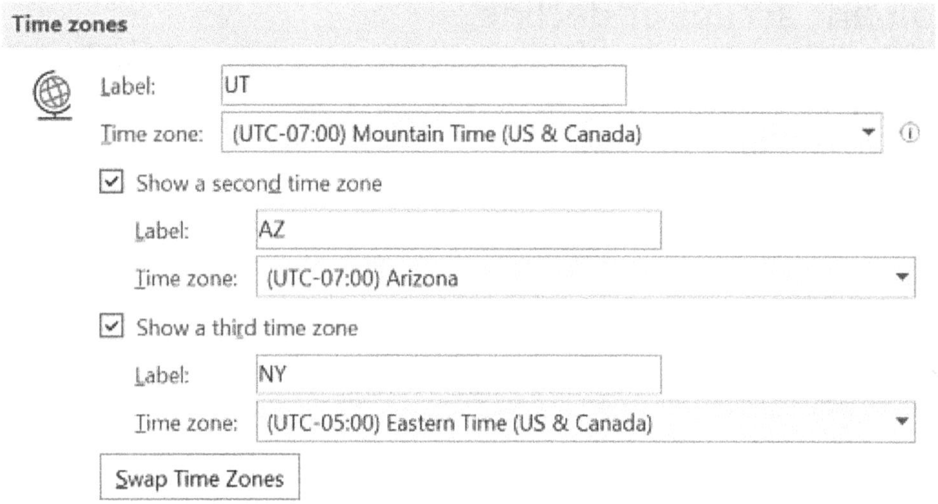

Time zones

Label: UT

Time zone: (UTC-07:00) Mountain Time (US & Canada)   ⓘ

☑ Show a second time zone

Label: AZ

Time zone: (UTC-07:00) Arizona

☑ Show a third time zone

Label: NY

Time zone: (UTC-05:00) Eastern Time (US & Canada)

Swap Time Zones

Figure 6.7 – Time zones

I have found this to be a game-changer in keeping up with what time it is in Arizona. Arizona does not have daylight savings time. Time zone in the USA changes every 6 months – half the year is the same time, and the other half of the year is an hour different.

Scheduling assistant

Scheduling assistant will let you view when people are available on their schedule before you plan a meeting or event. You will be able to view others' calendars to help schedule events with no conflicts. Remember that this information is only as good as the actual information that gets scheduled. More on **Scheduling assistant** will be covered in *Chapter 11, Sharing Mail, Calendars, and Contacts*, on sharing with Outlook.

The **Scheduling assistant** area on the **Calendar** tab allows you to turn on or off the **ScreenTips** to show. This makes it so that when you hover over an appointment in the Calendar, a short description will show with details. **Show calendar details in the scheduling grid** makes it available to others on your exchange network. By default, these two options are turned on. Turn these off if you want added privacy for your calendar.

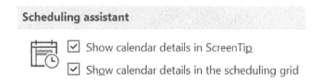

Scheduling assistant

☑ Show calendar details in ScreenTip

☑ Show calendar details in the scheduling grid

Figure 6.8 – Scheduling assistant options

Automatic accept or decline

It is now, more than ever, easy to decline meetings that you cannot fit into your schedule. By clicking on the **Auto Accept/Decline...** button, you can have Outlook automatically decline those meeting proposals for you if they conflict with another Calendar event. This can be a real timesaver if you are confident your calendar is up to date.

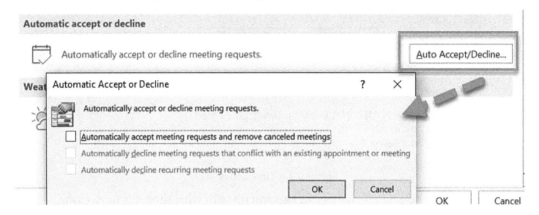

Figure 6.9 – Automatic accept or decline

Weather

With the help of the **Weather** section, you can toggle the weather bar on the Calendar and also choose how you would like to view the temperature in the Calendar window. By turning on this feature, you will see a bar at the top of your calendar with weather information listed.

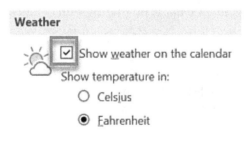

Figure 6.10 – Weather options

Appointments, meetings, and events

When it comes to working on your calendar, the most important topic is creating appointments, meetings, and events. The difference between **Appointment** and **Meeting** is that an appointment only involves you, not others, and a meeting involves other people as well. All-day events will show up at the top of the day with a bar indicating that the event takes all day.

For appointments, I would recommend you mark yourself as busy if you are sharing your calendar with others. Appointments are straightforward to set up. Click on the day in the Calendar that you want to place the appointment on and either double-click on the day or click on **Home | New Appointment**. If you want an all-day event, this can be done in the exact same way but then check the **All day** box for the event.

When viewing your calendar, you have a small monthly calendar that appears in the navigation pane on the left. In this calendar, you can select days that you want to view. Click the date or hold the *Ctrl* key down and select multiple days. You may choose every Friday in a month, for example, if you are trying to schedule a lunch appointment with a peer, or you could select the first week of January and then hold the *Ctrl* key to select the first week of February to locate the best day for a webinar in the first weeks of each month, as shown in this example.

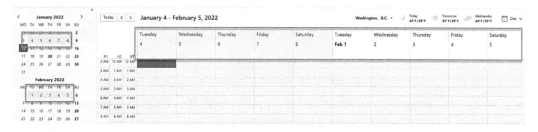

Figure 6.11 – Navigating Calendar

Once you've identified the date, you can simply double-click on the time of the event or day and the **New Appointment** dialogue box will open to schedule your appointment, or check the **All day** box to schedule an all-day event.

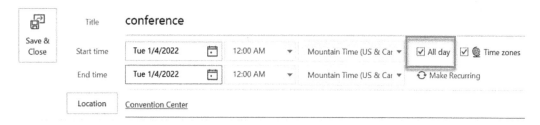

Figure 6.12 – All-day event

When setting your dates in these windows, you can use natural language dates. Try typing the following:

- `In seven weeks`
- `Second Monday in July`
- `Christmas`
- `Thanksgiving does not work but you can type the fourth Thursday in November.`

Give it a try – it is a real timesaver!

Recurring appointments

If you have meetings or events that happen at regular intervals, you will want to enter them into your calendar as a **recurring appointment** or **recurring event**. When you create the appointment or meeting, click on the **Recurrence** button on the **Appointment** or **Meeting** tab ribbon.

Figure 6.13 – Recurrence button

There are three settings you can adjust in the **Appointment Recurrence** dialogue box:

1. **Appointment time**: Specifies the **Start**, **End**, and **Duration** along with your time zone selections.

2. **Recurrence pattern**: Specifies whether the recurrence should be **Daily**, **Weekly**, **Monthly**, or **Yearly** and specific settings to go along with each selection.

3. **Range of recurrence**: Specifies a **Start** date for recurrence and determines whether it should **End by** a specific date, **End after** a specified number of occurrences, or have **No end date**.

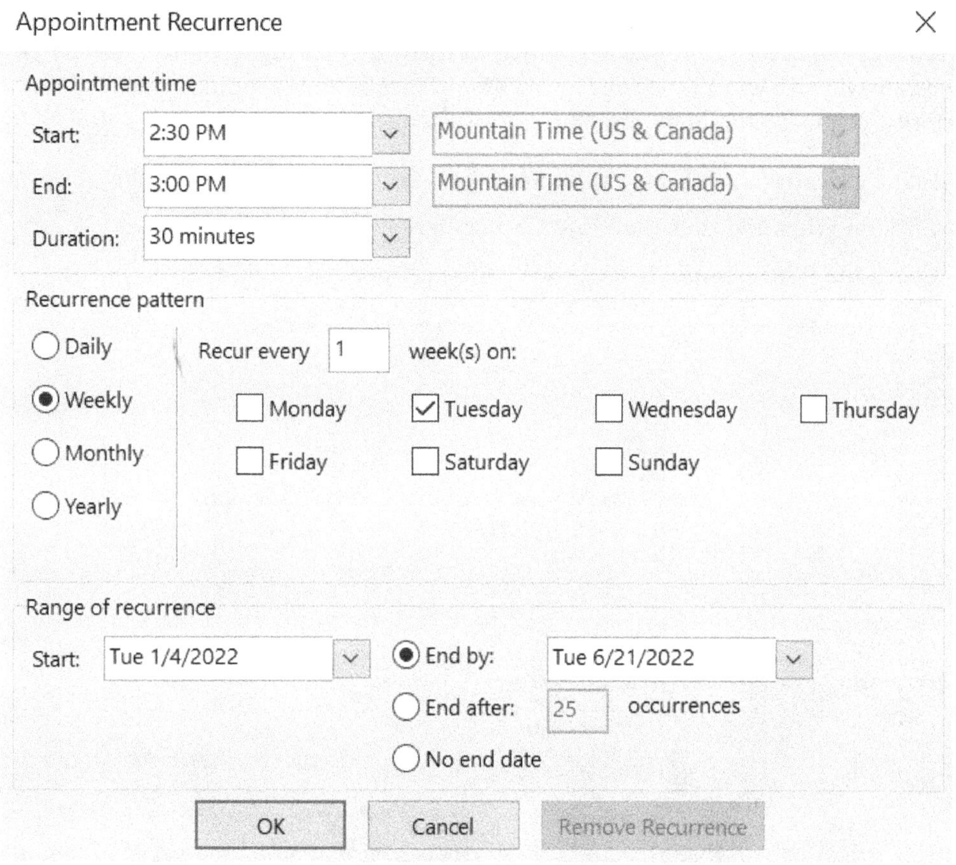

Appointment Recurrence   ✕

Appointment time

Start:	2:30 PM ⌄	Mountain Time (US & Canada)
End:	3:00 PM ⌄	Mountain Time (US & Canada)
Duration:	30 minutes ⌄	

Recurrence pattern

○ Daily   Recur every 1   week(s) on:

◉ Weekly   ☐ Monday   ☑ Tuesday   ☐ Wednesday   ☐ Thursday

○ Monthly   ☐ Friday   ☐ Saturday   ☐ Sunday

○ Yearly

Range of recurrence

Start: Tue 1/4/2022 ⌄   ◉ End by: Tue 6/21/2022 ⌄

                            ○ End after: 25   occurrences

                            ○ No end date

[OK]   [Cancel]   [Remove Recurrence]

Figure 6.14 – Appointment Recurrence

Recurring appointments are great for annual events such as birthdays or a meeting held every other week on the same day, or even the first week of a new month. This tool is a great timesaver.

Prioritizing appointments

Is your calendar swamped with appointments and meetings? Do you hesitate to say "no" to another appointment request?

Outlook's default priority field has three settings: **low, normal**, and **high**. Applying one of these settings will allow you to sort tasks by priority level. Viewing by priority level over the due date will give you a little edge in the importance of your appointments. To view the priority, you may filter high- and low-priority items:

1. In the Calendar, click **View | View Settings**.

2. Click on **Filter** and click the **More Choices** tab.

3. Check the **Whose importance is** box and select **normal, high**, or **low**.

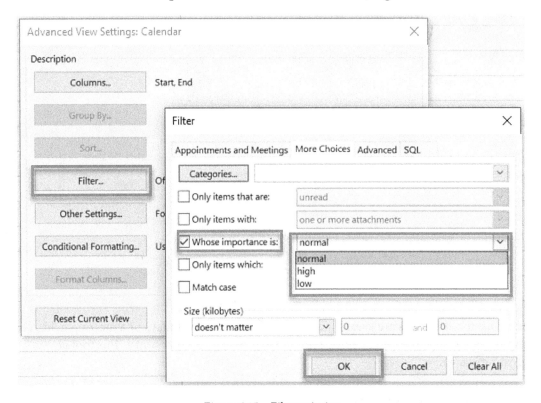

Figure 6.15 – Filter priority

It's best to view the filtered appointment by clicking **View | Change View | List**. Turn on this filter when you need to prioritize your emails according to your high-priority appointments and you'll know which appointments you can reschedule or should not reschedule based on the priority level you assigned. If you are not currently applying a priority to your appointments, they will all show in this filtered list as **normal** priority so using this list view to show the filter will not be as effective. If you are currently setting priorities on your appointments by using this filter, you will instantly know which appointments you can or cannot reschedule based on the priority level that you applied.

Multiple calendars

If you are combining various activities together on one calendar, you may want to consider creating additional calendars tailored to your lifestyle. I have found this extremely helpful as I start working on a new project because I will create a new calendar on which I schedule only activities related to that specific project. I have also found it nice to not have to display the Calendar all the time and I can hide it if no activity is happening for a while or delete it altogether once my project has been completed. If my project gets busy all of a sudden, I will use the **Overlay** option to be able to see my calendar combined with my activities on my other calendars. How busy you get or how overwhelmed you get maintaining your calendar will determine when you need to start keeping separate calendars.

1. To create additional calendars, click the **Calendar** button in the navigation pane, then click **Folder | New Calendar**.

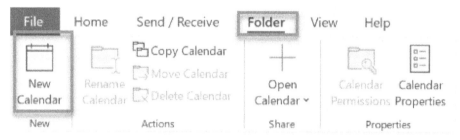

Figure 6.16 – Create a new calendar

2. Give the Calendar a name in the **Create New Folder** dialogue box and the calendar will by default be created in the **Calendar** folder.

3. Enter a name for the new calendar and, unless you prefer a different location, it will automatically have selected **Calendar Items** from the **Folder contains** dropdown and it will be placed in the *Calendar folder*.

4. Click **OK**. You can now view the new calendar in the **Calendar** view from the navigation pane.

Figure 6.17 - Create New Folder

Creating separate calendars can be very useful for keeping all your appointments and your thoughts organized. Now we will discuss how you can easily view your calendars in different ways to help you quickly view your calendar entries. You can view the calendars you create either as a single calendar or together in a side-by-side view or overlay view. You can choose the view you want based on your liking.

Viewing side-by-side calendars

Once the new calendar is created, its name will immediately appear in the navigation pane. You will see a box next to the name of the calendar. By clicking on this box, the calendar will appear in the view within the **Calendar** workspace. By default, your calendars will appear side by side.

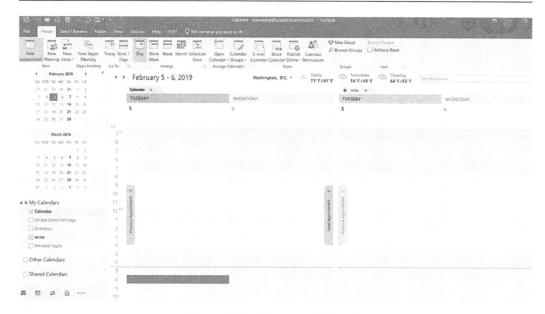

Figure 6.18 – Calendars side by side

I like this side-by-side view because it allows me to compare calendars and also focus on one calendar over another within the same workspace. You can hide any displayed calendars by deselecting the calendar's checkbox in the navigation pane or clicking the **X** that appears on the right side of the **calendars** tab in the workspace window above the calendar days.

Sharing calendars with coworkers who share the same Exchange account will be discussed in *Chapter 11, Sharing Mail, Calendars, and Contacts.*

Viewing overlay calendars

Outlook has an **Overlay** feature within the Calendar to be able to view two or more calendars together by layering them. This view will make it so that you can view all of your appointments or events together in one calendar. To activate this view, click **View | Overlay**. Repeat the step again to turn off **Overlay**.

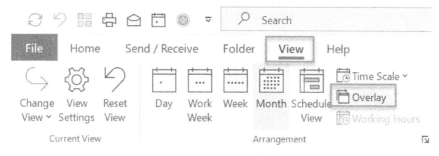

Figure 6.19 – Overlay

In order to help you differentiate the appearance of items in the Calendar, in the **Overlay** view appointments are color-coded. All items not on the primary calendar (usually the calendar opened first) will appear slightly transparent, indicating that it is not the primary calendar. For example, you could view your main calendar normally, and when you overlay a calendar that you have been made a delegate of, that calendar will have transparent headings so that you know the items are not on your personal calendar, as in *Chapter 11, Sharing Mail, Calendars, and Contacts.*

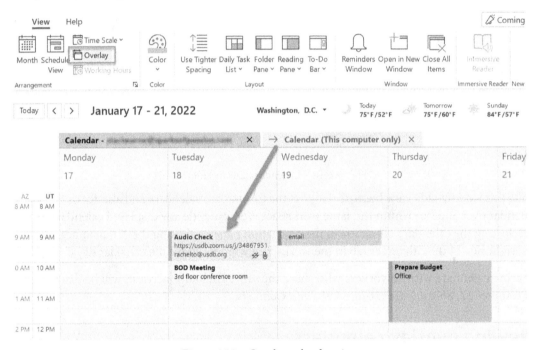

Figure 6.20 – Overlay calendar view

I like to activate **Overlay** on my calendars when I want to find an open available time on multiple calendars to schedule an event. It saves me a lot of time not having to open and close multiple calendars.

> **Note**
> To view a calendar in a separate window, as a separate calendar, you can right-click on the calendar name in the navigation pane and select **Open in New Window**.

Printing calendars

It's always nice to rely 100% on being able to access your calendar information online. But there might be times when you want to print out your schedule. Having a busy day can also mean your phone or computer battery may die or you may leave it behind somewhere when you find you need it. As a safeguard, I suggest you create a printout of the day, week, or month depending on your business needs. This could end up being a real frustration saver.

Printing out a calendar is straightforward. **File | Print** will give you the printing features for a quick printout. *Ctrl + P* is the shortcut for printing.

You have six settings for printing a calendar. If no details are entered on the calendar, it will print the calendar in **Daily Style**:

- **Daily Style**: This style prints a selected day of the calendar, which will include time and time zone information, calendar events, and the daily task list and notes.

Figure 6.21 – Daily Style view

- **Weekly Agenda Style**: Prints a selected week on one page. Shows each day in a separate box and daily events.

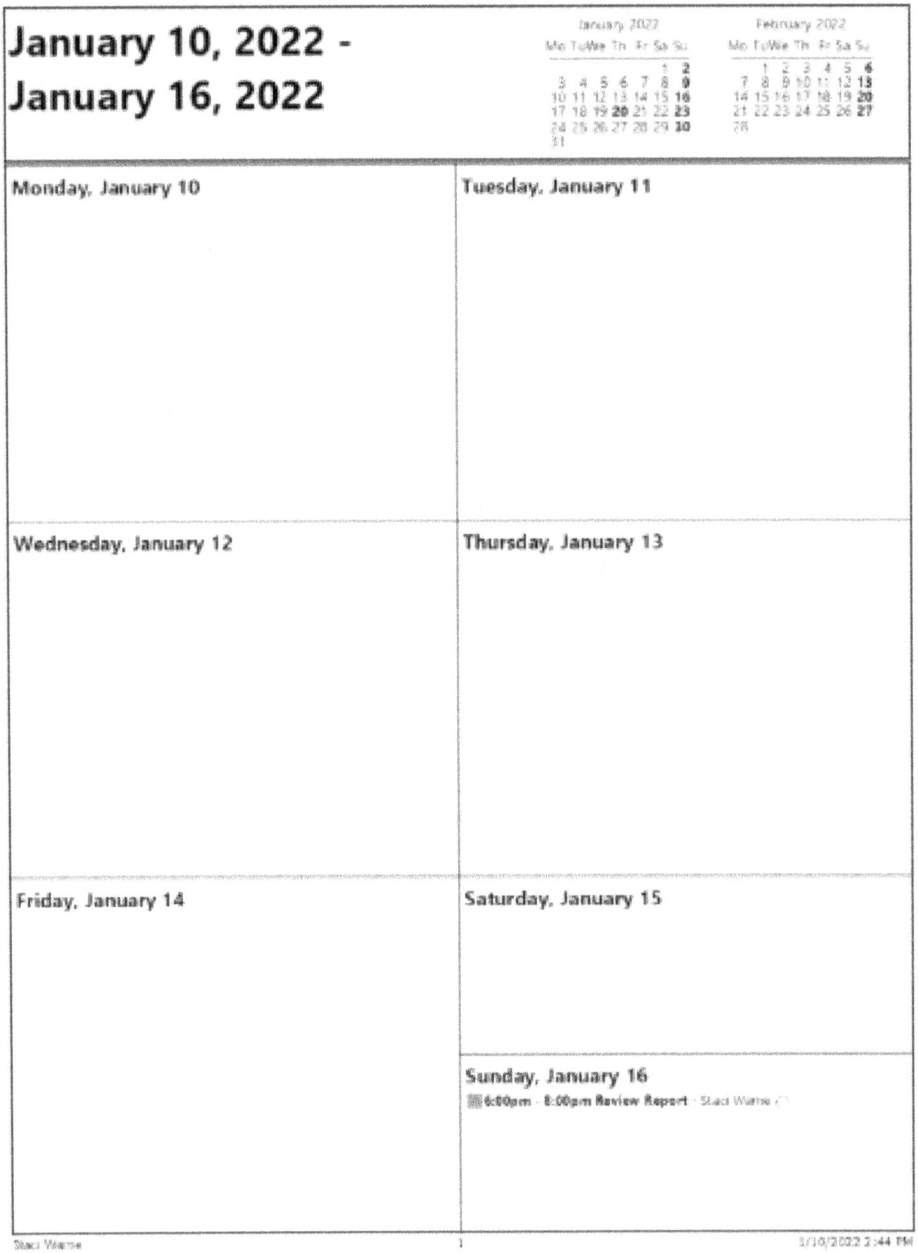

Figure 6.22 – Weekly Agenda view

- **Weekly Calendar Style**: Prints a selected week showing time and time zones and events for that week within the calendar.

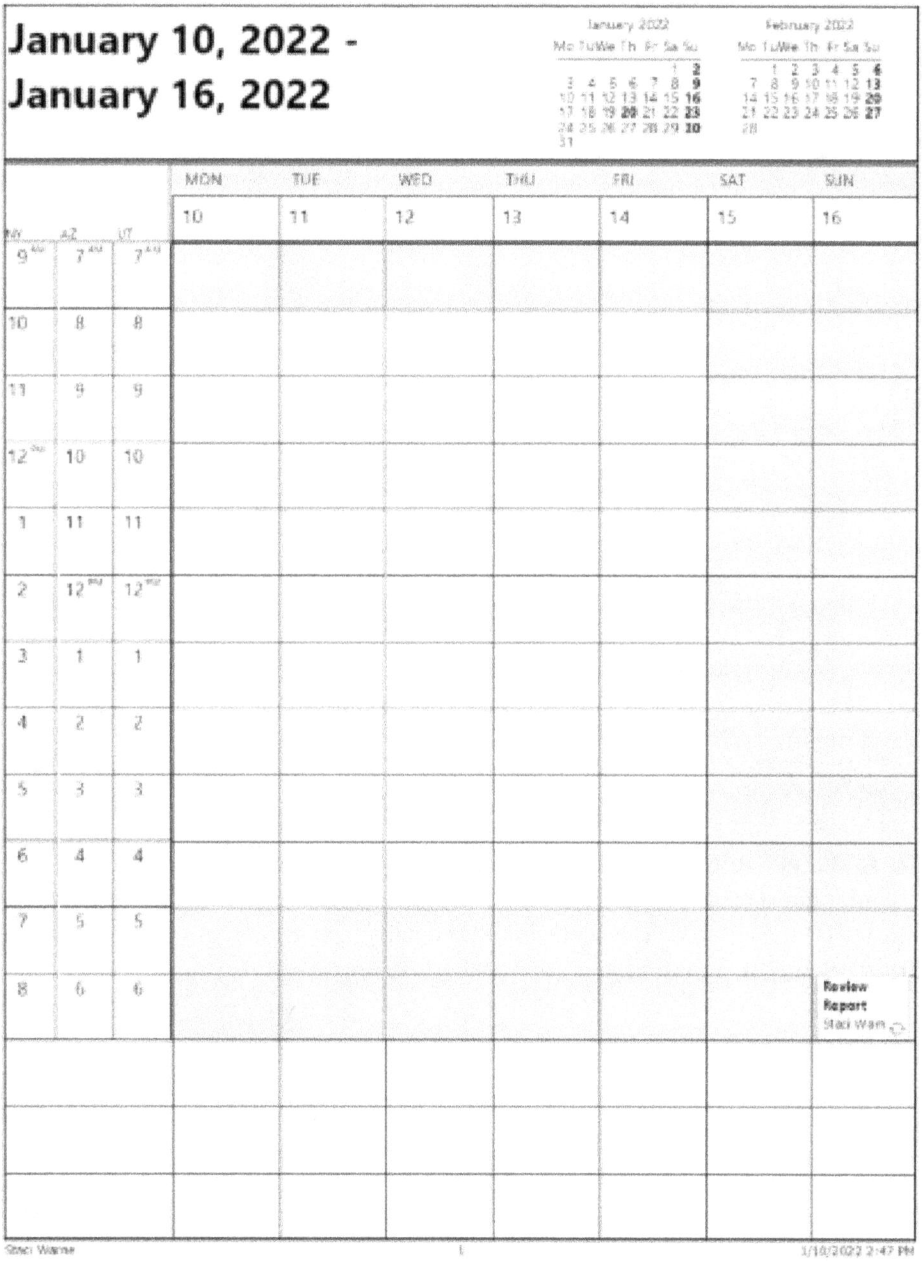

Figure 6.23 – Weekly Calendar view

- **Monthly Style**: Prints a selected month in a calendar view style showing events listed within the days of the month.

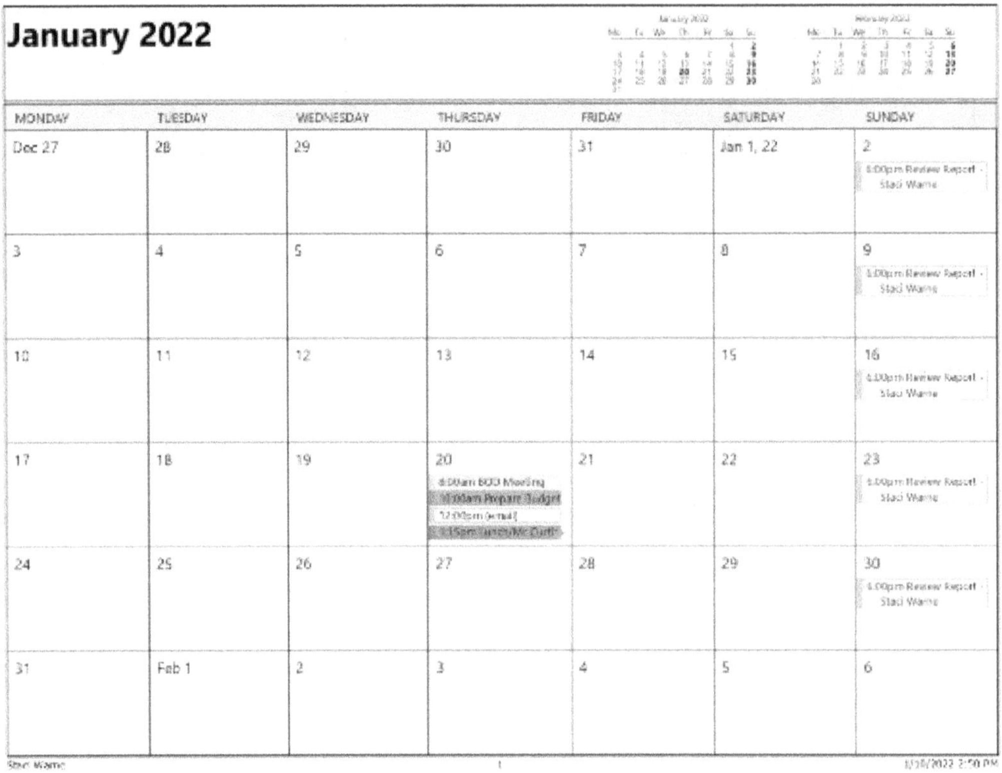

Figure 6.24 – Monthly Style view

- **Tri-fold Style**: Prints selected dates in a tri-fold style to allow the user to fold the calendar like a brochure. Includes days with time zones and times and events for the day on the left fold. The centerfold has a daily task list and a weekly calendar is displayed on the right fold.

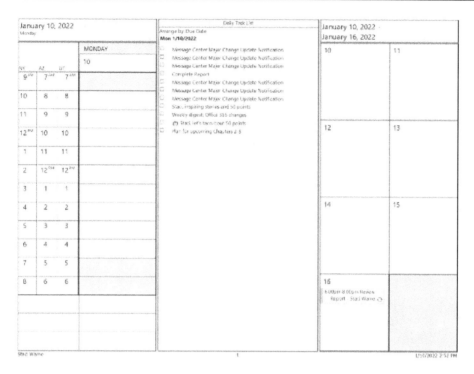

Figure 6.25 – Tri-fold Style view

- **Calendar Details Style**: Shows an email that has been brought into the calendar to display the details of the day and the email is what will be displayed.

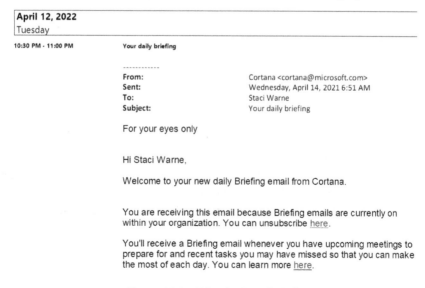

Figure 6.26 – Calendar Details Style

After selecting the setting style that you want to print your calendar in, you should then look at **Print Options**. Click on the **Print Options** button above **Settings** in the **Print** window.

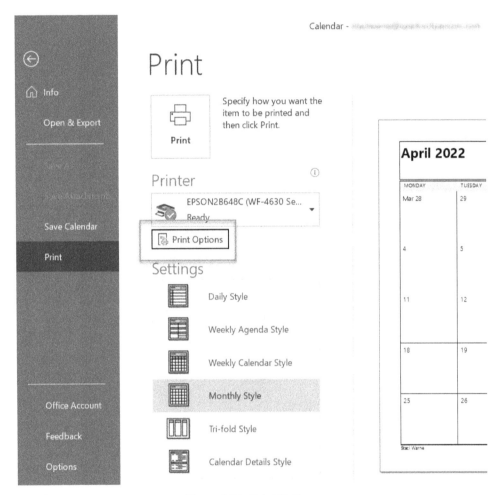

Figure 6.27 - Print Options

In the **Print** dialogue box, for each of the six styles, once selected, you can choose various additional settings for your printing preference. Click the **Print Options** button located above the **Settings** selections. In this box, you can change the printer, choose your **Print style** preference, select a **Page range** option, such as **Pages:** 2 - 3, or even select a date for **Print range**.

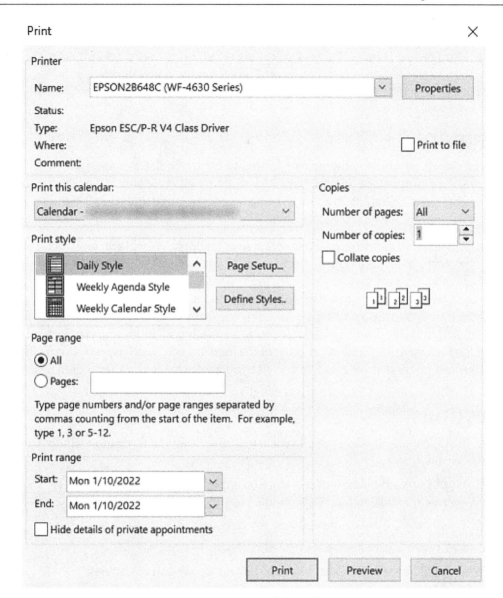

Figure 6.28 – Print dialogue box

Two options that are overlooked in this **Print** dialogue box are the **Hide details of private appointments** option at the bottom of the box, which you can select to have private appointments not show up on the printout, and the **Print to file** box at the top right of this box, which you can use to print to the computer and save it on your PC instead of printing it out on paper.

Printing a specific day or range

A handy feature when printing Outlook calendars is the ability to first select the day or days that you want to print and then select **File | Print**. By doing this first, only the selected day or selected range will be printed and you won't have to specify the style.

Summary

As you can see, there are so many reasons for you to use Outlook Calendar, and harnessing the power of Calendar features is just another example of using an electronic calendar. You can use Outlook as a tool to help you get organized and complete things you need to get done and stay on task at the same time.

In the next chapter, we will discuss the people side of Outlook. We will see how Contacts are an important part of keeping you connected with your friends, coworkers, and new and old acquaintances you have in your life. You will learn how you can efficiently add and handle new contacts. You will also learn best practices for organizing those contacts rather than be individually or within a group. You will learn what the **People Pane** is and how it can help you stay connected to your contacts socially and, most importantly, how to back up those contacts so you don't lose any of the information. Lastly, we will discuss the various address books that are available and give you guidance on how they should be used.

Questions

1. In the Calendar, why does the current calendar show in the navigation window on the left side?

2. How can I turn off the reminder feature on appointments? I don't want every appointment I make to have a 15-minute reminder set.

3. Can I have my Outlook tasks show on my calendar?

4. Can an email be converted into a meeting request?

5. Where is the **Board (Kanban)** view on the desktop version of Outlook?

Answers

1. The two calendars that are on the left side in the navigation pane are a way to navigate and select the days you want to view in the main **Calendar** window. You can use the arrows to navigate to other months, and when you change the month of the calendar, the other bottom calendar will change as well. You can also click on a date in these calendars to navigate to that date in your main **Calendar** window or even select two or more dates (hold down the *Ctrl* key) to compare them side by side. This is a very useful tool that many users do not use because they don't know of its power.

2. Click the **File | Options | Calendar | Calendar Options** section and *uncheck* the **Default reminders** box, or you can change the reminder time here as well.

3. Yes. Click **View | To-Do Bar | Check To-Do**. This will add the calendar to the **To-Do Bar** that will appear on the right side of the calendar.

4. Yes. Select the email that you want to convert to a meeting request, then click **Home | Reply with Meeting** (*Ctrl + Alt + R*). This creates the **New meeting** request with the message recipient on the **To** line and the email message included in the body of the meeting request.

5. As of now, the **Board** view is only available in the **Calendar** view of Outlook on the web. It is not yet on the desktop versions. If you like Kanban boards, then you may want to sign in to Office 365 on the web and give this a try.

Further reading

-   How to use the **Board** view:

    https://www.howtogeek.com/752967/how-to-use-board-view-in-microsoft-outlook-calendar/

7
Contacts in Outlook

A person either inside your organization or outside of your organization could be considered a **contact**. **Contacts** in Outlook is a repository where you can store information about the people you want to contact. This information could be mailing addresses, email IDs, names, personal notes, or even an entire email message with information that you want to associate with that contact.

Where do you want to store your contact information? Within your computer, on the cloud, or on your phone or tablet? You need to know this to decide how you want to store your addresses with the **Outlooks Contacts** feature, otherwise known as **Outlook People**. We will discuss how to efficiently add new contacts or create a contact group, as well as where to find contacts if your corporation uses Exchange or simply keeping the list in your address book. We will also show you how to manage your contacts and view them in multiple ways.

In this chapter, we're going to cover the following topics:

- Adding new contacts
- Contact groups (distribution lists)
- Views
- Viewing a contact's address on a map

Adding new contacts

Most of us have a pile of business cards that we got at some convention, or various other places, that we need to get into our contacts in Outlook. Outlook is a great place to manage all those cards. It can be a time-consuming endeavor uploading all of them, but the payoffs could be large. There are several apps that you can get on your phone that will allow you to snap a picture of a card and sync that picture with an Outlook contact. If you receive a lot of business cards, you may want to consider using one of these apps. In Outlook, to enter contact information, click **People | New Contact** and enter the information that is available.

Adding a contact from an email message

Let us understand how to add a contact from an email message:

1. Open the message so that the person's email ID is shown.

2. Right-click the email ID that you want to create a contact out of and click **Add to Outlook Contacts**.

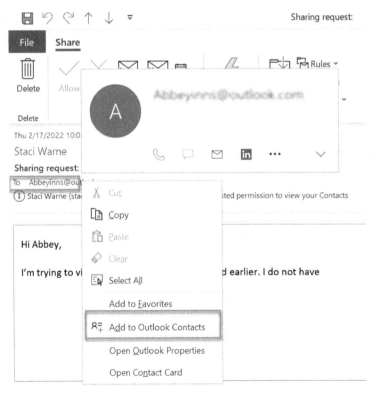

Figure 7.1 – Right-click menu for adding a contact from an email

3.   In the add new contact window, enter the details for your contact.

Figure 7.2 – Adding a new contact entry

4.   Click the **Save & Close** button on the **Contact** tab in the ribbon when the entry is complete.

I have found that this is the quickest way to insert a contact, especially if you do not have all the details for them. This is quick and can easily be done within seconds once the email message has been opened.

Business cards

20 years ago, I never imagined that I would be giving my business card out electronically instead of a paper business card. You can create a business card in Outlook to send through your emails so that the recipients have your contact information just as they would if you handed them a physical business card, and it includes the same information if not more.

Default business cards

An electronic business card is created when you add a new contact in Outlook. An electronic business card is also created in the background for each contact. Outlook gives us different views to display contacts in the workspace. To view your contacts as business cards, open the **People** or **Contacts** workspace and click **Home | Business Card**.

Figure 7.3 – Business card view

Only the fields that you populate with data will be displayed within the business card view or any other view. Each business card will include the contact's name, picture, phone numbers, email ID, company name, job title, and more, and you can edit this information to your own liking. If a field is left blank, it will not appear on the business card. I would recommend that you do not overdo adding fields to the business card. Think of adding content as you would on a real business card with just the necessary information to show on the card. Otherwise, the card will have too much information to view nicely on the card. If you need to make changes to a business card, you can edit it, as we will show next.

Editing a business card

To edit a business card, first open the business card by double-clicking on the preferred card in the workspace. This will show all the details pertaining to the selected contact.

All you need to do is click **Contact | Business Card**. The **Edit Business Card** dialog box will open, showing several options available for you to choose from for editing the business card.

Figure 7.4 – Editing a business card

Now, let us understand the components shown in *Figure 7.4*:

1. This is a preview of how the business card looks if sent to another recipient.

2. The **Fields** section is used to add or remove fields to or from the card. The items you see in this box are going to show on the card if the fields have data in them to display. When you highlight one of these fields, you can click **Remove** to remove the field from this list. Click the **Add...** button to see a list of available fields that you can add to the card.

Figure 7.5 – Adding fields to a business card

3. Below the **Fields** list are buttons to arrange the fields how you would like them to show on the business card. Select the field you want to re-order and then click the *up or down arrows* to place it where desired within the **Fields** list.

4. The **Card Design** area of the **Edit Business Card** dialog box has the controls for adjusting the layout of the card. You can change the layout position of the image as well as the background color that you want to be applied to the card.

    Click on the **Change...** button to select a picture to display on the card if you desire.

5. In the center of the right section of the dialog box are the **Edit** options for the fields that are listed on the left. When you select a field on the left, you can use these controls to adjust the font, text, label, and colors for the selected field.

6. The **Reset Card** button allows you to reset the card back to the default settings. Use this if you have made changes to any items in this dialog box to reset all adjustments with just one click. It's a quick way to go back to the start and redesign a new look or branding.

You can set up several business cards if you prefer and select the card you want to attach to an email. You must right-click on the desired card and then click **Forward Contact | As a Business Card**. The business card will be included as an attachment in the new message that is created.

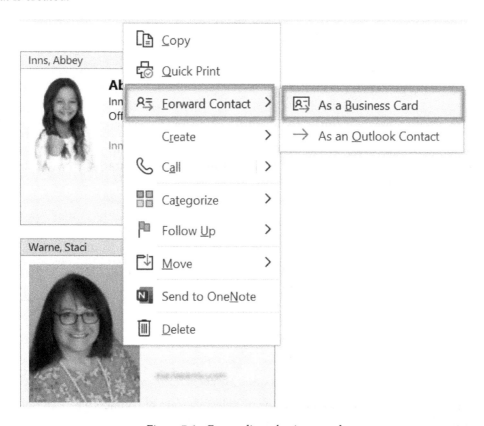

Figure 7.6 – Forwarding a business card

These steps only apply to a single business contact, as shown. The **As a Business Card** option will be grayed out if the business card is a contact group, which will be discussed in the next section.

Contact groups

Do you find yourself emailing a group of people all the time? Doing these repetitive tasks over and over again can really take up a lot of your time. Outlook's contact groups will free up a lot of your time once you get the groups set up and you will find this setup very easy. By setting up an Outlook contact group, instead of selecting multiple contact names you want to include in an email you are composing, you can select a single contact group instead. To create a contact group, take the following steps:

1. From the **People** button on the navigation pane, click **Home | New Contact Group**.

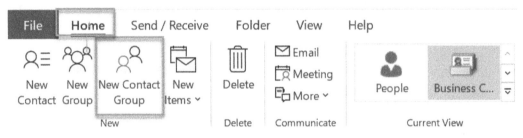

Figure 7.7 – New Contact Group

2. In the **New Contact Group** window, enter a name for the new group.

3. Click **Contact Group | Add Members**. Select where you are getting the members from by selecting one of the three choices: **From Outlook Contacts**, **From Address Book**, or **New E-mail Contact**.

Figure 7.8 – Add Members

4. You can select these names one by one; to select a group of contacts, you can hold down the *Ctrl* key and select each name individually, or if the names are all together, you can click the first name and press and hold the *Shift* key and select the last name, and the entire group will be selected. When the names are selected, click on the **Members** button to populate the members into the **Members** field. If you double-click on one of the names, it will populate in the **Members** field as well.

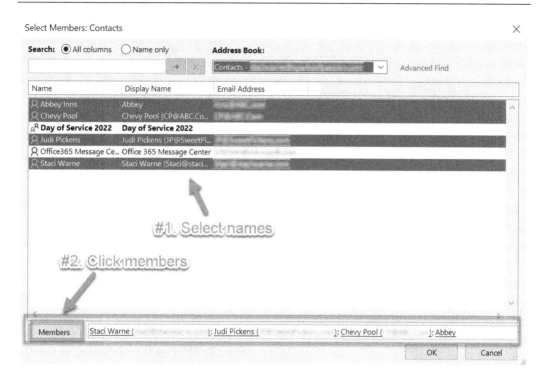

Figure 7.9 – Selecting member contacts

As members are selected from the various methods, the contact will be added to the **Contact Group** window after clicking **OK**. You will see the names appear in the **Members** box, as shown previously.

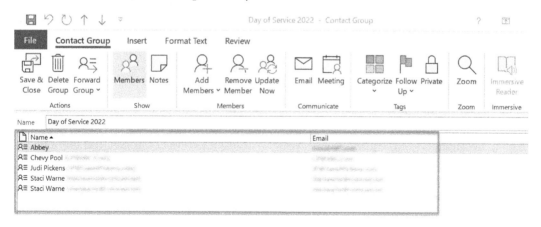

Figure 7.10 – Contact Group

5. Click **Contact Group | Save & Close** to save the new contact group. Your new contact group will now show as a separate item in the **People** workspace in all views.

Figure 7.11 – People workspace, business card view

When in the business card view, the business card for a contact group will not have a picture field. It has a generic picture and shows the name of the contact group and the text **Group**. You cannot edit the information shown on the card as you can with individual contacts.

> **Note**
>
> Don't confuse a contact group as described in this chapter with a group inside of Outlook. A group is a collection of people put together to work on a common project or event. To set up a group, click **Home | New Group** in the **People** workspace. This feature is described in *Chapter 13, Collaboration and Integration within Outlook.*

Update Now

Contact groups, also known as distribution lists, do not automatically update as changes are made to your address book. By using the **Update Now** feature, Outlook will scan through the members of the group and update all necessary contact information for you. Click **Contact Group | Update Now**.

Figure 7.12 – Update Now

This action will synchronize the details of the distribution list members with the information stored about them in the address book. In the following figure, an error appears because one of the contacts in the group had been deleted previously:

Figure 7.13 – Update, contact not found

As employees come and go within jobs, I have found that having Outlook synchronize my groups has helped me eliminate the bounced-back messages that I would get if an email ID was no longer active.

Managing contact group members

You can manage contact groups by updating the members as they come and go. I've not worked with a group yet where I did not have to remove a member or add a member over time:

1. To manage a contact group, you first have to open the **People** workspace in any view that you prefer.

2. Double-click on the contact group that you want to manage or view. You could also select the group and hit *Enter* on the keyboard.

3. Click **Contact Group | Add Members** or **Remove Member**.

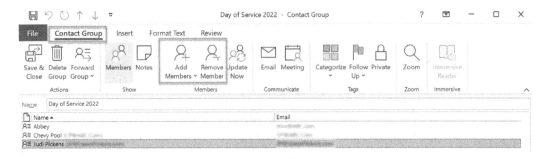

Figure 7.14 – Add Members or Remove Member

4. Selecting the **Add Members** or **Remove Member** button in the previous step will open the **Contact Groups** detail window on the **Contact Group** tab to manage the members in the group.

    The same steps can be used to add members using the **global address book** or **Contacts address book** or for creating a new contact as we did when creating the **Contact Group**.

5. Save the changes by clicking **Contact Group | Save & Close**.

Sending a message to a contact group

Sending a message to a contact group is where the real time savings happen. Instead of choosing each individual ID that you want to send the message to, just select the contact group name and all the contacts you added as members of the group will be added to the email. If you put them on the **To** field, they will be able to see who else the email is addressed to, so you may want to include them in the **Bcc** line if you have security concerns where you want to prevent everyone in the group from seeing this information.

Compose the email as you normally would for a new email and insert the group contact name in the address fields instead of typing in each individual email ID.

The following steps will show additional methods that are unique to contact groups:

1. Open the contact group that you want to send an email to.

2. Click **Contact Group | Email**. A new message window will open with the **To** field populated with the name of the contact group that you want to send an email to.

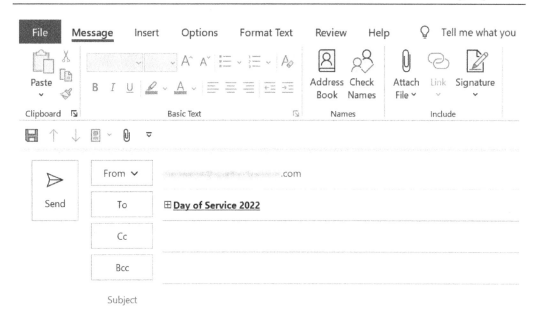

Figure 7.15 – New email to a contact group

You have the option to leave the name of the contact group in the **To** field or click the plus sign next to the contact group name and it will expand to show the recipients' names and email IDs, as shown:

Figure 7.16 – Expanding the contact group to show email IDs

If you choose to leave the name of the contact group in the email's **To** field, the recipients will have the names of each person of the group showing in the email they receive, not the name of the contact group that you created.

Forwarding a contact group

There may be times when someone else will need to send an email to your distribution list. Your contact group can be shared with them by you forwarding the contact group to them. This is another time-saver as the person will not have to individually add all the names from your group to a new email. To forward a contact group, take the following steps:

1. Open the **People** workspace by clicking on the **People** button in the navigation pane, and then select and open the contact group.

2. Click **Contact Group | Forward Group | As an Outlook Contact**.

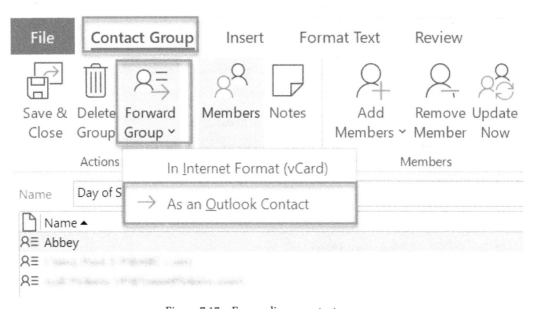

Figure 7.17 – Forwarding a contact group

> **Note**
> An alternate method to forward a contact group is to right-click the contact group and click **Forward Contact | As an Outlook Contact**.

The contact group will be inserted as an attachment in a new email message, and you can fill in the required fields for sending a message as usual.

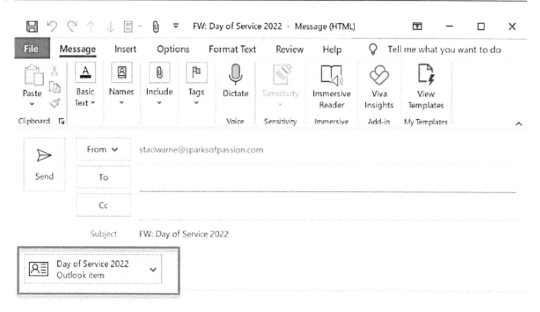

Figure 7.18 – Contact group attachment

When the recipient or recipients of the email open the email, they can save the attachment with the help of the **People** button using the drag-and-drop techniques shown in *Chapter 1, Getting Started with Outlook*.

Deleting a contact group

You may find that you have duplicated a contact in error and need to delete one of the duplicates or you no longer need a contact group.

To delete a contact group, select the contact group that you want to delete, and you can try one of these actions:

- Click Del on the keyboard.
- Go to **Home | Delete**.
- Right-click on the **Contact Group | Delete**.

It's easy to create, manage, and delete contact groups. If you need to send emails over and over to the same people, creating a contact group will be a true time-saver. The way you view your contacts is another time-saver for the way you work. Viewing only the **Contacts** data that you need and filtering out the rest will be discussed in the next section.

Views

By default, you will see your personal contacts inside of Outlook. You can view other address books by first clicking on the **Contacts** object, then in the **Find** group on the ribbon, selecting **Address Book**. Use the drop-down list under **Address Book** to see all the address books and contact lists in your organization group.

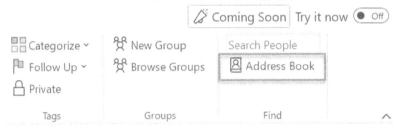

Figure 7.19 – Address Book

Viewing contacts

Once you enter your contact information, you can see the information arranged in several different views. This is a quick way to get an overall picture of your contacts. You can also manually type in addresses or contacts to add these contacts to your personal contact list. The contacts that you are seeing are only your personal contacts, not your list of corporate contacts. If you are able to access those contacts, you will see how to view them next. To change views, take the following steps:

1. Click the **Contacts** object, then click **View | Change View**.

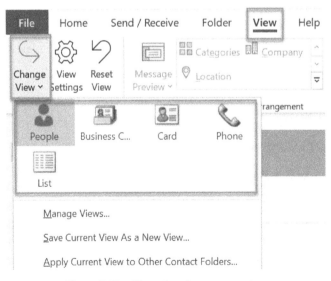

Figure 7.20 – Changing the contacts view

You can change the way you view your contacts from the standard view of **People**. While in the **People** view, click **Home | View** and choose from the following views:

- **People**
- **Business Card**
- **Card**
- **Phone**
- **List**

2. Click on each of these views and notice how the names or cards look on the screen.

Don't worry about changing views; you don't lose the actual cards, you are just viewing them in a different way. For instance, if you are going to be setting up a calling campaign, the phone list view would be helpful for seeing multiple phone numbers for a contact.

> **Note**
> An alternate method to use when changing the view from **People** is to click on the drop-down button in the **Current View** section on the **Home** tab.

Managing views

Views allow you to look at your data in different ways within Outlook. At times, you may find that the default views do not give you the exact data that you want to view. You can use **Manage Views...** to create a more customized view of your Outlook contacts, which may be adding fields or simply changing the fonts or placement and fields in the view.

Let us understand the steps to manage views:

1. Select the **Contacts** button on the bottom of the navigation pane.
2. Click **View | Current View | Change View | Manage View...**.

3. From the **Manage All Views** dialog box, you have options for creating a new view, copying a view to update it, or modifying, renaming, or resetting a view. The **Reset** button will only appear if the view selected is a view created by Outlook (if it is a custom view, the button will appear as **Delete**).

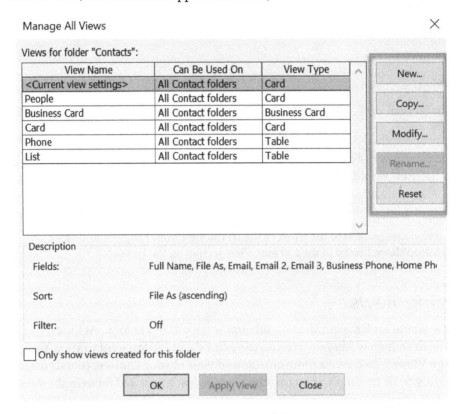

Figure 7.21 – Manage All Views

Now, let's understand the **New...** view.

Understanding the New... view

To create your own custom view in the **Contacts** workspace, take the following steps:

1. Click **New...** in the **Manage All Views** dialog box.

2. Enter a name for the new view, as shown in *Figure 7.22*.

3. Select the type of view that you want.

4. Choose the preferred folder option for viewing the new view. You are selecting whether you want the view to be available to everybody, just you, or all contact folders. The default is **All Contact folders**.

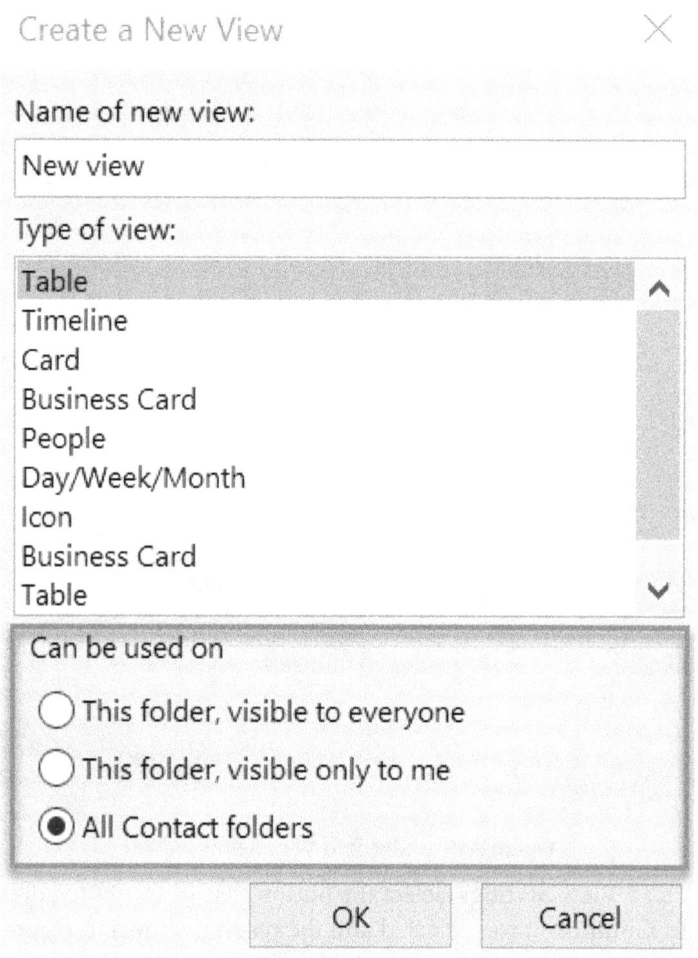

Figure 7.22 – Create a New View

5.   Click **OK**.

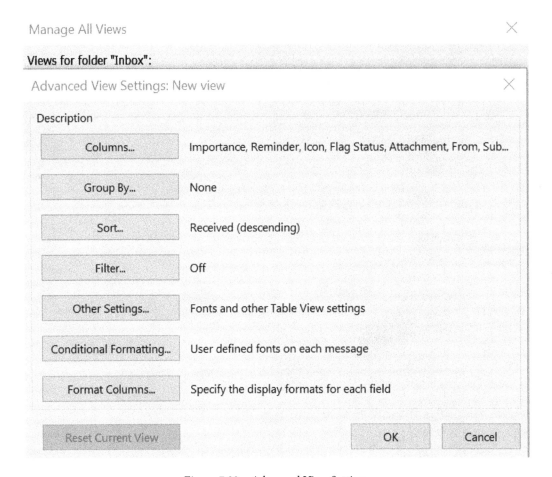

Figure 7.23 – Advanced View Settings

6.   From **Advanced View Settings**, select the button that you want to adjust or select (for example, **Columns...** was selected and the result is shown in *Figure 7.24*):

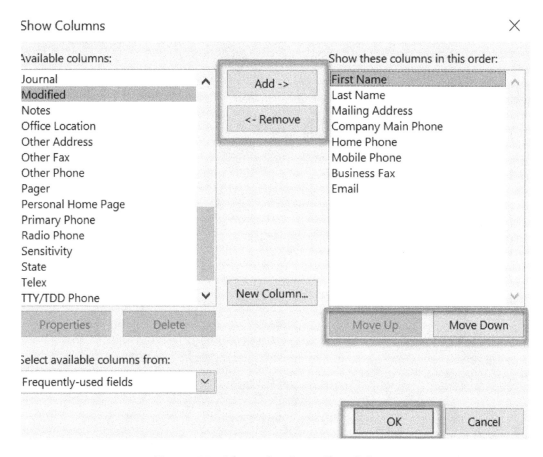

Figure 7.24 – Advanced settings – Show Columns

7. The left side of the **Show Columns** dialog box shows all the available fields and the right side shows all the selected fields to show in the new view. You can select a field and either add or remove it from the list on the right. You can select a field on the right and use the **Move Up** and **Move Down** buttons to position the field in the desired order. Click **OK**.

8. Adjust all settings desired in the **Advanced View Settings** dialog box. Each button will have a unique dialog box relating to the items to adjust.

9. When you have adjusted all items, you can click **Apply View** and the view will now show in the **Contacts** workspace. This view will also be available as a button to select on the **Home** tab in the ribbon in the **Current View** section.

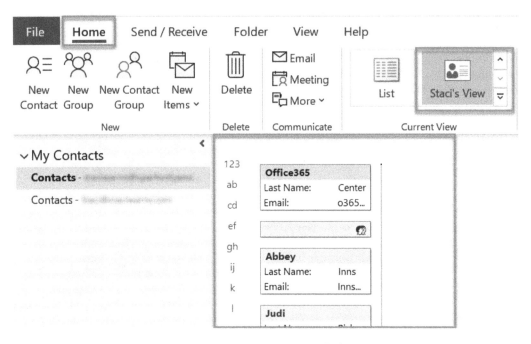

Figure 7.25 – New view applied

Although I like how the views are designed, you may find that the fields are not appropriate for your work, or you may have created some additional custom fields that you would like to show. By managing views, you can create those custom views to display the data that you need.

Let's now discuss the remaining four buttons in the **Manage All Views** dialog box.

To make it easier to create views, we have the ability to use the following buttons when setting up a custom view. When using **New...**, we have to select all the fields that we want to set up. When using the other buttons, we can use a template that is created for a table and adjust the template settings accordingly. This is handy if you want all the fields to show in the table view but maybe just want to add a calculated field or a few additional fields to that view. Let's discuss how you would use these additional buttons:

- **Copy...**: Select the view that you want to copy from the **View Name** field. This is your original template. Click **Copy...**. Enter a name for the new view and click **OK**. Carry on from *step 6* in the section about **New...** discussed previously.

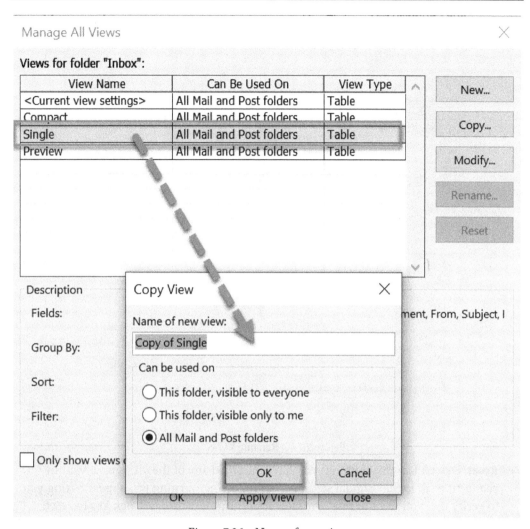

Figure 7.26 – Name of new view

- **Modify...**: Select the table that you want to modify from the **View Name** field. Click **Modify...** and you will be able to modify the table selected in the **Advanced View Settings** dialog box. Carry on from *step 6* in the section on **New...** discussed previously.

- **Rename...**: Select a view from the **View Name** field. Click **Rename...** and enter a name for the view in the **New name of view** field. Click **OK**.

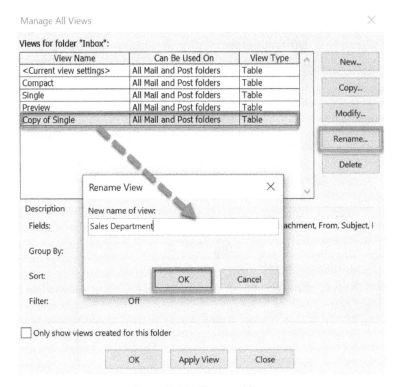

Figure 7.27 – Rename View

- **Reset/Delete**: Use this button if you have modified any of the views and want to change it back to the original settings. The following warning will appear asking you to verify that you want to reset the view to its original settings. Click **Yes** to reset:

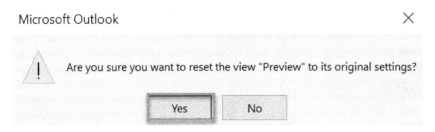

Figure 7.28 – Resetting a view

If there is not an original template made for the view, which would be the case for a view you created with the **New...** button, then the **Reset** button will display as **Delete** as there would not be a view to reset to.

Next, we will discuss the **Global Address List** (**GAL**) and how you can also customize this address list to your liking.

Viewing the GAL

The GAL is used by any company that hosts its email system using Microsoft Exchange. This gives you the benefit of a centrally managed address book for the entire company. This list is uploaded and managed by your IT department and will be stored on the Exchange server. Using the GAL means you do not have to add every user in your organization to your contact list, but you do need to know how to access this information.

When you start composing an email, you can either type in the name of the person you'd like to send it to or click on the **To** button to open the selected names and contacts dialog box to select the names from the contact list. To access the GAL, click on the drop-down arrow in the **Address Book** section and choose **Global Address List**. You will see your entire list of employees listed here and you can select the email IDs that you want to include in your email here.

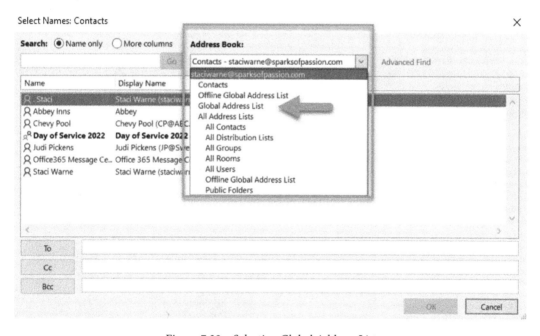

Figure 7.29 – Selecting Global Address List

If your system gets slow when selecting email IDs from the GAL, or if your company moves to another email system, you add the address list to your locally stored contacts folder in Outlook. To do this, follow these steps:

1. Open a new email window inside Outlook.

2. Select **Global Address Book** from the drop-down menu.

3. Highlight all the entries in the GAL or the entries that you want. To export the entire GAL, press *Ctrl + A* to select everything. To manually select the range, click on the first entry, then hold down the *Shift* key and click on the last item.

4. Right-click the highlighted items and select **Add to Contracts**. This could take some time depending on the number of contacts you've selected and your network speed.

5. Once complete, you can select the email IDs from the contacts list instead of the GAL.

Viewing a contact's address on a map

When you are viewing the contact information, to the right of the address is a **Map It** button.

Figure 7.30 – Map It on a contact

Once you click on **Map It**, you will be taken to **Bing Maps** with the address of your contact shown in the window. It will identify as much information as possible. You can also click on the **Directions** button to get detailed driving directions to this location. This is such a time-saver compared to how we found locations 20 years ago.

Figure 7.31 – Bing Maps

The Bing Maps feature is an add-in that is already installed within Outlook and is part of the Office add-ins. If you do not see this feature, your administrator might not have enabled this feature through the Office add-ins for Outlook.

Summary

Outlook is a great email service and its ability to manage and organize more than just email is incredible. In the end, it's up to you how much you want to utilize all of its capabilities. It's great as a stand-alone email platform, but add the power behind the calendar and **Contacts** and it is a great productivity tool. In this chapter, we discussed several features that show you the power behind the **Contacts** feature. Use this to keep track of not only your company through the GAL or keep your contacts close to home with the **People** feature. Either way, you won't be searching too far or too long to find an email address.

I love saving time and in the next chapter, I will show you some additional time-saving tips and tricks that you can use while working with Outlook notes. If you like the sticky notes that people use on their desks, then you will love this electronic version to use with Outlook. I especially like placing notes on my desktop within Windows to keep track of and take notes for several of my projects. Keep reading and I'm sure you will love this little-known secret as well.

Questions

1. I'm running Outlook 365 and I can't find the **People** pane. What should I do?

2. How can I use the favorites section on the **To-Do** pane?

3. Can I email all my contacts at one time through Outlook?

4. I have too many contacts; how I can organize them?

5. What do I need to do to sync my Outlook calendar with my Outlook phone calendar? I can see my emails fine but not the calendar.

Answers

1. The social connector, which people also refer to as the **People** pane, is available in versions 2016 and earlier. Microsoft has retired that product now in Outlook 365 as of late July 2020.

2. You can show people in the favorites section of the **To-Do** pane. Right-click on the sender's email address and choose **Add to Favorites**. You will see the person's picture and email address available for use in Outlook. The search box in the favorites will allow you to find people in your emails. Once you click on them in the favorites, you can email them from the open dialog box.

3. Yes, this can be done with a mail merge, with limitations; refer to *Chapter 5, Outlook Mail Merge.*

4. The easiest and fastest way to organize your contacts is with categories, which allow you to apply color to contacts. For example, you can use red for family and blue for coworkers, or something that makes sense to you. Then, you can sort by color and focus on the group you want. Refer to *Chapter 4, Organizing Your Outlook Environment,* for a detailed explanation of categories.

5. It can be assumed that you are using either a POP or IMAP account for email, as was discussed in *Chapter 3, Managing Email Accounts.* POP accounts will not sync anything; IMAP will sync email and folders only. Contacts and calendar items can only be synced with an Exchange account, which is included with a Microsoft 365 subscription, as well as Google Sync.

8
Outlook Notes

It is time to unclutter your monitor and trash those sticky notes. Outlook Notes will give you the confidence to do that. Notes are *electronic sticky notes*, often referred to as digital notes, and are a version of the traditional sticky notes that we all have that love/hate relationship with. I used to have these sticky notes all over my monitor, on the walls, on my calendars, and just about everywhere that I could put them. I can laugh at myself now to think that I used a sticky note on my calendar to remind me of some details. Is that not what a calendar is for? I finally started using Outlook Notes and got all those physical sticky notes off my desk. Digital notes reside on the right side of my desktop inside Windows.

In this chapter, we're going to cover the following topics:

- Creating a new note
- Organizing notes
- Displaying notes on the desktop
- Sending notes

You can access these notes on your screen while working and use them to jot down text, directions, data lists, phone numbers, information from the web, emails, and more. You may want to consider leaving a note open while working, which will allow you to interact with and even copy and paste information and pictures as needed. You will learn how to not only create, organize, color code, and email these notes to others, but also how to save them inside Outlook as well as on your desktop.

Creating a new note

Let's learn how to create a new note in this section:

1. Click on the **Notes** object in the bottom section of the navigation pane of Outlook. If you do not see the **Notes** button on this pane, click on the **...** button, and in the new selection, click on **Notes**.

Figure 8.1 – More objects

Instead of selecting **Notes**, you should set it up on your navigation pane so that the **Notes** object is easily accessible next time.

2. To do this, select **Navigation Options...**:

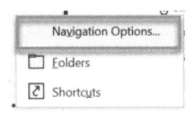

Figure 8.2 – Navigation Options selection

3. In the **Navigation Options** dialog box, set **Maximum number of visible items:** .

The maximum number you can set is *eight objects*, and this includes the **More** button. I have found that I like displaying six items, and I think having more than six items makes the buttons a little too small for my liking. Also, you can use the **Move Up** and **Move Down** buttons after selecting one of the objects to place them in a particular order from left to right on the navigation pane:

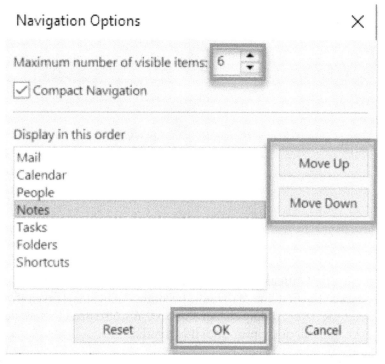

Figure 8.3 – Navigation Options dialog box

Once **Notes** has been selected, the **Notes** window will open. This resembles a yellow sticky note that you might have sitting on a desk, monitor, mirror, or wherever.

A note, as shown in *Figure 8.4*, will have these five characteristics, as numbered in the following screenshot:

- **Notes menu**: Use this menu for **Save As**, **Delete**, or **Forward** functions for any note. You can also use this for **Cut**, **Copy**, and **Paste** operations or for assigning a **Category** color, or simply for **Save** and **Close** operations.

- The move handle or title bar at the top of the note allows you to move the note around on the screen.

- This **X** is the close button to close the note.

- This is the resize handle that you can click on and drag to resize the note. You may also resize the note on the sides of the note like you would in a window.

- The date and time when you last modified the note will appear in this section at the bottom of the note.

To use this note, simply start typing in it. The first line that is entered in the note will be used as the title of the note, so don't make it too descriptive. Use it like the subject of an email.

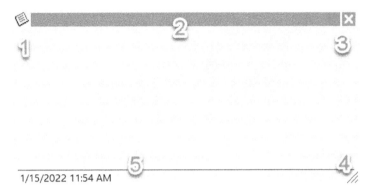

1/15/2022 11:54 AM

Figure 8.4 – Note

There is no versioning for Outlook Notes, and when you close the note, it will automatically be saved. The first line of the note becomes the filename (even if you leave it blank), and to edit the name, simply change this text. You also need to have data in the note window, or the title will not appear until it is entered.

Note

To create a new note, you could also click on **New Note** in the note window, or a quicker method is to press *Ctrl* + *Shift* + *N*. When you press *Ctrl* + *N*, a new item for the app that you are in will open. For example, if you are in an email, you will get a new email window; if you are in the calendar, you will get a new appointment. Adding the *Shift* key makes it works differently, as this shortcut key is reserved for **New Note** no matter which app is active. Try it out, it's one of my favorite shortcut keys!

Organizing notes

Hopefully, by now you have taken down all your paper notes and created digital notes in Outlook. Now it's time for us to organize these notes so that we can find what we need quickly. I recommend that you use the first written line of the note to help you organize your notes as well. You could enter the first word as the intended action of the note. Use terms such as To-do, Call, Reminder, and Lunch as possible ideas, and try to stay consistent in your naming, which will help you refer to your notes in your free time. For instance, if you only have 10 minutes, you could look at a note whose first line/word action helped you complete that task in 10 minutes. One example could be the call item, which would allow you to find a note and make a quick call.

There are multiple ways to organize your notes, and the top three ways I suggest are as follows:

- **Categories**: If you apply a category to your note by *right-clicking* on the note and selecting **Categories**, apply a color so you can quickly search by category. All the category colors will be grouped together. Click on the **Categories** menu in the notes list to group all the same colors together:

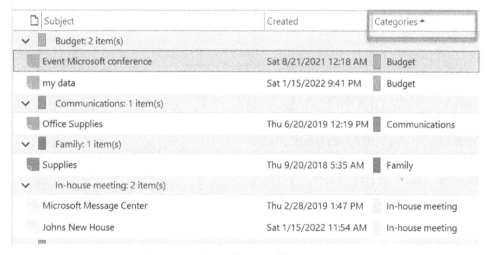

Figure 8.5 – Notes list sorted by Categories

- **Current View – Icon**: In this view, you can click on a note and drag it where you want in the notes window. You can arrange these in whatever order makes sense to you.

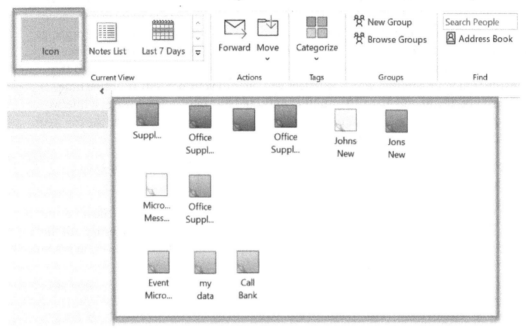

Figure 8.6 – Notes Icon view

- **Folders**: Create a folder in the notes navigation pane. To do this, *right-click* on the **Notes** folder and then click on **New Folder…** when prompted to enter a name for the new folder. You can now drag icons to the desired folder. Use this folder to view those notes that you have placed inside.

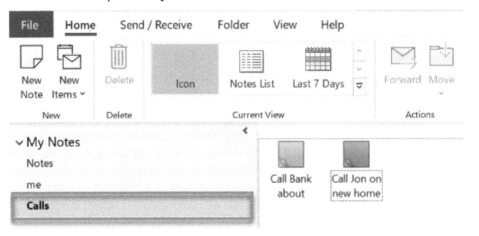

Figure 8.7 – Notes folder view

It does not matter which of these or other methods you choose to organize your notes. If you are comfortable with and can remember how to access your notes, it is the best method for you.

Displaying notes on the desktop

If you would like to have notes available to you on the desktop, you can save notes outside of Outlook and open them without opening the main Outlook application:

1.   To do this, click **Menu | Save As** on the **Note**.

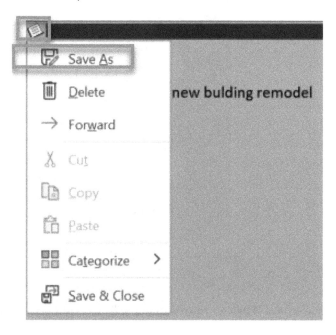

Figure 8.8 – Menu item on note

2. A Windows dialog box will open and allow you to choose a location to save the note. Choose the `Desktop` folder to display the **Notes** on the desktop.

Figure 8.9 – Desktop notes

> **Note**
>
> The version and style of Windows you're running will determine how the notes appear on your desktop.

Let us understand another convenient way to get a note on the desktop.

1. Press and hold the *Ctrl* key while you click on the note and drag it to the desktop. This will create a copy on the desktop without having to get the menu icon on the note.

2. When you open the saved note on your desktop, you can edit and add to the note.

3. When you add to this note, it will not synchronize with the note in Outlook. When you edit the note in Outlook, it will also not synchronize with the note on the desktop. Decide where you want to store this note and use the note from that location.

Now let us understand how to send notes.

Sending notes

Use the **Forward** button to send a note to someone else through email or another channel:

1. Select the note and click on **Home | Forward**.

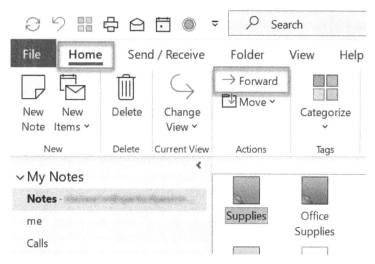

Figure 8.10 – Forward selected note

2. The selected note will be an attachment in a new email.

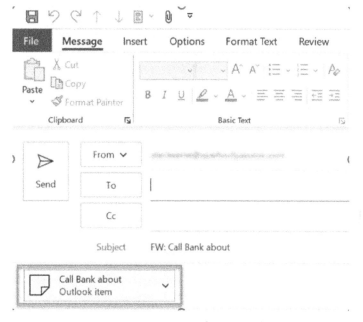

Figure 8.11 – Forward note email

If the recipient opens the email through an application such as Gmail, it will be opened as a plain text email, but if opened in Outlook it will be treated as a note. This makes sending a quick note to your co-workers in the office very useful.

Summary

The next time you want to jot down a note on a piece of paper, do it on an **Outlook note** instead. Use notes for anything you would write on paper or for items you need to use again on the computer, such as reminders, ideas, addresses, and directions. Outlook Notes is very convenient for saving information that you may need later. You learned in this chapter not only how to create a note quickly with *Ctrl + Shift + N*, but also how to organize and send notes through email to recipients. This is a quick and efficient way to get information stored on your computer for use now or later without having to keep track of paper, which risks the loss of the note as it could be thrown away by accident.

In the next chapter, we will discuss creating **tasks** to help you be proficient in your daily work. You will learn how tasks are stored in Outlook's default folders. You will learn several tips and tricks on how to turn Outlook into a powerful task manager to enhance your daily productivity.

Questions

1. Is there a shortcut key to move to notes?

2. What are the sticky notes that I see on my Windows computer?

3. How do I change the font in my notes?

4. Can I retrieve a deleted note?

5. Can I open the notes folder in a new window?

Answers

1. *Ctrl + 5* is the shortcut key combination to open the Notes workspace.

2. Sticky notes appear on Windows computers as well as inside OneNote and the OneNote app. When you add a note inside OneNote – a sticky note on your phone, for example – that note will automatically sync with Outlook. If you turn on the sync feature and select your Microsoft 365 account on the Windows sticky notes, the notes created will also sync with OneDrive.

3. In Outlook 2010 and 2007, you can change the fonts in the notes by clicking **File |
    Options | Notes and Journal**. This option was taken away in Outlook 2016 and later
    versions. The default font in these later versions is 11-point Calibri.

4. You can retrieve a deleted note as long as it still resides in your deleted folder in the
    navigation pane. Click on the **Mail** button on the navigation pane, then open the
    contents of the **Deleted Items** folder. You will find your deleted notes in this folder
    as well. To retrieve the note, move it to another folder.

5. To open the Notes folder in a new window, click on the **Notes** button in the
    navigation pane to display the notes in the workspace. Right-click on the Notes
    folder, which displays your email ID located on the navigation pane for the notes,
    and click **Open in New Window**.

9
Tasks and To-Dos

A task is something that should be done, and completing the task or tasks is one way to show that you have achieved an objective. This could be anything from going to a meeting or preparing a report. Any item that you feel needs to be placed on a list so that you will remember to complete it, by setting a reminder or assigning it to another person, is a task.

Our minds can only remember so much information, and there is nothing wrong with needing a little nudge to remind you to complete something. Outlook is the best tool to help you stay on top of deadlines, not forget an event, or manage your team activities without skipping a beat. It also allows you to create your own tasks and recurring tasks and, better yet, view those tasks within your calendar. This is a hidden secret of Outlook.

In this chapter, we're going to cover the following topics:

- To-do list versus tasks
- Creating new tasks
- Recurring tasks
- Assigning tasks
- Replying to a task assignment
- Task status reports
- Creating task folders
- Viewing tasks in the calendar

Staying on top of your tasks will take a little practice. Once you learn how to put all these techniques together and work hard to complete your to-do lists, you will be surprised by how much you will accomplish.

To-do list versus tasks

There are tasks you can create inside of Outlook and there is a to-do list. What is the difference? This can be very confusing to navigate. It's important that you understand the difference between these two features. Let's dive in and cover them now.

To-do

When a flag, as mentioned in *Chapter 4, Organizing Your Outlook Environment*, is added to an email, the item is linked to the to-do list that is viewable if the **To-Do Bar** option is turned on from **View** | **To-Do Bar** | **Tasks**.

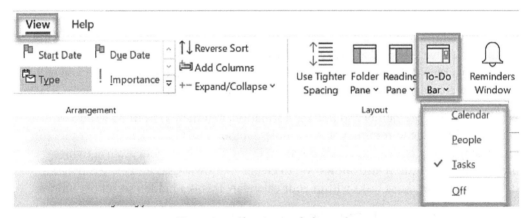

Figure 9.1 – Showing to-do bar tasks

The to-do bar will indicate what needs to be done so you can view the items in one location.

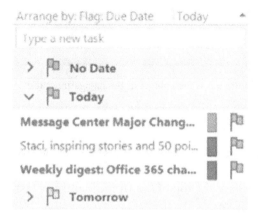

Figure 9.2 – To-do bar tasks

This is a convenient list and it is especially helpful to be able to refer to all your items in one place. The items on the to-do bar include the following:

- Entered tasks
- Appointments
- Email messages you have flagged

This can be a little confusing because you are not actually placing these items here. The main purpose of the to-do bar is to help you remember items you have flagged to complete today or on a future date within your emails.

When a flag is created, Outlook also adds the item or email to the to-do list in the task object where it is also saved.

Tasks

To view and manage tasks, click on the task button at the bottom of the navigation pane.

Figure 9.3 – Task object in the navigation pane

Within the tasks workspace, you can create new tasks, manage your tasks, and select a task to assign to others to complete.

You can use the navigation pane to the left of the task workspace to view the to-do list, tasks, and folders you have created to store and organize your tasks. The task workspace will display the flagged emails at the top of the window and any tasks will be displayed below the emails that are marked as *flagged*.

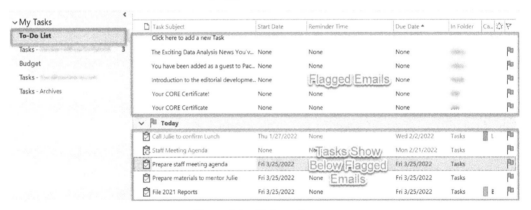

Figure 9.4 – Task workspace

> **Note**
> Tasks and flagged items are not stored in the to-do list. They are added to the default **Task** folder.

Creating new tasks

To help manage your tasks in Outlook, use the tasks workspace. This workspace allows you to not only create new tasks but also assign tasks to yourself or others for completion.

The task request form is used to create a new task, assign a task to another user, and request updates. To display this form once you have activated the task object, click **Home | New Task**.

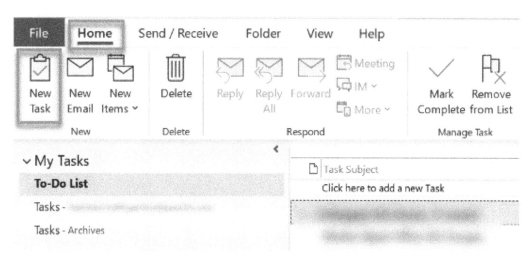

Figure 9.5 – Creating a new task

Use this task request form to not only create a new task but also store information pertaining to the task.

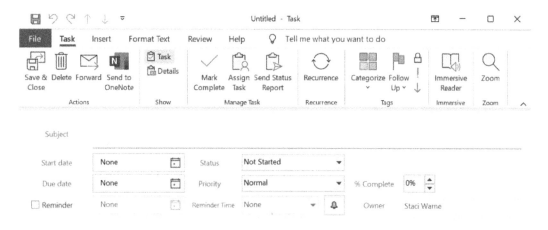

Figure 9.6 – Task request form

> **Note**
> Display the task request form from the email workspace or any other workspace by clicking **Home | New Item | Task**.

Tasks are not linked to an email message through flags and are able to hold details such as **Start date**, **Due date**, and **Reminder**. The following figure shows the task request form that is available to store this information. Some people choose to record all the information you see here, while others choose to record a name in the **Subject** field and nothing else. It's up to you how detailed you would like to get.

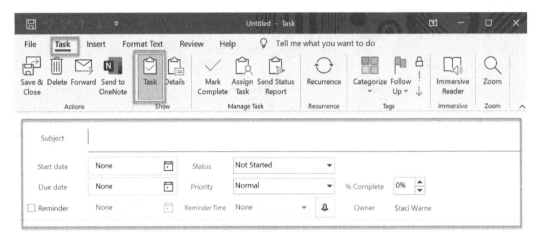

Figure 9.7 – New task

To keep even more information about the task, click the **Task | Details** button.

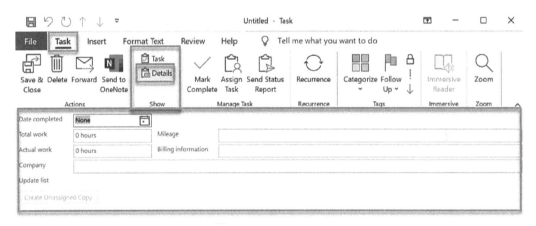

Figure 9.8 – Task detail information

In the details section of the task, additional information is stored in the fields, which include **Date competed**, **Total work** (hours), **Mileage**, **Actual work**, **Billing information**, **Company**, **Update list**, and an area for **Create Unassigned Copy**.

> **Note**
>
> When you receive a task request, the text boxes with the task data will appear shaded until you accept the task. This gives you control of the tasks you accept.

Recurring tasks

A recurring task in Outlook is a task that you create once and then have that task recreated automatically after a designated time interval. You can set any task that has been created into a recurring task by clicking on the **Recurrence** button located on the **Task** tab

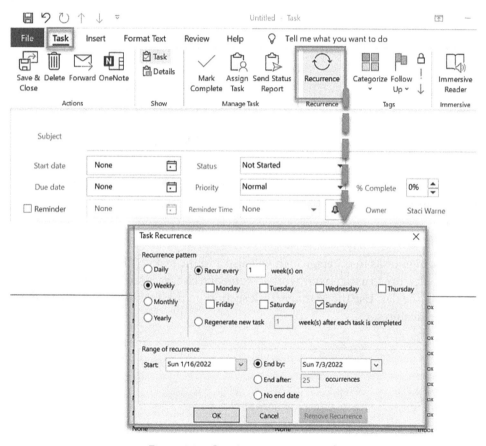

Figure 9.9 – Creating a recurrence task

It is important for you to realize that recurring tasks do not work the same as a recurring appointment for your calendar. Recurring tasks are not static tasks like an appointment. Once you set a recurring task, Outlook displays the current or original task. Once you mark the original task as complete, the next-occurring task will appear in your task window.

Click **Home** | **Mark Complete** to have the task show as completed, and a *strikethrough* line will appear on the task, or it will not show on your screen, depending on your settings.

Figure 9.10 – Mark Complete

Outlook has the tasks set up like this because it assumes that you don't want to move on to the next task until the current task is completed. This may not be your intention but that is the logic that Outlook uses.

Assigning tasks

You can also assign tasks to others, which will also add the task to their task list. You will find this a nice feature to assign your work to someone else, as it seems we never have enough time in the day. Use the **Manage Task** section on the **Task** ribbon to access these more advanced features.

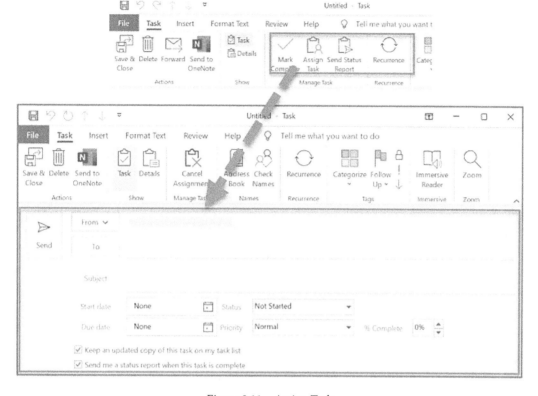

Figure 9.11 – Assign Task

Status of a task

There are five status levels to choose from when you assign a task to yourself or others. The **% Complete** field and content of the task can be changed based on the status chosen. The following table lists the status levels and the settings that will be automatically applied:

Status	Description	% Complete
Not Started	Default status applied if no status is selected	0%
In Progress	Indicates task is being worked on	0%
Completed	Indicates that a task is complete	100%
Waiting on someone else	Indicates that a task needs more work or work is needed by someone else	0%
Deferred	Task is on hold until a later date	0%

Table 9.1 – Status options

The following figure indicates the Status drop-down to set the status:

Figure 9.12 – Status field

The **% Complete** field can be changed as needed to apply to the status of the assigned task. After completing the message and filling in the remainder of the fields as appropriate, click **Send** and the message will be sent to the recipient of the assignment.

Replying to a task assignment

When a task has been assigned, the recipient of the task will receive a message notifying them that a task has been assigned to them. They can click the buttons on the **Task** ribbon to **Accept** or **Decline**, or they can assign the task to someone else.

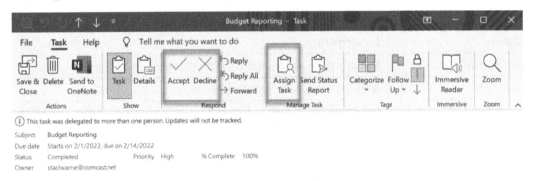

Figure 9.13 – Accepting or declining a task

The following table indicates what action will be taken depending on the option you choose: **Accept**, **Decline**, or **Assign Task**:

Selection	Action Taken
Accept	• Your response will be sent to the email ID of the person who sent the assigned task. • The task will be sent to your task list. • You can now include this in your working task list as any other task.
Decline	• Your decline response will be sent to the email ID of the person who sent the assigned task. • The task will be deleted from your message list, allowing the task to be assigned to another recipient.
Assign Task	• Opens a new email message with the task information available to assign the task to another person. • A message will be sent back to you, not the original sender/assigner, letting you know of their response.

Table 9.2 – Action for selected task

Upon accepting an assigned task, you will be able to track and complete the task as you would any other tasks that you create in the *Task* folder. You will also be able to tell that this is an assigned task by the icon that appears in the icon field in the task workspace.

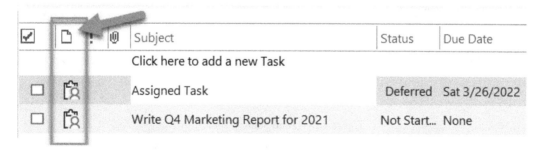

Figure 9.14 – Sort icons in the task workspace

Clicking on the icon shown in the header section of the preceding screenshot will sort your tasks and place all of your assigned tasks at the top of the list for easy accessing or locating the assigned tasks.

A task status report

One advantage of assigning a task to another person is the ease of sending and receiving a status report of the assigned task. When they open the task, they can prepare and send a status report that will be delivered to you, who assigned the task. This report will include all details pertaining to the task, such as the following:

- Start Date

- Due Date

- Status

- % Complete

- Actual work

- Requested by name

To send a *status report* for a task that was assigned to you, open the task and click **Task | Send Status Report**. A new email message will be generated with the status information included in the body of the message along with a subject line indicating that it's a task status report. After entering the recipient, click **Send** and the status report will be sent.

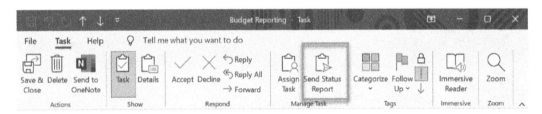

Figure 9.15 – Send Status Report

The *status report* will look just like an email message and will also include the status information. If you prefer, you can also include a message within the email before clicking on **Send**.

Task folders

You create task folders to organize your tasks in the same manner as you do with file directories. You can create tasks under each task folder that is showing in the navigation pane. To create a task folder, take the following steps:

1. Create folders in the **Tasks** navigation pane to organize your tasks.

2. Right-click on a task folder in the navigation pane and enter a name for the folder. The default is to list new tasks under the task folder. You can create several folders to help you organize tasks. This is the same process as creating folders to organize your emails and is specific to the task object.

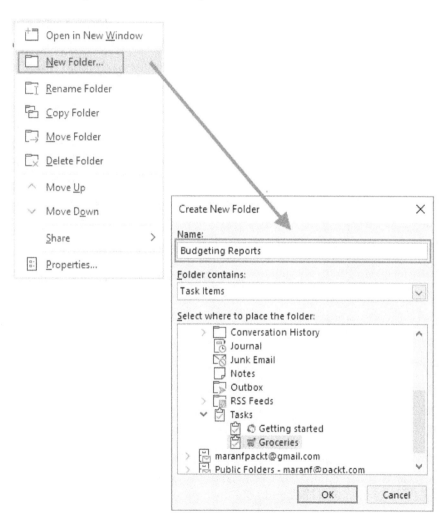

Figure 9.16 – New task folder

Task folders are containers to store your tasks under for organizational purposes. These folders can be very useful when you create several different tasks and allow you to click on the folder to view all the tasks associated with the selected folder. When you are in the task view, you can use these folders to view the tasks that have been assigned to the folder. If you are in another view, such as the calendar view, you may find it is easier to use that selected view to see your tasks, as will be shown next.

Viewing tasks in the calendar

Displaying your tasks on the calendar is a hidden secret in Outlook in my opinion. This is one of my favorite ways to see my tasks and keep me working in my calendar. This stops me from getting distracted by incoming emails. When you are on the **Day** or **Week** view in the calendar, you can view your tasks at the bottom of the calendar:

1. To turn on this feature, click on the calendar object in the navigation pane, then click **View** | **Day** or **Week**, as shown in the following screenshot.

2. Next, click **Daily Task List** | **Arrange By** | **By Start Date** or **By Due Date**, as shown in the following screenshot. There is also an option to turn on **Show Completed Tasks** for viewing the tasks you have already completed for that date as well. This helps me feel like I have completed something in the day; they will be displayed in the grid with a strikethrough.

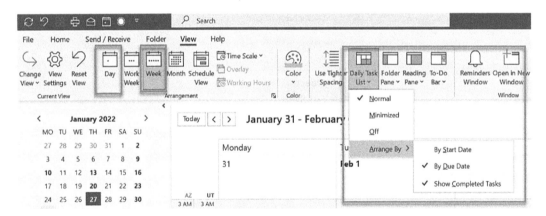

Figure 9.17 – Daily Task List | By Due Date

Your tasks will be displayed in the bottom section below the calendar. As you scroll through the calendar dates and times, the window will display the available tasks for you to always have handy in your view. You can position your mouse pointer on the line between the two windows and click and hold the mouse to make the window larger or smaller for your preferred view.

I like to have it small on the screen, and then I can make this window larger when I am ready to work on my tasks.

You can also double-click on a task in this view to open the **Task** window for more details. This is a quick way to see any emails or notes that you may have attached to the task.

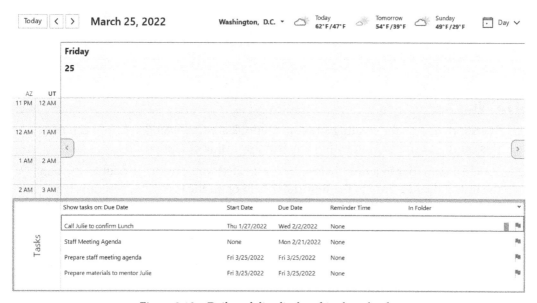

Figure 9.18 – Daily task list displayed in the calendar

I hope you will try out this handy tip. I have found it to help my productivity increase as I can use this while working in my calendar to quickly look at more details about my tasks without changing views.

Summary

Tasks have so many useful features that can really help to increase productivity. They are a hidden secret in Outlook, and it will benefit you to learn how to manage your tasks and always have them available to track what needs to be done. This could be through flagged emails or tasks that you create, or better yet, create and assign to another person. By tracking your tasks at a high level, as you have learned to do through this chapter, you will find that you are less likely to forget any highly important items that must be completed.

In the next chapter, we will discuss the different ways that you can simplify your Outlook search. Once you learn how to master these search techniques, you will no longer feel like you must create hundreds of folders to organize your emails yourself. Outlook search has gone through a complete overhaul in the past few years and with the many tips and tricks you are about to learn, you will quickly find any item you need.

Questions

1.   What are the shortcut keys for creating a task in Outlook?

2.   How can you set a reminder on your tasks?

3.   Can you rename a task?

4.   How do you set tasks to appear at the top and not the bottom of the to-do bar?

5.   I would like my task icon to appear at the left of the mail icon on the navigation pane, is this possible?

Answers

1.   The shortcut keys for creating a task in Outlook are *Ctrl + Shift + K*. You can use this shortcut combination within any window inside of Outlook.

2.   To add a reminder to a task that is already created, you can either double-click on the task and add a time to the **Reminder** field or, in the task view, you can right-click on the flag for the task and click **Add Reminder...**, and then set the time for the reminder in the **Custom** dialog box in the **Reminder** section.

3.   To rename a task, right-click on the task name and click **Rename Task**. You can then change the name of the task as desired as the **Name** field will be in edit mode. Click **Enter** when done.

4.   You can make the to-do bar display a combination of calendar items, people, and tasks. The items that show at the top will be the first items you select and will appear in the order selected. To have your tasks appear at the top, simply unselect all the current options and reselect the items again in the order that you want them to appear.

5.   Yes, you can change the settings for how the icons appear in the navigation pane. Click on the **...** icon, then click **Navigation Options....** Select the desired object in the **Display in this order** box in the **Navigation Options** dialog box and then click the **Move Up** button as needed to move the selected object to the top of the list. Click **OK** and the selected icon will show as specified.

Part 4:
How to: Share, Search, and Archive in Outlook

If you are tired of searching for items and wading through thousands of emails to find an important email, this section is for you. You will learn how to set up a search the first time by narrowing down the details of the item you are looking for, and you will be amazed at how few seconds pass as you locate that much-needed document. You will then learn how you can share this or other information between different people and/or different accounts. When your mailbox is overflowing with emails that you don't want to delete, you can set up an Archive to guarantee that email will still be available when you need it, not only this week but years into the future. This section contains the following chapters:

- *Chapter 10, Save Time Searching*
- *Chapter 11, Sharing Mail, Calendars, and Contacts*
- *Chapter 12, Archiving and Backup*

10
Save Time Searching

Many of us have a hidden fear of hitting the *Delete* button. We all fear that one day, we might need that important email and we won't be able to find it if we delete it. As our inboxes become larger and larger, the fear escalates about what we feel should be deleted. As time passes, our inbox gets out of control.

How can you ever find that important email that was stored days, years, or decades ago? Since Microsoft released the latest updates for the **Search** feature back in 2019, you can get rid of that fear of losing an email.

This chapter will discuss how to utilize the Outlook Search feature so you will feel confident in keeping any email you think you may need later. However, if your computer is running out of storage space, you might want to use the cloud for your email storage.

In this chapter, we're going to cover the following topics:

- Using Search

- Instant search

- Advanced Search

- Settings and indexing

- Search syntax and operators

Using Search

With an Outlook account, you are allowed 15 GB of email storage space per account. Microsoft 365 subscribers are allowed 50 GB of space, but many accounts have more storage than this. I have 1 TB of storage on the cloud with my subscription. With this much storage for our emails, most of us have no reason to delete any of our emails for storage reasons.

In most cases, you can now keep all the emails you want as not only can the cloud manage this, but Outlook's Search feature has been vastly improved. When I need to search for an old email, I usually find it by simply typing an email ID or topic in the **Search** box and my email will appear, without using the advanced search feature.

The **Search** box is at the top of the Outlook window in the title bar, to the right of **Quick Access Toolbar**, if you have this toolbar docked above the ribbon, as shown in the following screenshot:

Figure 10.1 – Search box

You can access this from any object with *Ctrl + E*. When you click in the **Search** box, on the left, you will see **Current Mailbox**, which is the default. This indicates that the search will only search in the mailbox that is showing currently, which for most people would be the inbox. To change this, click on the arrow to the right of **Current Mailbox** and a drop-down menu will appear where you can broaden the search by selecting your preference. If you are not sure where the required email is stored, click on **All Mailboxes** or **All Outlook Items**:

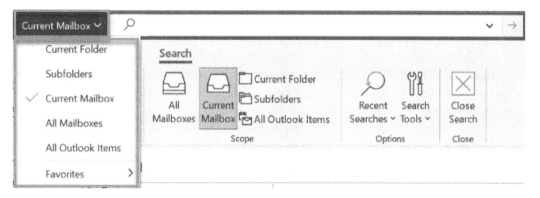

Figure 10.2 – Search location options

Search, in my opinion, cannot get any easier than this, but it does, which you will see as we continue. There are two different types of searches you can perform:

- Instant search
- Advanced Search

I will explain these two types of search and you can decide when to use each type depending on your needs at the time.

Instant search

Instant search is the **Search** box in the title bar of your Outlook window, as shown previously. This **Search** box is always available, and you don't have to click any specific area to activate it. It is available in all the Outlook objects, such as you saw previously in **Mail**, as well as **Calendar**, **People**, **Tasks**, **Folders**, and **Notes**. It's available all the time, no matter what object you are working on, in Outlook 2019 and later as well as Outlook for the web. Older versions of Outlook will have this **Search** box above the workspace window.

1. Once you click on the **Search** box, a drop-down menu appears with possible suggestions of what you may be looking for. This box will consistently change as you continue to enter your desired search. The following figure shows the three sections that might appear if items are available to search for in these areas. In this example, when I click in the box, my previous search terms, as well as people I have previously emailed, appear in this drop-down box, and you may see **Recently Used Actions**, **Suggested Searches**, and **Suggested Actions** show as suggestions as well. This list is dynamic and will change as necessary.

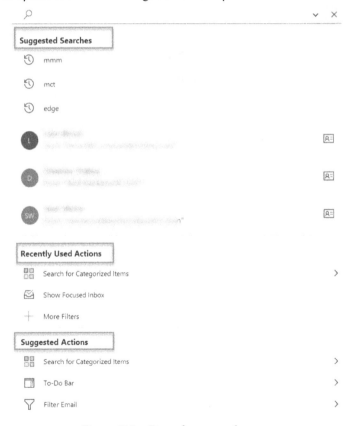

Figure 10.3 – Drop-down search menu

2. The next step in finding your item is to simply type in what you are looking for. I've found it helpful to keep my eye on the drop-down box as I am typing. The more I type, the more information will appear and disappear from the suggested items.

3. After you have entered your text, assuming you didn't find your item in the drop-down box, click *Enter*.

Outlook will now have populated the workspace with possible solutions as well as activated the **Search** tab.

For the following example, I searched for the words `microsoft edge`. My workspace now shows not only **Microsoft Edge**, but also other items with the word **Microsoft** as well. If I had just searched for `Edge`, I would have gotten other emails as well referring to my car, as I own a Ford Edge car and I have received emails from the car dealership from which I purchased my car. Later, in the *Search syntax and operators* section, I will give you some suggestions on how to type in your search to narrow down the results.

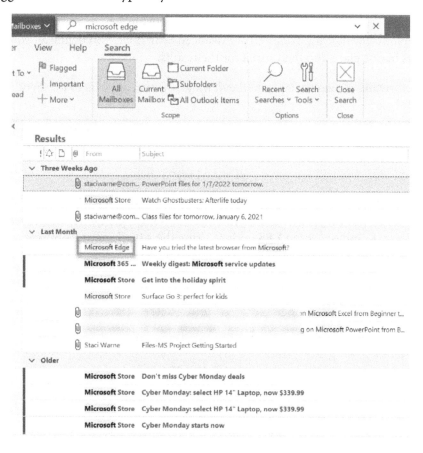

Figure 10.4 – Search results

You may feel that you want to narrow down the search even more, and you can do this from the ribbon. Using the tools on the ribbon, you can refine your search even further:

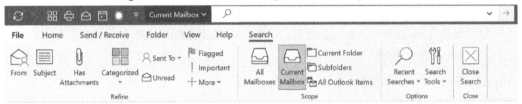

Figure 10.5 – Search tab

You have buttons including **Subject**, **Has Attachments**, **Categorized**, and more. By choosing **All Outlook Items**, Outlook will not only search your mail but will also include your Calendar and other objects.

Advanced Search

Using Advanced Search is an even more efficient way of using Search and you will have even more options for filtering your items. Advanced Search lets you define all your requirements in one place and then run it for the results:

1. To use **Advanced Search**, click on the *down* arrow that appears to the right of the **Search** box.

    The following figure has **Advanced Search** open, so you will see the arrow pointing up. To close this view, you can click on this arrow again.

2. Once opened, you will see some predefined search fields.

    Choose all the options that apply and enter the information as needed. For example, if you wanted an email with an attachment, you could click on the dropdown by **Attachments** and select the **YES** option. Using the **Attachment Contains** option, you can type in words that are included in the attachment.

    Your available options will be different depending on the object you are in when you select **Advanced Search**.

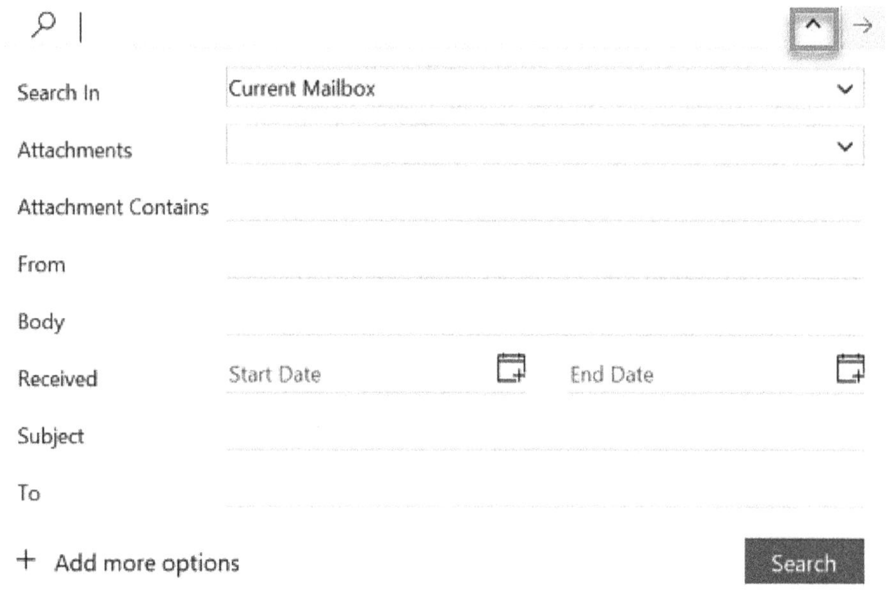

Figure 10.6 – Advanced Search

3. For **Advanced Search**, you were probably thinking there would be more options than shown in this box. If you click on the **Add more options** button in the bottom-left corner of the box, you will see even more:

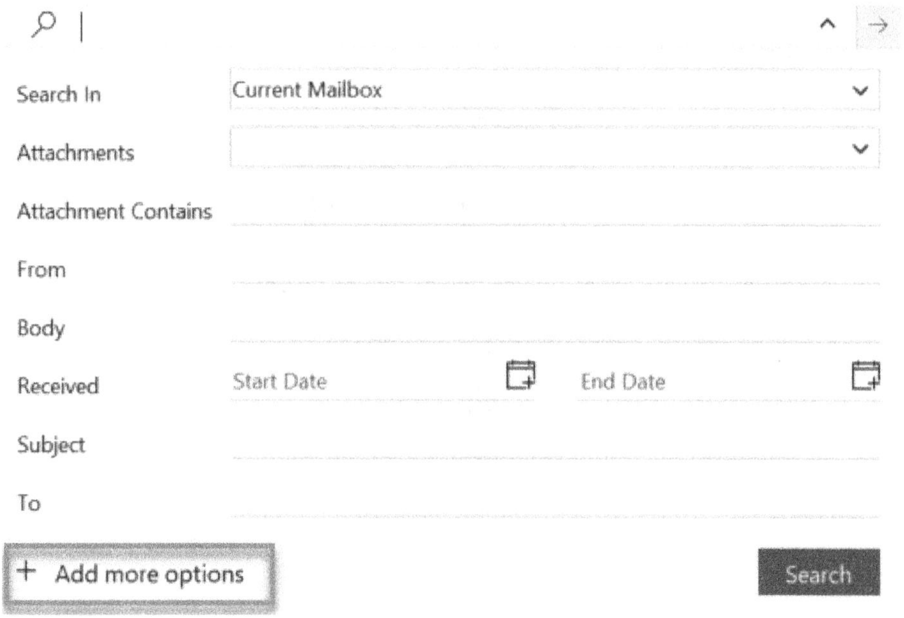

Figure 10.7 – Add more options

4. Once this is done, the **Advanced Search Options** box list will be displayed, and you can click on the box next to the item you want to specify information for.

5. Click on the empty box and that item will appear in the list. For example, if you selected the **Bcc** field, then the list would show that field with a box next to it to fill in an email ID that you were searching for. This opens several additional possibilities.

For more options, click on **Add Form Field**. This will open a window to select all the available different form fields, and even your own custom forms will appear here. As you can see, Search has endless possibilities:

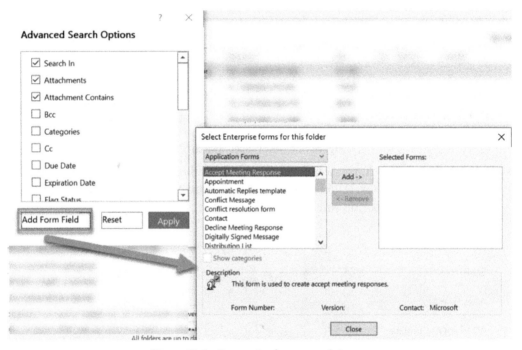

Figure 10.8 – Enterprise forms search items

How specific you get to find your item is up to you. You can search as granularly as you need. Start out very broad and keep adding to it. Within seconds, you should find what you need, which will probably have you wondering whether you need all your created custom folders anymore. This will be discussed in *Chapter 16, Managing Your Day System*.

Settings and indexing

With all Office applications, we have default options, and these have been discussed in previous chapters of this book. There are options for **Search** as well:

1. Click **File | Options | Search**. Let's explore a few of these settings:

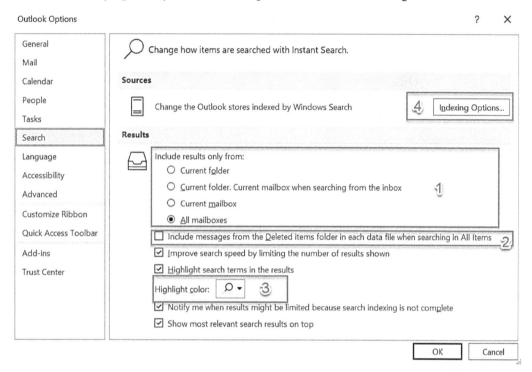

Figure 10.9 – Outlook search options

2. **Include results only from**: If you choose the **All mailboxes** option, your search will take a little bit longer as it searches everything.

3. **Include messages from the Deleted Items folder in each data file when searching in All Items**: Check this box if you want to include the **Deleted Items** folder in **All Items**.

4. **Highlight color**: Yellow will be used unless you change this color.

5. **Indexing Options…**: Indexing will help you get faster search results. It does not just pertain to Outlook Search, but it helps with any search you do in Windows.

Indexing means going through all your files and messages and any content on your computer and cataloging this information. This process is similar to an index of a book but, instead of manually finding that index in the back of a book, you are searching for it electronically. If Outlook Search doesn't find what you want, then indexing may not be working properly.

6. To do some troubleshooting, you can click on the **Indexing Options...** button:

Figure 10.10 – Indexing Options

7. Verify that **Microsoft Outlook** is in this list and that **Indexing Complete** is stated at the top of the **Indexing Options** dialog box.

8. Click on **Microsoft Outlook** and then click on **Modify**:

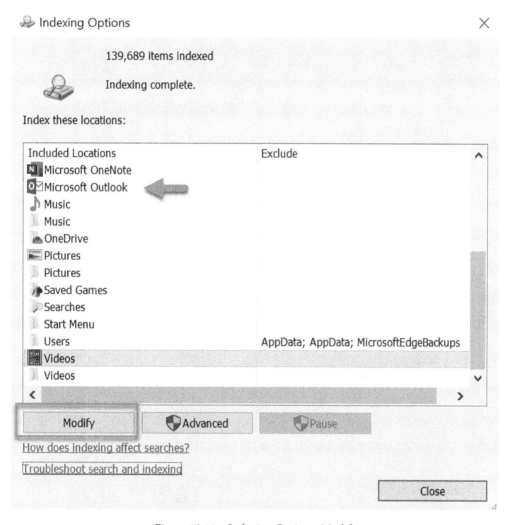

Figure 10.11 – Indexing Options, Modify

9. Verify that the **Microsoft Outlook** selection box is checked. If not, check the box and click **OK** so that indexing is performed on Outlook:

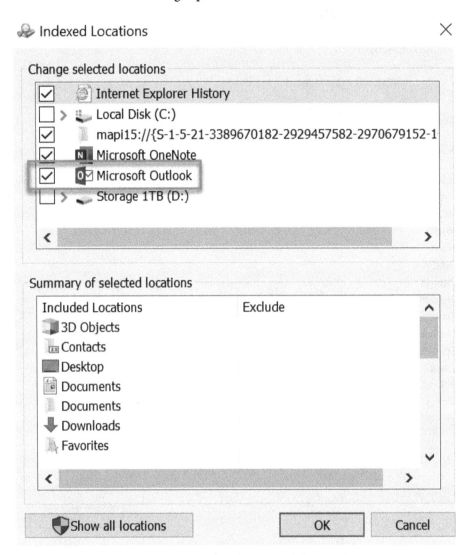

Figure 10.12 – Indexed locations

10. To troubleshoot indexing problems further, open the **Options** window for indexing. To do this click **File | Options | Search | Indexing Options…**:

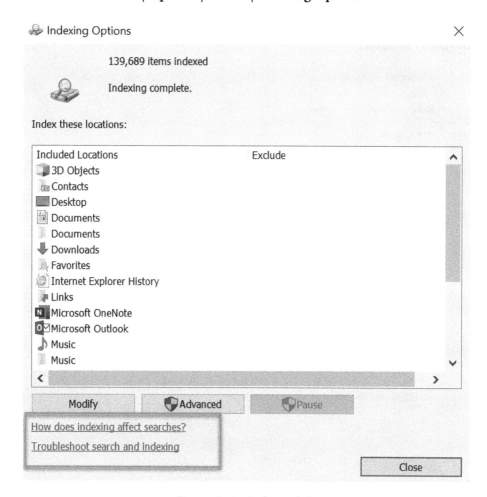

Figure 10.13 – Indexing help

The bottom-left corner of this box has two links to get help from Microsoft.

11. Click on the **How does indexing affect searches?** link for help on understanding how indexing works, and click on **Troubleshoot search and indexing** for the troubleshooter to open, where there will be a tool that will repair indexing on the computer. You will need to be signed in as an administrator for this tool to work.

If you find your search results are still not complete, you should rebuild the Outlook index. You can identify the need for this by noticing that you are not seeing the expected results of your searches, or you are seeing partial or no items returned with a search. A rebuild will restart the indexing of all your data files and completely rebuild the search catalog.

Rebuilding the Outlook index

You can rebuild the index and override the original index settings:

1. To do this, click on **File | Options | Search | Indexing Options | Select Outlook | Advanced | Rebuild:**

Figure 10.14 – Rebuild index

A message will tell you that you are about to start rebuilding the index and some functionality will not be available to you in the **Search** feature until the index rebuild is complete:

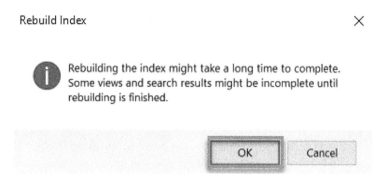

Figure 10.15 – Rebuild index running

2. The **Indexing Options** box will now indicate that the indexing is in progress, as shown here:

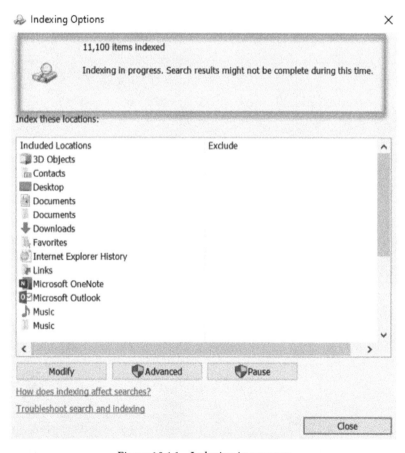

Figure 10.16 – Indexing in progress

Once this is complete, you can run a search to ensure it is working correctly.

Search syntax and operators

If you had problems searching for emails over a decade ago, you need to realize that Search has become a lot more robust. Locating emails and other items has become even easier if you use the right terms. There is, however, more to Search than just typing in a word in the **Search** box and pressing *Enter*. Let's now learn how to enter your search terms the right way.

The following table gives examples of what you can enter in the **Search** box without using the Advanced tools. By learning these techniques, you will speed up your search requests and fine-tune the process.

This is not a complete list. For more information on Search syntax for Outlook, refer to the *Further reading* section at the end of this chapter.

Outlook Search Syntax		
Operator	Example	Notes
Subject	Subject:Edge	Finds the word Edge anywhere within the Subject line.
From	From:@abc.com	Finds @abc.com in the From line. The following are examples: help@abc.com Staci@abc.com support@abc.com
To	To:Staci@abc.com	Finds emails with email ID to Staci@abc.com in the To field.
Cc	CC:Staci@abc.com	Finds emails with email ID to Staci@abc.com in the Cc field.
before	before:received<12/31/2021	< Less than > Greater than <= Less than and equal to >= Greater than and equal to
after	after:received>12/31/2021	
Combine before and after	Received<12/31/2020>01/01/2020	Finds emails sent or received during 2020.
date	Date:received<=12/31/2021 received:"last week" before:December 2021 after:last month	Less than = before Greater than = after Date = mm/dd/yyyy "yesterday" "last week" Other words: today, tomorrow, yesterday, this, next, last, past, coming, week, month, year, this week, next month, last week, past month, coming year, Sunday, Monday, Tuesday, Wednesday, Thursday, Friday, Saturday, January, February, March, April, May, June, July, August, September, October, November, December, January 2020, December 2020, June 2014, and so on.

size	size:<5MB	Empty: 0 KB
	received:>=lastweek	Tiny: 0-10 KB
	received:>11/31/2020	Small: 10-100 KB
	received:=>1-11-2021	Medium: 100 KB-1 MB
		Huge: 16-128 MB
	size:>=5MB<=10MB	Gigantic: >128 MB
	Or use	< smaller than
	Size:>5MB..10MB	> greater than
	Or use	<= smaller than or equal to
	size:>5MB<10MB	>= greater than or equal to
folder	folder:archive	Finds email located in the Archive folder only.
has:attachment	hasattachment:true Has:attachment	Finds mail messages that have at least one file attachment.
hasattachment:false	hasattachment:false	Finds mail messages with no attachments.
AND (uppercase)	Microsoft AND Edge Cat AND Dog	Both words must be present.
OR (uppercase)	Microsoft OR Edge Cat OR Dog	Finds either word; does not have to contain both words.
NOT (uppercase)	NOT category:red	Excludes certain search results.
[ ]	Birthday [06/01/1995]	Finds an item in which a certain value is not set.
"Text with spaces"	"Microsoft Edge"	Finds both words that are enclosed within the double quote marks.

Table 1.1 – Outlook Search syntax

Summary

Using **Search** is the fastest way to search for previous emails or other items that you need to find. Everyone learns their own style of how they want to find items, and I have found this even depends on what I am looking for. You can start by scanning folders, or you can choose to sort and filter the inbox, but if you are like me, you will go to **Search** first. I have found it to be the fastest option that works every time.

In the next chapter, we will discuss the different ways you have for sharing **Mail**, **Contacts**, and **People** with others in your organization. You will learn the steps necessary to give permission to other users, and what is necessary for sharing to occur.

Questions

1. How do I permanently delete an email I no longer need?

2. What is the difference between **All Mailboxes** and **All Outlook Items** when performing a search by location?

3. How can I set the default **Search** location to **All Mailboxes** so I don't have to change it each time?

4. Is there a limit to how many search results Outlook will provide?

5. I want to clean up some space on my computer and I noticed I have emails in my **Deleted Items** folder. Can I delete these emails?

Answers

1. When you delete an email from the inbox, it gets placed in the **Deleted Items** folder by default. This will reside in the **Sent Items** folder for 30 days unless it is permanently deleted. To delete permanently, select the message, and click *Shift + Delete* on the keyboard.

2. **All Mailboxes** will include a search in all your emails within your mailboxes. **All Outlook Items** will search your mailboxes, Calendar, and Tasks.

3. You can change this in the **Options** settings for **Search**. Click **File | Options | Search**. Under the **Results** section for **Include results only from**, select **All mailboxes| OK**.

4. Yes, the Outlook limit for search results is to display 200 items with Outlook default settings.

5. Yes, you can delete the entire contents of the **Deleted Items** folder at once or you can select each email and delete it individually. Emails will stay in **Deleted Items** for 30 days, but you can change this setting by going to **File | Options** for emails going forward. To delete all emails currently in the **Deleted Items** folder, right-click on the **Deleted Items** folder and select **Empty Folder**.

Further reading

*   *How to search in Outlook:*

    ```
    https://support.microsoft.com/en-us/office/how-to-search-
    in-outlook-d824d1e9-a255-4c8a-8553-276fb895a8da
    ```

11
Sharing Mail, Calendars, and Contacts

When was the last time you waited until noon to open your email? Many people try but very few actually manage to do that. For most of us, checking our email is the first thing we do when we get up or when we get to the office. One of the biggest advantages of sending email is that delivery is fast. In contrast to traditional mail services, we can send emails 24 hours a day, 365 days a year. We can check and read our emails at any hour of the day on any day of the year too. But is that really to our advantage and is it productive?

Many productivity gurus will tell you that scheduling a time to read your email will help you save time. I believe this is true and I encourage everyone to do this. I also believe asking for a little help is a good solution, which opens up concepts we will cover in this chapter on sharing your **mail**, **calendar**, and **contacts** with others to help you manage and monitor them. Many executives refer to such "others" as assistants.

In this chapter, we're going to cover the following topics:

- Sharing mail, calendars, and contacts
- Permissions
- Changing/editing delegate permissions
- Requesting sharing

Sharing mail, calendars, and contacts

When we think of sharing our Outlook objects, such as email, calendars, or contacts, we think of giving the other person or assistant our personal email ID and password so that they can access our account and do everything inside our Outlook account. This is a possibility, but it also can leave you at risk of having your account compromised. The results of this action could be in the form of data leaks, loss of reputation, financial losses, and, depending on the severity of the actions, possibly even prison.

Sharing passwords is never a good idea no matter how well you trust the person. In most businesses, the sharing of passwords would violate the business's information security policy and procedures. Luckily, Outlook has a feature to share access to your Outlook account.

In Outlook, the term **delegate** refers to any user who has access to another user's mail folders. This can enable them to receive, respond to, and send emails and perform other actions on that user's behalf. The delegate must be within your **Exchange** account and available in your **Global Address List** (**GAL**). The access selected will grant the person assigned as the delegate the right to act on your behalf within their profiles.

1. To assign rights to a delegate, from the account that you want to give the delegate access to, click **File** | **Info** | **Account Settings** | **Delegate Access**.

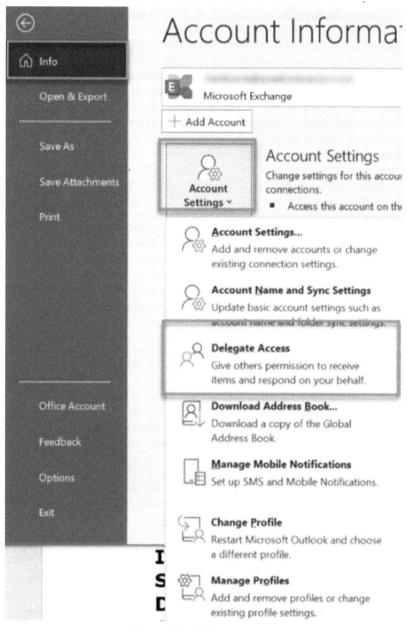

Figure 11.1 – Delegate Access

2. In the **Delegates** dialogue box, click the **Add…** button.

> **Note**
>
> If another delegate has been assigned previously, the email ID of that person
> will be listed in the white box in this window. We will discuss this later in this
> chapter.

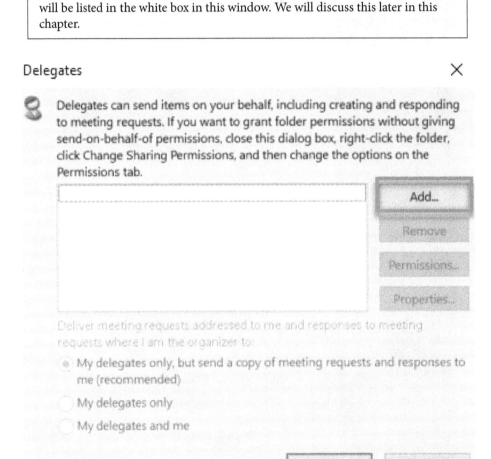

Figure 11.2 – Delegates Add… button

3. Once you click the **Add…** button, the **Add Users** dialogue box will open.

4. In this **Add Users** dialogue box, you can search for a delegate's email ID by using the
    All Columns or **Name only** options.

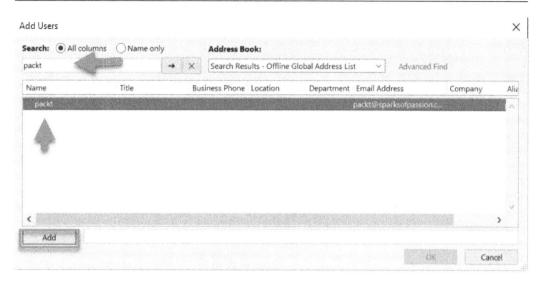

Figure 11.3 – Add Users

5. Once you have typed a name into the search box, click the **Add** button toward the bottom of this box. The name will appear in the field to the right of the **Add** button.

6.   Click **OK**.

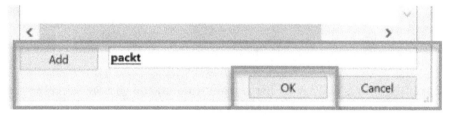

Figure 11.4 – Adding a name to add a user

If the name is in the Exchange account assigning the delegate, then you will get a **Delegate Permissions** dialogue box, otherwise, you will get the following error box.

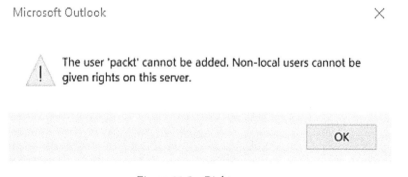

Figure 11.5 – Rights error

244 Sharing Mail, Calendars, and Contacts

There is nothing you can do to correct this error except give the delegate an email ID on your server for your business account. This will have to be done by the administrator for your company's M365 account. Click **OK** for this box to go away and you will be back to the **Delegates** dialog box where you can type in the correct email ID of the delegate you want to enter.

Permissions

Permissions allow the delegate to have specific rights when using your account or accounts. You control the level of rights they have by assigning permissions:

1. In the **Add Users** dialogue box, type in the last name of the person you would like to make a delegate in the search box.

   This person, as stated before, must be a user in your GAL. You may have to select the GAL from the dropdown in the **Address Book** section, as shown in the following figure.

Add Users

Figure 11.6 – Add Users

The available names will appear in the main window, and you can select the person you want as the delegate from this list.

2. You can either double-click on the name or click once on the name to select it and then click the **Add** button, as seen previously. After selecting the name (or names) to set as a delegate, click on the **OK** button.

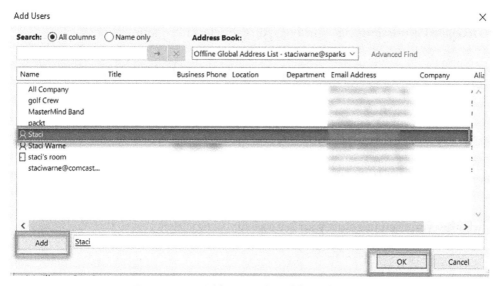

Figure 11.7 – Add Users selected from the GAL

> **Note**
>
> Next to the **Add** button in the textbox, be sure that only the name of the delegate is selected so as to not duplicate anything. If any of these names are not in the Exchange GAL, you will get an error box.

3. If the user is identified in the GAL, you will see the following **Delegate Permissions: Name** dialogue box. You can set up the delegate's permissions in this box.

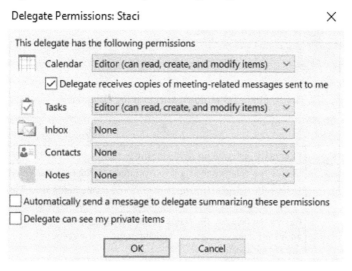

Figure 11.8 – Delegate Permissions: Name

4. When you click on the drop-down arrows by each of the object types in the
    Delegate Permissions dialogue box, you can select from four options:

    - **None**

    - **Reviewer**

    - **Author**

    - **Editor**

    These types are explained in *Table 11.1 – Permissions*.

    Be very selective with the rights you want to grant to delegates, and I would
    recommend that you occasionally re-evaluate them throughout the year to see
    whether you want to adjust your settings for each delegate.

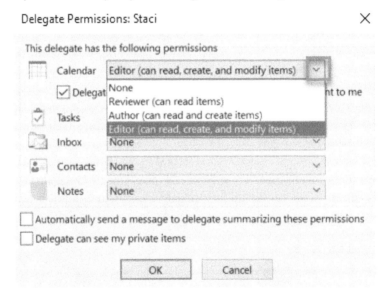

Figure 11.9 – Drop-down selection for Calendar

Delegate Permissions	
None	Grants the delegate no rights for the item.
Reviewer	Grants the delegate the right to read items in the object selected.
Author	Grants the delegate the rights to read and create items as well as to change or delete only items that they created in the object selected.
Editor	Grants the delegate the rights to not only read items in the account but, in addition, change, delete, and create items on the account holder's behalf in the object selected.

Table 11.1 – Permissions

5. Beneath the **Calendar** selection, there is the checkbox **Delegate receives copies of meeting-related messages sent to me**.

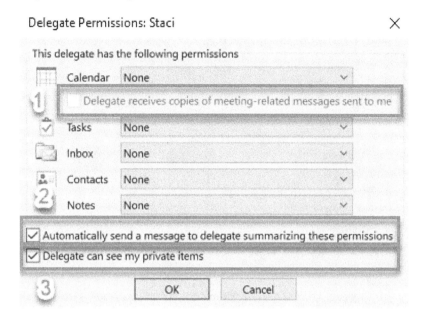

Figure 11.10 – Delegate extra permissions

- **Point 1**: This is indicated by the number one in the preceding figure. Checking this box will send a copy of any emails relating to any meetings scheduled for the email ID. Often, the delegate will also be responsible for monitoring all entries on the calendar. Giving this permission is an easy way to keep the delegate involved and informed.

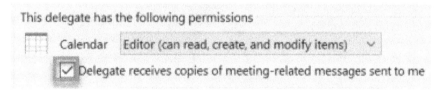

Figure 11.11 – Delegate receives copies

- **Point 2**: The second checkbox in *Figure 11.10* is **Automatically send a message to delegate summarizing these permissions**. If checked, an email will be sent to the delegate indicating the permissions that they have been granted. I have seen it happen that the delegate has been given authority but had no idea because communication was not followed through. This ensures that the delegate will be notified via email automatically.

- **Point 3**: The third checkbox is **Delegate can see my private items.**

Figure 11.12 – Delegate permissions and private items

> **Note**
>
> To ensure that delegates can't read the items that you have marked as private, do not grant them **Reviewer** permissions in your calendar, contacts, or **Tasks** folder.

6. Once you have completed granting permissions in the **Delegate Permissions** dialogue box, click **OK** for the permissions to be applied and, if selected, an email will be sent to the delegate automatically.

    The following figure is an example of the email that will be sent to the delegate.

You have been designated as a delegate for Staci Warne

Staci Warne
To   Staci

⟵ Reply   Reply All   → Forward   ··

Sat 2/5/2022 7:02 F

This message was sent automatically by Microsoft Outlook to inform you that you have been designated as a delegate. You can now send messages on my behalf.

You have been given the following permissions on my folders:
Calendar:	Editor (can read, create, and modify items)
Tasks:	Editor (can read, create, and modify items)
Inbox:	Editor (can read, create, and modify items)
Contacts:	Editor (can read, create, and modify items)
Notes:	Editor (can read, create, and modify items)

To open folders for which you have permissions, click the File Tab, and on the Open tab, click Other User's Folder. You will also be receiving copies of meeting requests sent to me and will be able to respond to them on my behalf.

You will be able to create and modify Meeting Workspaces on my behalf.

Figure 11.13 – Delegate email

Viewing delegated folders

Let's take a look at the delegate permissions that enable you to view the objects of the user that has granted you the permissions.

To view the objects of the user, click **File | Open & Export | Other User's Folder**. From the drop-down arrow, select the folder you wish to view.

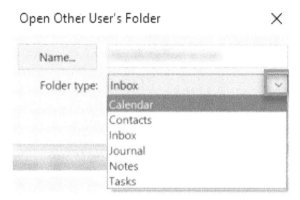

Figure 11.14 – View another user's folder

The shared user folder will be opened in the shared folder and, depending on your permissions, you can perform tasks inside of the folder.

Inbox permissions

If you have permission to send emails on behalf of the user, you will see the new mail window shown in the following figure.

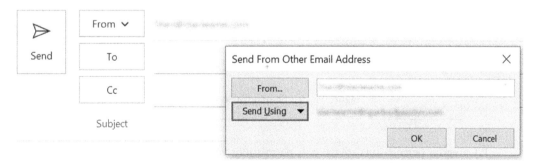

Figure 11.15 – Send From Other Email Address

The **Send From Other Email Address** dialogue box will have a **From...** box showing the message will be sent from your email ID and the **Send Using** box will indicate that you are sending it from the email ID shown.

Calendar permissions

To view calendar items after opening the shared folder as seen previously, on the selected calendar, perform the following steps:

1. Click on the **Shared Calendars** item that appears in the navigation pane.
2. Click in the blank box next to the calendar that you want to view.
3. Once clicked, the calendar will be shown in the work area.

Figure 11.16 – Shared Calendars

Note

If **Calendar permissions** are the only permissions you are granting to a delegate, you can click on the **Calendar** object. Then, click **Home | Share Calendar**. Choose the calendar you want to delegate and make the necessary adjustments through the **Calendar Properties** dialogue box.

Contacts permissions

Shared contacts will appear as shown previously with calendars. There are a few rules you will need to be aware of with contacts:

- Contacts you add or edit will not appear in your contacts but will appear in the sharing person's contacts. You can edit and delete their contacts.

- You can use search to find their contacts. Type Delegated Contacts in the search box and select the name of the person who delegated the contacts to you.

Changing/editing delegate permissions

To change any of the permissions that have been assigned to a delegate, take the following steps:

1. Click **File | Account Settings | Delegate Access**, as shown in *Figure 11.8 – Delegate Permissions*.

2. Uncheck the boxes next to the permissions for the Outlook folders the delegate has access to, or check a box if you want to give permissions for that folder.

3. Check the box **Automatically send a message to delegate summarizing these permissions**.

> **Note**
> To remove all the delegate's permissions at once, don't click **Permissions** in *step 1*; click **Remove** and skip the rest of the steps.

Request sharing

If you need permissions for sharing and you do not have them, you can have Outlook generate an email to request this action from a user that is on Exchange. This example will show asking permission to share a user's contacts.

1. Click **Home | Open Shared Contacts**.

Figure 11.17 – Open Shared Contacts

2. Enter the email ID of the person whose contacts you want to share in the *Open Shared Contacts* dialogue box.

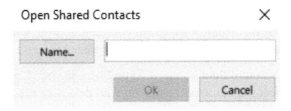

Figure 11.18 – Enter name in Open Shared Contacts

3. Exchange will not recognize the permissions granted for your request and will ask **Do you want to ask <the name requested> to share his or her Contacts folder with you?**

Figure 11.19 – Error viewing folder

4. Click **Yes** to have an email created.

The email will be addressed to the recipient that you are requesting permissions from as shown.

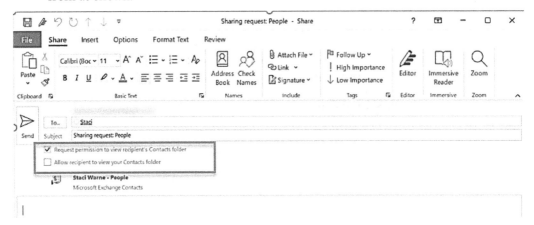

Figure 11.20 – Email generated to request permissions

5. You can customize the email with a message if you prefer. The checkbox **Request permission to view recipient's Contacts folder** is selected by default. You also have an option below this: **Allow recipient to view your Contacts folder**. You must click in this box to allow this action, which will also open another dialogue box, asking if you want to do this and indicating that the permissions granted will be **Reviewer (read-only)**, which will have buttons for **Yes** and **No**.

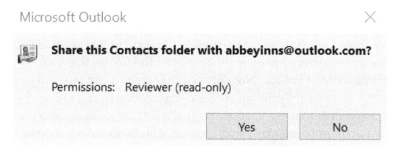

Figure 11.21 – Share Contacts via email

6. The following figure is the email that will be sent to the recipient once you click on the **Send** button in the generated email.

Figure 11.22 – Email requesting permissions to view

The recipient of the email will need to request to grant delegate permissions to the user as described earlier in this chapter. There is a link in the email to access help online for these steps.

> **Note**
>
> Not all objects will have the **Open Shared…** button on the **Home** ribbon.
> To do the same steps as indicated for the **People** object previously, you can
> right-click on the item in the navigation bar and click **Share (Item)** from the
> drop-down menu, such as **Share Notes** or **Share Task**.

Summary

Having a person known as a delegate in Outlook is the same as having an assistant that
helps you control your incoming mail, but they control the folders that you have delegated
to them to maintain within Outlook. Not only can they receive and respond to your
emails but they can also control your calendars, events, contacts, and tasks, all without
you giving your passwords to them to access your account. By delegating to them, they
will use their own account to maintain your account. This is one of my favorite tips for
saving time with Outlook and I have found it to be a real productivity booster!

In the next chapter, we will discuss archiving and backing up your Outlook items. Is your
data protected in M365? We will discuss how secure your data is in Outlook and what
you need to be aware of. After applying the techniques in the next chapter, you will feel
confident that your email is secure and protected, and you will be able to locate any email
quickly after archiving and backing up your items.

Questions

1. I have several administrators that update my calendars and emails and occasionally
   a meeting change will happen and only half the recipients will see the change. Why
   does this happen?

2. I can't click on the **Share your Calendar** button. Why not?

3. How do I share my calendar via email?

4. How do I enable sharing of my calendar in the M365 admin center?

5. I keep getting an error when trying to share my calendar and want to try updating
   Outlook. How do I run an update?

Answers

1. Unfortunately, giving authority to several people is not a great idea. Remember that with delegates, the last change wins. If an executive accepts a meeting invite and then a delegate declines the invite, the last change will win. In this case, the delegate would overwrite the executive's authority. You need to have one person who is responsible for making any changes to appointments.

2. If the **Share your Calendar** button is grayed out and you cannot click on it to activate the command, it's most likely because the administrator of the account or IT department has prevented you from sharing calendars.

3. If you don't want to assign a delegate for others to view your calendar, you can email the calendar.

    I.   Click **Calendar | E-mail Calendar**, enter the calendar's name and the date range that you want to email, and click **OK**.

    II. The new email will open the address of the recipient or **To** field. Add any message and click **Send**.

    III. The recipient of the email will see a snapshot image of your calendar.

4. Sign in to Office 365 on the web (`www.office.com`). Click **Admin | Settings | Org settings | Service Tab | Calendar**. From this calendar page, select the settings you want to allow the user to share the calendar.

5. Open Outlook and click **File | Office Account | Update Options | Update Now**.

12
Archiving and Backup

Billions of emails are sent every day! The average worker receives over 100 emails per day. With Outlook currently being one of the top communication tools used in business, these numbers will continue to rise.

The question we usually face is, when do you delete an email and when do you save it? My friend recently told me she had over 16,000 unread emails in her inbox, and her inbox is still growing. How many times do you glance at an email and not read it completely because you know the content, but you just don't feel good about deleting it? You never know when you may need that email, which just escalates the problem of never having control of your inbox.

As we go through this chapter, you will be guided to take control of your inbox and learn about the following topics:

- Cleaning up email clutter
- Archiving
- Saving emails outside of Outlook

- Backup in Outlook

- Exporting and importing

- Restoring .pst files

I'm not proposing that you should start deleting all your old emails, but taking control of your inbox means learning how to **clean**, **archive**, and **back up** your email to stay in control and still have confidence that you will be able to find an email when you need to. By successfully using the tools described in this chapter, you will also have conquered a very important step in *Chapter 16, Managing Your Day System,* in the *Manage your day system* section.

Cleaning up email clutter

It can get very confusing when considering how to effectively archive and back up your files in Outlook. You may have the following questions:

- Are my files backed up to the cloud?

- What happens to my emails when I archive them?

- If I archive my emails, will I still see my emails?

- If I archive, will I still need folders?

- Should I back up or archive?

Before you start to consider using the **Archive** and **Backup** tools, I would suggest you look at your inbox to determine how much space you have free in your account. Click on any account in the *navigation pane*, and then click **File | Info**. You will be able to view the size of the mailbox in this window.

Account Information

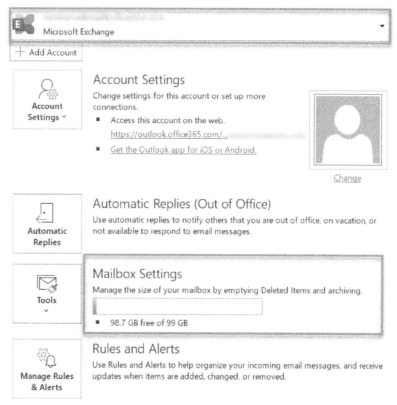

Figure 12.1 – Mailbox size

If the **Mailbox Settings** section does not show this information, it is because you are looking at an account that is not an Exchange account, and that information is not available to you within Outlook:

1. To view the size of the *Exchange* account, click **Tools | Mailbox Clean Up... | View Mailbox Size....**

Figure 12.2 – Mailbox cleanup

2. In the **Folder Size** dialog box, you can view how large your account or folders within the account are.

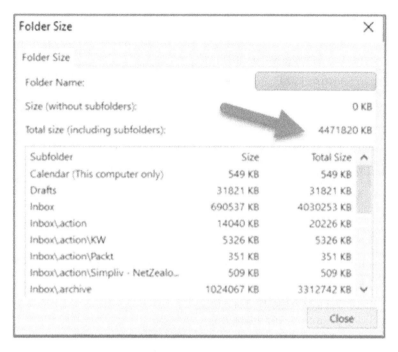

Figure 12.3 – Folder Size

The size of the folders will be shown in *KB* (kilobytes). You may want to convert this number to *GB* (gigabytes), which is a more recognizable format for most people. If you are low on storage space, this number will give you an idea of how much space you will need to free up to allow your mailbox to not exceed your limits.

3. The following table illustrates how to convert KB to GB:

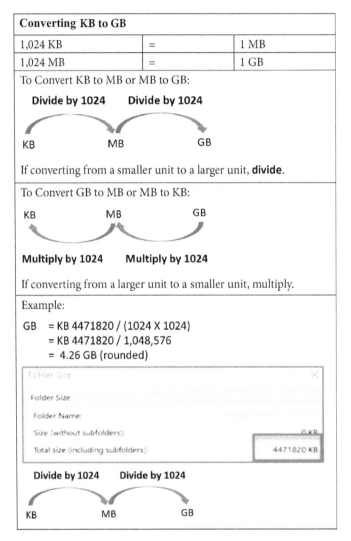

Converting KB to GB		
1,024 KB	=	1 MB
1,024 MB	=	1 GB

To Convert KB to MB or MB to GB:

Divide by 1024   Divide by 1024

KB   MB   GB

If converting from a smaller unit to a larger unit, **divide**.

To Convert GB to MB or MB to KB:

KB   MB   GB

Multiply by 1024   Multiply by 1024

If converting from a larger unit to a smaller unit, multiply.

Example:

GB   = KB 4471820 / (1024 X 1024)
        = KB 4471820 / 1,048,576
        = 4.26 GB (rounded)

Folder Size   ×

Folder Size

Folder Name:

Size (without subfolders):   0 KB

Total size (including subfolders):   4471820 KB

Divide by 1024   Divide by 1024

KB   MB   GB

Table 12.1 – Converting KB to GB

If your email starts to slow down and get sluggish when sending and receiving emails or working with your calendars, then you will want to look and see how much remaining storage you have for your account. I have generally found if you are using more than *2 GB* of storage in your accounts, Outlook will slow down.

4. To clean up your folders, click on **File | Info | Tools | Mailbox Cleanup…**. This is the same process as shown previously for looking at the size of an **IMAP** or **Pop** account, which you can view when you click on the **View Mailbox Size…** button.

Figure 12.4 – Mailbox Cleanup items

Other options you will be able to use to help with mailbox cleanup are as follows:

- **Find items older than** and **Find items larger than**: Toggle between the two options and type in either the days or size of the files you want to locate. The previous example shows the amount of **1240** KB, which will find all items over 1 GB.

- The **AutoArchive** button: Clicking on this button will automatically send your files to the `Archive` folder, which will be discussed later in the *Archive* section of this chapter.

- **Empty** and **View Deleted Items Size…**: Clicking **Empty** will permanently delete any items in the Deleted items folder. You may want to view these items in the *navigation pane* before clicking on this button. Once the button is clicked on, everything in the Deleted Items folder will be permanently deleted and a warning box will appear, asking you to confirm that you want to do this action. Click **Yes** to continue to *delete* these items, and click **No** to *cancel*.

- **Delete all alternate versions of items in your mailbox** is a way of handling conflicts that occur when multiple edits take place on items. Outlook will make the best choices for you in determining which files you want to keep when conflicts are present. Clicking **Delete** will allow Outlook to make those choices. Clicking **View Conflicts Size…** will allow you to view the folder size before deciding whether you want to use the **Delete** button.

Using **Mailbox Cleanup** is a faster way to clean up your folders, and I find it very helpful in quickly getting my inbox under control. If you don't want to delete the email items completely, then I recommend using the **archiving** features in Outlook because you will still be storing those emails in your system, rather than deleting the items permanently.

Archiving

So, why **Archive**? Back in the day, when email was first invented, it was very expensive to keep a backup of all your data, let alone all your emails. That is why **Archiving** was created. Archiving keeps our mailboxes small and moves out old emails to a separate data file, referred to as a .pst file. Storage sizes generally provided now, in the cloud, have lots of available space, and Microsoft **OneDrive** accounts are so large that it's no longer a big concern. OneDrive account sizes are as follows:

- Outlook.com – 15 GB cloud storage (free account)
- M365 Family – 6 TB (1 TB per person) cloud storage
- M365 Personal – 1 TB cloud storage
- M365 Enterprise - 1 TB cloud storage
- OneDrive for Business (Plan 2) – unlimited cloud storage

With the various M365 plans, you also have the option of purchasing additional OneDrive storage. Refer to the *Further reading* section in this chapter for a link to OneDrive plans and M365 subscriptions, and be aware that these storage amounts can often change.

With this vast amount of cloud storage available, why worry about archiving? The most important reasons I think are *compliance* and *legal* ones. Each country and industry will have its regulations and standards that must be followed for the security and retention of emails. With a tax audit or legal proceeding, you might have to go back to past emails and find related items. Another reason would be productivity. The more you have in your inbox, the slower your computer/Outlook will perform.

> **Note**
>
> The *50 GB* option is not available in trial subscription accounts with *M365*. The increase of space from the free *15 GB* option will not start until the trial subscription is over and the paid subscription has started.

There are three ways to archive in Outlook:

- **Archive**
- **AutoArchive**
- **Online Archive**

I will explain these three ways to help you choose which method or methods will work for you.

Archive

In Outlook 2016, a new **Archive** button appeared on the **Home** tab. This button moves your selected message from the inbox to the **Archive** folder. This is not an `Archive` folder; it's a folder that has been created by M365, under the inbox.

Figure 12.5 – The Archive button

No real archiving is being completed with this step, but it is decluttering your inbox. I have heard this button referred to as *fake* archiving. Using this method will not reduce the size of your mailbox because it just resides in a different folder.

An advantage of this method is that email will not be cluttering up your inbox, and you will still be able to view the contents of this folder through Outlook on the web and with your Outlook mobile phone apps.

> **Note**
> Instead of using the button on the ribbon, you can use the shortcut keys
> *Backspace* to archive and *Delete* to delete the selected message.

AutoArchive

AutoArchive was introduced in Outlook 2003. It was created to help with the slow performance of overflowing mailboxes. **AutoArchive** is always running in the background, looking at all your mailbox folders. It will physically move your old emails from your folders to a separate data file on your computer, also known as a `.pst` file.

When the following dialog box appears, Outlook is prompting you to use **AutoArchive**.

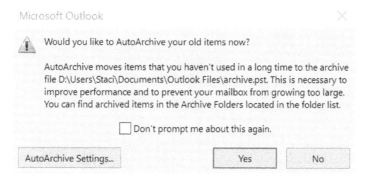

Figure 12.6 – The AutoArchive warning

Once your emails have been auto-archived, they will reside in a separate group in the folder pane, as shown here.

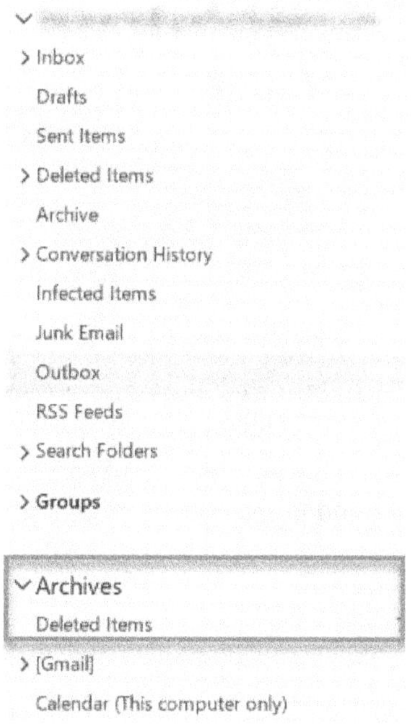

Figure 12.7 – The archive group

This **Archives** folder is stored locally on your computer. These folders will not be saved to the cloud and will not be available on your phone apps.

You also have controls for setting up what you want to be auto-archived. *Right-click* on a folder to set the properties for that specific folder.

Click the **Default Active Settings…** button to set up additional **AutoArchive** actions, or select the radio button for the **Archive this folder using these settings:** option, as shown here.

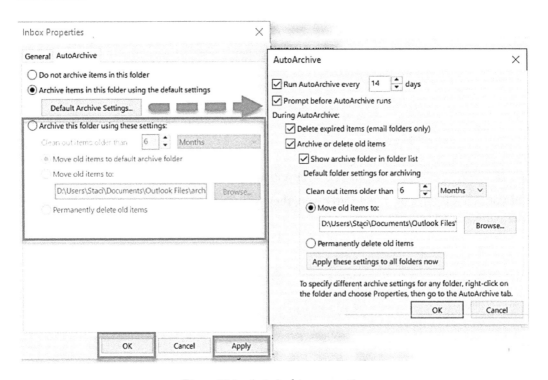

Figure 12.8 – AutoArchive properties

At first, **AutoArchive** is not the most intuitive, but once you set it up the way you want and know that it is running quietly in the background, you will feel confident that your archive mail will be assessable. If you have limited mail server storage available to you, it is the best way to automatically get old items out of your folders where they are taking up space continuously.

Online Archive

This is the newest method for archiving and is also referred to as *in-place archiving*. This is the archiving that happens when you save to the cloud. Instead of saving your old items on your local drive, your emails will be saved in the cloud. This method was created to replace **AutoArchive**, which stores your files on your local computer. To access **Online Archive**, you must have an *Exchange account*, and more information can be found through the link in the further reading section of this chapter.

If your administrator has activated this for you, you will see it in the navigation pane as a separate group for **Online Archive – email ID**. Through the settings provided by your online *Exchange admin*, you will have the items to be archived sent to this `Online Archive` folder.

The advantage of this method is that all of your emails will be available to you on any device if it has an internet connection.

Backing up Outlook

If you are using M365 for Outlook, you can feel confident that your files are being *backed up* to the *cloud*. If you want another safeguard, you may want to consider backing up your Outlook objects via another method as well. There are two methods for backing up your files. One is **exporting**, and the other is to save emails outside of Outlook, which can mean having a backup copy on another computer, an external hard drive, or a folder such as the desktop on your computer. I also have found it handy to back up my Outlook files to a *USB drive*, as they get very large, and it is handy just to store this away from the computer or even use it to import those emails into another computer, not on your M365 account. You can have your *cloud backup* and *offline backup*.

Exporting and importing

Using the **Import/Export** feature in Outlook is a quick way to back up all your objects to a `.pst` file. Once exported, you can store the file on your computer or an external storage device, or even another computer:

1. To export the files, click on **File | Open & Export | Import/Export**.

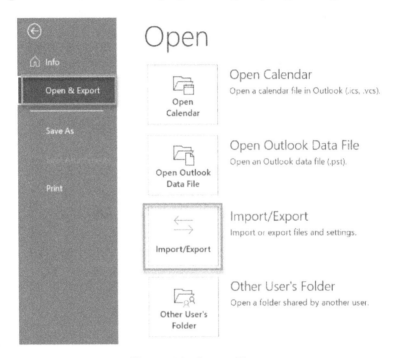

Figure 12.9 – Import/Export

2. The Import and Export Wizard will open. Select **Export to a file | Next >**.

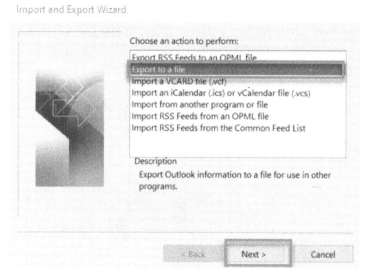

Figure 12.10 – The Import and Export Wizard

3.   Select **Outlook Data File (.pst) | Next >**.

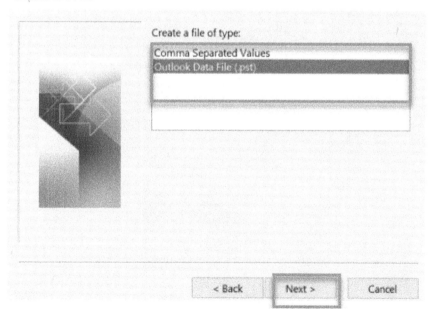

Figure 12.11 – Export to a File

4. The next step of the Wizard is to select the item that you want to export. Select the name of your email ID, as shown in *Figure 12.12*, or you can select an individual item, such as **Inbox** or **Contacts**. Also, check the **Include subfolders** box if desired. This is especially important if you created subfolders underneath the **Inbox** folder or other folders.

5. After making the desired selection, click the **Next >** button.

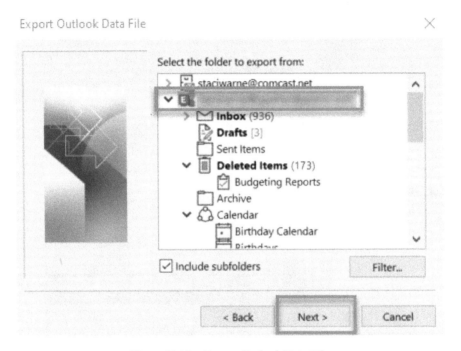

Figure 12.12 – Export Outlook Data File

6. In the next step of the Wizard, the default location for the backup will be shown in the **Save exported file as:** box. Click on the **Browse…** button and select the location or folder in which you would like to save the backup .pst file.

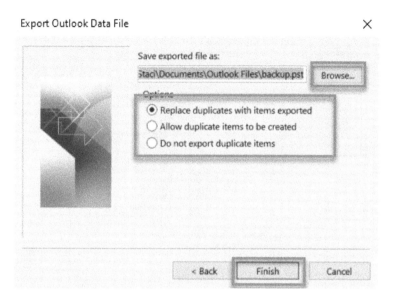

Figure 12.13 – Export Outlook Data File – Finish

You may choose to *save the export* on the computer you are using or to an external device, such as a *USB drive* or *external hard drive*. (Before saving to an external device, be sure that the size of the external drive is large enough for the data you are exporting.)

7. Click **OK** after entering a name or accepting the default name, and the path you selected will show in the **Save Exported Data File** dialog box. Select the option you desire for duplicate entries and click **Finish** to complete the Wizard.

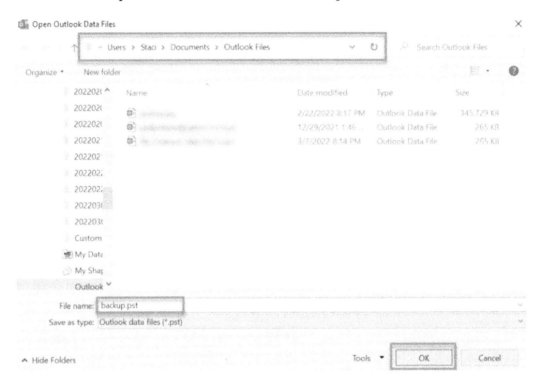

Figure 12.14 – Saving the Outlook .pst data file

You will then be asked to enter and verify a *password* so that the file is password-protected when opening and importing the .pst file into Outlook. If you do not want a password, leave the two boxes blank, and click **OK**, which will finalize the steps for the *Export Wizard*, and your file will be saved or backed up to the location that you specified.

This method is most desirable if you want to select all the objects within Outlook, your inbox, and subfolders, or just your contacts or tasks.

To access these files, refer to the section in this chapter on restoring a .pst file.

Saving emails outside Outlook

Saving emails outside Outlook is an easy way to save your emails onto your computer, simply by *saving* that item to a *folder* by clicking on **File | Save As**.

Follow these steps to save your email to another location:

1. Open the message you want to save.

2. Choose a location in which to save your email message and enter a name for the file.

3. Ensure that you are saving the email as the type of file you want in the **Save as type:** drop-down list.

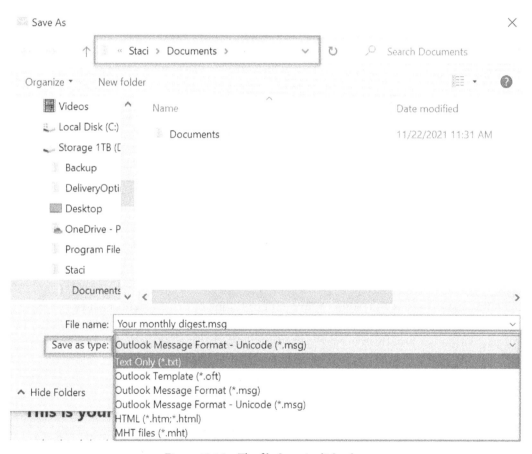

Figure 12.15 – The file Save As dialog box

When you open up one of these files, it opens by default in Outlook. These file types can also be opened in other applications or used within code if needed for the web.

The possible file **Save as** types are listed in the following table:

File type	Used for
Text Only (*.txt)	This type has all the formatting removed from the message and only retains the text.
Outlook Template (*.oft)	Use this for messages you want to repeatably use in Outlook. This type will save text, formatting, and attachments.
Outlook Message Format (*.msg)	This type can only be read by Outlook. It will keep attachments, text, and formatting intact.
Outlook Message Format – Unicode (*.msg)	This is Outlook's default setting and is best used for international characters that are readable by versions of Outlook that require a different language.
HTML (*.htm;*.html)	This saves the file in a format that can be displayed on the web/ in a web browser. File attachments are not saved in this type. Using this type will also create a separate folder that will hold supporting files that are needed for the HTM file.
MHT files (*.mht)	This file type is identical to the HTML file type, except that a folder is not created. The contents of the file will be saved as one file. Applications that can display HTM and HTML files in addition to MHT can be used with this file type.

Table 12.16 – File Save As types

One of the reasons you would want to save a file with one of these types is to save the email into a folder with other items related to the message. This allows you to organize the email with other files from other applications, such as *Excel*, *PowerPoint*, and *Word*, enabling you to locate emails related to a project in one location.

When you open one of these files from within a folder, such as your *desktop*, by default, the item will open inside Outlook with the message in view.

> **Note**
>
> Although PDF is not a file **Save As** type for Outlook, you can save the email as a PDF file by choosing **File | Save As | Print**, and instead of choosing a printer, choose the **Microsoft print to PDF** option.
>
> Click **Print**, and then save the file to the location you desire as prompted.

Restoring a .pst file

When you set up an Outlook account (excluding an Exchange account), a `.pst` file is automatically created. This `.pst` file is known as an *Outlook data file*. This name will typically be your email ID name with the `.pst` extension (for example, `staci@staciwarne.com.pst` or `archive.pst`):

1. To locate the data file that has been automatically created, click **Home | New Items | More Items | Outlook Data File…**.

Figure 12.17 – The Outlook data file

2. The **Create or Open Outlook Data file** dialog box will open, showing the locations of the `.pst` files on your computer. To create a new data file or `.pst` file, change the name of the file (leaving the `.pst`). If you want to have a password associated with this file, check the **Add Optional Password** box.

3. Select the `.pst` file that you want to restore if the file was saved previously, which will show in the main window of the **Create or Open Outlook Data File** dialog box.

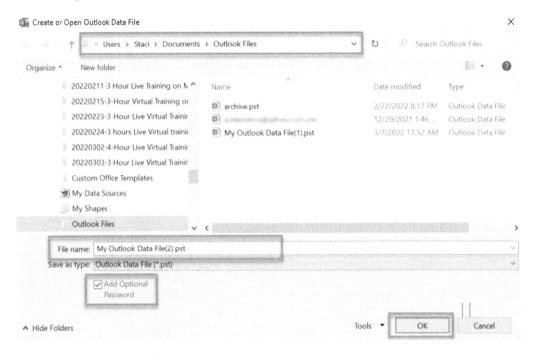

Figure 12.18 – Create or Open Outlook Data File

4. Once you click **OK**, the **Add optional password** dialog box will show, asking for a password to be assigned. Type the password again in the **Verify Password:** field to ensure that you have typed the password correctly and the two passwords match.

Figure 12.19 – Add optional password

5. Once this password is assigned, to use the saved `.pst` file, you will need to know the password that was assigned and enter it to use the `.pst` file.

    Your actual passwords are hidden in the **registry**, and you cannot just access a list to recover these passwords. If you know the previous password and you saved it to the list, you can change the password by clicking **File | Account Settings | Account Settings | Data Files** and opening the name of the `.pst` file you are changing. In the **Outlook Data File** dialog box, click **Change Password….** Be sure to check the **Save this password in your password list** box to be able to change the password later.

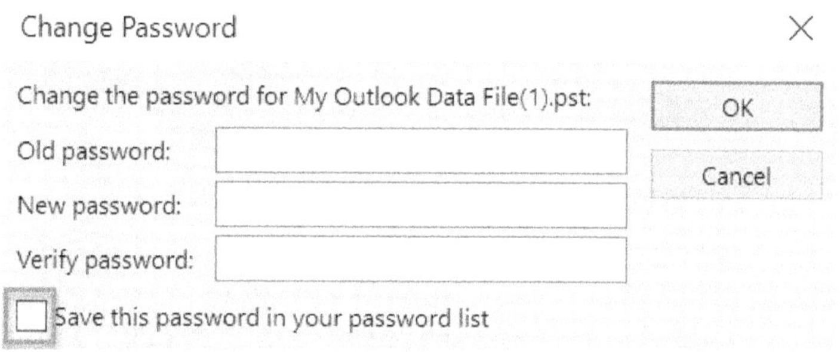

Change Password   ✕

Change the password for My Outlook Data File(1).pst: OK

Old password: [   ]

New password: [   ]   Cancel

Verify password: [   ]

☐ Save this password in your password list

Figure 12.20 – Change Password

Note

Outlook `.pst` data file passwords are not a safeguard to prevent a malicious attempt to access your email. For added security, you should also set up a password-protected Windows user account for any user accessing the computer.

---

6. Once you click **OK** to complete this restore, the objects will appear in the navigation pane in Outlook, and if you backed up the entire `Email` folder, you will see it under the **Outlook Data File** heading. When you expand the folder, the subfolders will show exactly how you saved them previously.

Figure 12.21 – The navigation pane – the restored .pst file

When you are done viewing these items, you can close the data file by *right-clicking* on the heading and selecting **Close "My Outlook Data File(1)"**. This will help to avoid looking at a duplicate item heading in the navigation pane.

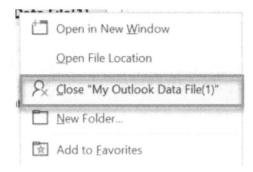

Figure 12.22 – Closing the Outlook data file

By closing the Outlook data files, you will not confuse the current files with the backed-up data files. If something did happen to the existing files, you can use this technique to bring in the backed-up files and use them as your data files within Outlook if your files became corrupted or were lost somewhere by accident.

Summary

Backup redundancy is never a bad thing if you want to feel confident that you will never lose any of your email items. Data centers are not 100% online all the time. In that rare moment when you need your email in one of these downtimes, you can feel confident in knowing that you will always have your items when you need them.

In the next chapter, we will discuss another one of Outlook's greatest strengths, the power to collaborate with others. Knowing which programs are available to collaborate with from within Outlook and how to access and use these other applications, such as OneNote, Teams, Viva, and your mobile phones, will not only save you time but also help you work smart with Outlook.

Questions

1. Why can I not see the **AutoArchive** option in the **Advanced** tab of the **Files | Options** dialog box?

2. My Outlook environment is running slower than usual lately. How can I fix this?

3. Why do I keep getting a message saying my *mailbox* is full?

4. How can I *repair* my Outlook 365 account?

5. What is a `.ost` data file? My file shows `.ost`, not `.pst`.

Answers

1. **AutoArchive** is on the **Advanced** tab underneath the Outlook start and exit headings. If you do not see this, it is probably due to your IT department in your organization not giving you the rights on the server to access this feature. Another reason for this is that you have an Exchange account, and online archiving has been enabled for you with automatic settings.

2. If your inbox is storing a lot of emails, usually because you never delete any messages, you will want to check the size of your folders. Click **File | Folder | properties | Storage**. If you have more than 2 GB of emails used, you need to archive some of your emails.

3. This message appears when your PST file has reached its maximum storage limit. To fix this, you can manage the mailbox size by clicking **File | Info | Tools | Mailbox Cleanup...**.

4. Occasionally, your files may become corrupt in Outlook. To repair them, click **File | Account Settings... | Select the account to repair | Repair...**. If you don't have access to Outlook, you can run a repair in the **Programs and Features** object in the **Windows Control Panel**.

5. A `.pst` file is a file that is stored on your computer. This is typically the case for files created before Office 2016. If your file is a `.ost` file, you have a file that is maintained on an *Exchange server*, and you will need to contact the administrator of your M365 account to maintain this file.

Further reading

- *Microsoft plans available for M365:*

  `https://www.microsoft.com/en-us/microsoft-365/buy/compare-all-microsoft-365-products`

- *How to manage .pst files in Microsoft Outlook:*

  `https://docs.microsoft.com/en-us/outlook/troubleshoot/data-files/how-to-manage-pst-files`

Part 5: Outlook Collaboration and Integration

Outlook's greatest strength is the ability to collaborate with others. Sharing information between Microsoft Exchange, Cloud Services, and other programs can make your day-to-day work faster, make you work smarter, and more efficiently. You will learn how to collaborate with programs through the cloud, through web pages, through an RSS feed, and other applications such as OneNote.

This section contains the following chapter:

- *Chapter 13, Collaboration and Integration within Outlook*

13
Collaboration and Integration within Outlook

Microsoft Outlook brings together the best tools for allowing us to collaborate with others. It is now easier and faster to connect with others anywhere in the world. Outlook has several applications integrated within its platform to make it more efficient when working with others and is very easy and intuitive to learn. You can now not only work with the best tools but also work and collaborate with others in real time.

By using Outlook, you can collaborate with anyone who has a computer, and I'm going to show you some of the apps that Outlook utilizes within the application for collaboration. In this chapter, we will be discussing the following topics:

- Cloud computing
- Outlook groups
- Mobile phones
- Add-ins
- RSS feed

Microsoft 365 subscriptions now have so many applications available to us that it can be hard to know which apps to use when. Let's dive into this chapter and learn which of these apps have direct collaboration and integration features within Outlook.

Cloud computing

Instead of storing all your data on your own physical computers, we have the option to use the cloud. What does this mean? The cloud is a means for us to store our data on off-site computers located in various locations around the world, known as data centers. This storage could consist of anything from software programs, data storage, or virtual machines to email servers, as with Outlook. The "cloud" is another word for "internet" as the data is transmitted through the internet through secure networks. In *Chapter 3, Managing Email Accounts*, we discussed the Microsoft Exchange protocol.

Exchange runs on the cloud in Microsoft's data centers and is what allows us to access our data anytime, anywhere, and on any device with internet availability.

Let's be honest, no one wants to work 365 days a year. However, we do want to have our data, and especially our email, available to us around the clock, 24 hours a day, and 7 days a week! That is what we will get by using Outlook.

To use the cloud within Outlook, you first will want to activate the cloud storage options to store your desired settings in the cloud.

Click **File** | **Options** | **General**. Click the box next to **Store my Outlook settings in the cloud**, then click **OK**.

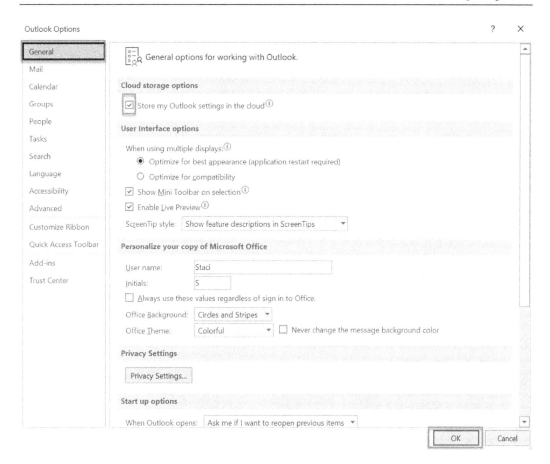

Figure 13.1 – Cloud storage options

Now, any activity that happens in Outlook will be available to you from the Outlook web application as well. Outlook will now start synchronizing any activity in Outlook to the web. This is the advantage of using cloud functions; you can get your Outlook emails and other items through the web on all your devices, such as other computers, tablets, and mobile phones, using your Microsoft 365 subscription. Once this synchronization is complete, you will receive a message stating Outlook has synced your settings from the cloud.

Let's discuss the different ways that you can collaborate, through the cloud, using OneDrive and Outlook.

OneDrive

OneDrive (formally called SkyDrive) is Microsoft's cloud storage. iCloud and Google Drive are similar offerings by Apple and Google. Saving your data to a OneDrive account allows you to access your files while away from your computer and collaborate with others by sharing these files with them.

OneDrive is preinstalled if you are using Windows 10 or newer. If you don't have Windows 10, you can download and install OneDrive. More information on this can be found in the *Further reading* section of this chapter. Once OneDrive is installed, you will be able to save and use files on any device from your OneDrive account, using an internet connection.

When you attach a document to an Outlook email message, that file is copied to the email to be sent to a recipient that you provide, as was described in *Chapter 2*, *Sending and Receiving Emails*. Once the document is attached, you can identify whether it is being shared in the cloud by the cloud icon that will appear in the icon for the attachment. If you select this document from your computer, a copy will be attached.

To collaborate with another user on the attached file, take the following steps:

1. Click on the drop-down arrow to the right of the attachment, then select **Upload | OneDrive**.

Figure 13.2 – Uploading an attachment to OneDrive

2. The icon will now have a cloud appearing at the bottom, indicating that the file is in the OneDrive folder on the cloud.

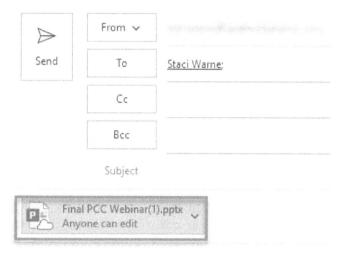

Figure 13.3 – Attached cloud file

3. Click the drop-down arrow again to set the permissions for the recipient of the attachment, indicating how they will be able to collaborate on the attached file.

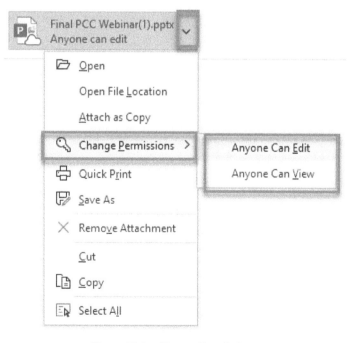

Figure 13.4 – Change Permissions

The default for uploading an attachment is the recipient that you are sending the email to will have permission to edit the document. Outlook will assume that you want to be able to collaborate and work on the document together with the recipient once the document has been sent.

The possible permissions to select are as follows:

- **Anyone Can Edit**

- **Anyone Can View**

The default selection is **Anyone Can Edit**. If you do not want the recipient to be able to make changes to the document, be sure to change this to **Anyone Can View**.

> **Note**
>
> If you are attaching files from a SharePoint site, you will have additional permissions of **Organization Can Edit**, **Organization Can View**, **Recipients Can Edit**, and **Recipients Can View** in addition to the **Anyone Can Edit** and **Anyone Can View** permissions.

4. The selected permission will appear in the attachment box so the recipient will be able to identify the permission granted to them. After entering the recipients for the new email, click **Send**.

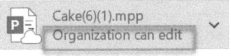

Figure 13.5 – Permission selected

5. The email will be sent to the recipient, informing them that you have shared a document with them. The recipient can view the file and permissions and click **Open** from within the email to view or work on the document.

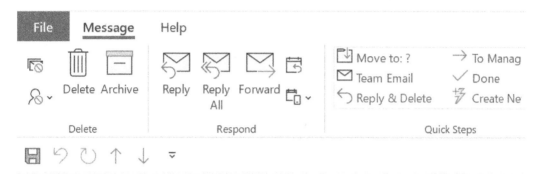

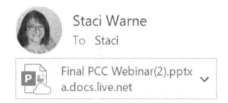

Figure 13.6 – Email – sharing a file

If permission was given for the document to be edited by the recipient, then the document will be updated in real time and the shared document will reside on the OneDrive of the person that shared the file.

> **Note**
>
> Sharing a file and setting permissions can also be done from the OneDrive folder in File Explorer. Right-click on the file and select **Share**. In the **send link** dialog box, enter the *email ID* of the user that you would like to share, enter a message, and select permissions. Click **Send** and the message will be sent to recipients.

We too are utilizing the sharing feature of OneDrive storage for the collaboration on this book. Together with the amazing team at Packt and the technical reviewers, we are all collaborating from different locations around the world and working on our files from within OneDrive in real time together.

Viewing and changing permissions in OneDrive

After you have shared files with others within or outside of your business, it's expected that people's jobs and roles performed within or even outside the company will change. You may find that sharing a document is no longer necessary or you may just want to change the permission options that were granted, as shown in *Figure 13.4*, originally.

To view or change these permissions, take the following steps:

1. Open OneDrive from within your Microsoft 365 account online. (`login.microsoft.com`)

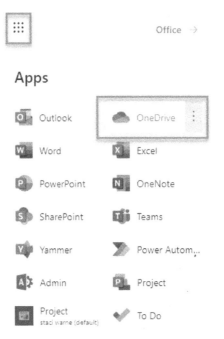

Figure 13.7 – Opening OneDrive from within Microsoft 365

2. Click on the **Shared** link located in the **Sharing status** column for the desired file, as shown:

Figure 13.8 – Shared icon for file

3. A **Manage Access** pane will open on the side of the screen. You will see the people that have shared access or any access to the file located in the **Direct access** section. Click the drop-down arrow next to the person that you would like to change permissions for and select the desired permission, as shown:

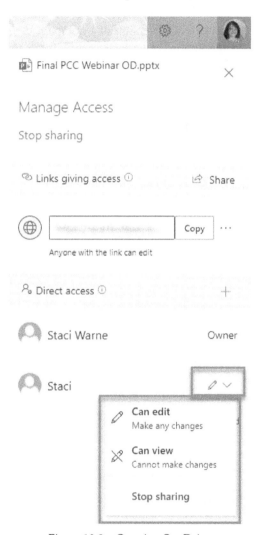

Figure 13.9 – Opening OneDrive

This pane can also be used to add or manage the files or folder permissions through the OneDrive desktop app for Windows 10. For other Window versions, this screen could look slightly different. Let's now look at another useful app used within Outlook to help you collaborate with others, which is one of my favorite applications that I have been using for over 10 years and is now integrated within Outlook.

OneNote

Great applications don't always work well together, but with Outlook and OneNote, it can't get a great deal better than this. I use OneNote as a place to write my notes and create content when I start a new project or create a new course. OneNote was released back in 2003 and is an application that allows you to capture information in one location and organize that information in an electronic version of a notepad. If you want to save paper and help the environment, I suggest you take a serious look into using this application. Although it has been around for almost two decades, many people have never used it.

Once you start a new project, I would suggest that you first open OneNote and create a new notebook for that project. There are several ways that you can organize notebooks to your liking and your imagination is the limit.

To create a new workbook in OneNote, take the following steps:

1. Open OneNote by clicking **Start** | **Programs** | **OneNote**.

2. To create a new notebook and save it in the cloud, click **File** | **New** | **OneDrive**.

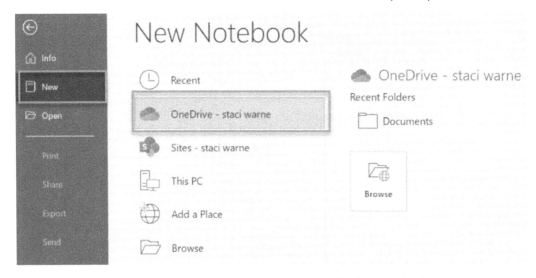

Figure 13.10 – Creating a new OneNote notebook in the cloud

3. Enter a name for the notebook and click **Create**.

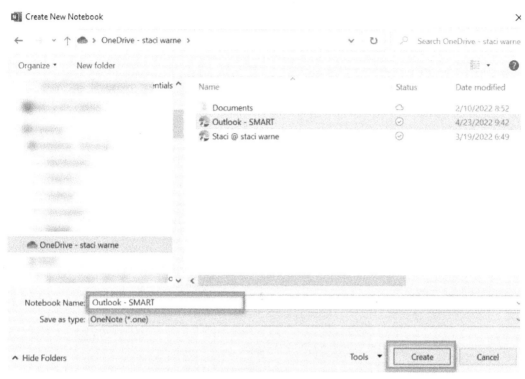

Figure 13.11 – Naming the notebook

4. If prompted, you can share the notebook by entering the email IDs of the individuals you wish to share the notebook with. Click **Not now**.

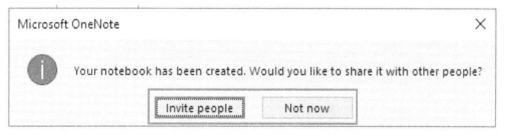

Figure 13.12 – Notebook created

5. You have now created a notebook and can start writing notes and adding sections at the top of the page (like adding chapters to a book). You can also add pages over at the right of the notebook. You can click anywhere on the page and start typing and you can copy and paste information from the internet or other locations and start building your notebook.

Let's now go to Outlook and see how it can be integrated with OneNote.

Activating Send to OneNote in Outlook

You will need to turn on the feature for Outlook to send information to OneNote.

To do this, click **File | Options | Advanced**. Scroll down to the **Other** heading and ensure the **Use Send to OneNote with OneNote for Windows 10, if available** text box is selected, then click **OK**.

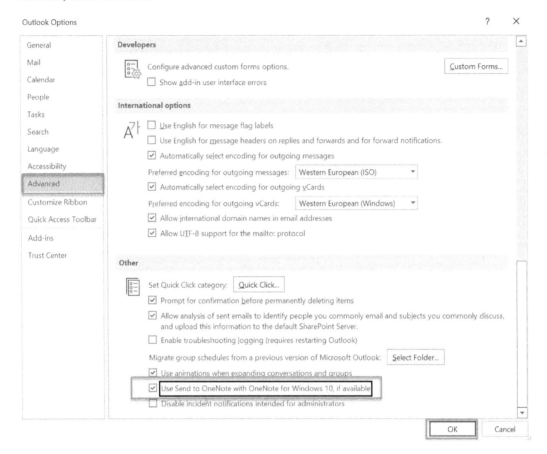

Figure 13.13 – Using Send to OneNote

If you are using an operating system prior to Windows 10, you will need to install the COM add-in for versions prior to Outlook 2016. I like to think that by activating this feature, you are turning Outlook into a project management application with OneNote integration.

Now, we will not only be able to share emails between the two applications, but we will also be able to integrate with Outlook's to-do list and calendar features as well.

Sending Outlook items to a OneDrive notebook

Let's now copy our email messages and meeting invitations to OneNote by using the **Send to OneNote** button:

1. Select the item or items that you want to copy into OneNote.

2. Click **Send to OneNote**.

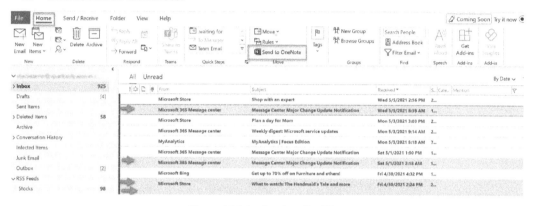

Figure 13.14 – Send to OneNote

3. From **Pick a section or a page in which to put the e-mail**, select the OneDrive location to save the information to and click **OK**.

Figure 13.15 – Selected notebook

4. Each of the email messages that were selected will appear as a separate page inside of the workbook. The first page is untitled but can be renamed as preferred. The other pages have for their titles whatever the subject of the email that was selected is. In this example, I selected email messages but had I selected a calendar item or task, they also would have been copied over.

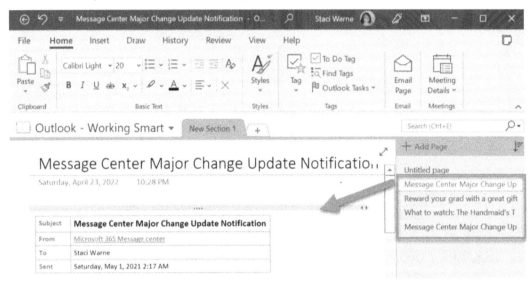

Figure 13.16 – Email copied to OneNote pages

If there had been any attachments in the selected messages, links would be available to open the attachment from this page.

Not only can we easily send information to OneNote, but OneNote also has the integration built into its interface to work with Outlook.

Let's demonstrate this by creating items within OneNote to integrate with Outlook.

Emailing notes to OneNote

Another great feature of OneNote is the ability to take meeting notes (or record meetings) and send that information through Outlook to your recipients. Usually, you would have to do this with copy and paste but this feature is also built into OneDrive:

1. Enter the meeting notes or information into OneNote on a page. When it's ready to send, click **Email Page**.

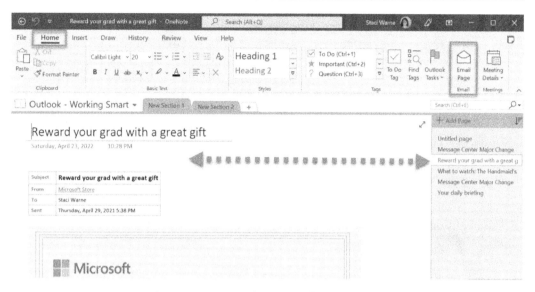

Figure 13.17 – Emailing a page from OneNote

2. Next, Outlook will open with the OneNote page showing in the email. If any email IDs are identified in the message, they will appear in the **To** section; otherwise, you will be able to enter the email IDs, as shown:

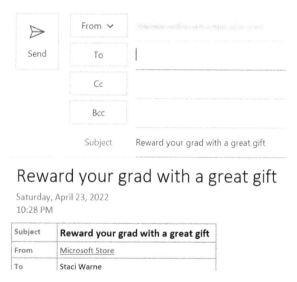

Figure 13.18 – New email page

No more copy and pasting and rearranging the email. This will automatically be laid out for you. I am always amazed at the new features that come out of Outlook and although this feature has been here for some time, it is really underused. Give it a try, I'm sure you will agree! Now, there is more; let's learn how to create a task out of a OneNote item.

Creating Outlook tasks from OneNote

There are several templates within OneNote to help you set up a quick page or, as in my case, use a template for your budget meeting. Once the page is ready, we can send this item to an Outlook task right from within OneNote:

1. Click **Insert | Page Templates**. Select the desired template from the right pane and fill in any data as needed.

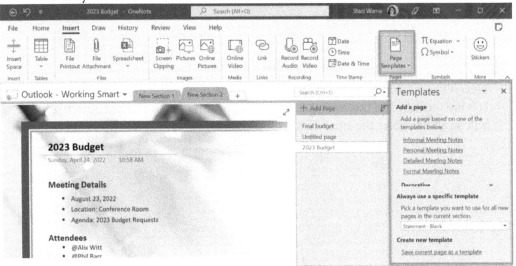

Figure 13.19 – Page Templates

I especially like using this for meeting notes. You should take some time to look through the **Insert** ribbon as there are some features I really like, such as the record feature, which not only records but also syncs the time with the recording. It's truly amazing.

2. Once the page is completed, you can send the page to an Outlook task by clicking **Home | Outlook Tasks** and then selecting the flag icon.

Figure 13.20 – Creating an Outlook task

3. Open the Outlook tasks pane and the task will now be in your task list.

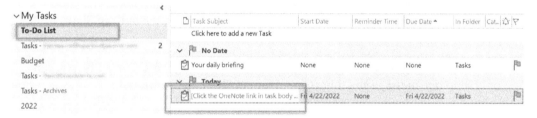

Figure 13.21 – OneNote created a task

4. Click on the task link to open the OneNote page with the details of the task in one place.

Outlook is a wonderful application but when you collaborate with OneNote within your Office suite, it can be powerful and such a great productivity tool that can save you hours and hours within your day.

Now, let's discuss the power of Teams and how it can enhance your collaborative experience even more.

Microsoft Teams

Microsoft Teams is part of the Microsoft 365 suite of applications and has been allowing teams to work together since 2017. It is a collaboration tool that is used online and is gaining in popularity among businesses. To use Teams, you need a Microsoft 365 license. There is a free version but it is very limited.

Outlook has built-in features to allow collaboration with Teams, and these Outlook features are what I will be describing.

Some of the advantages of using Teams are the following:

- Provides a platform and a central location for groups of people to collaborate on a subject.
- Using chat within teams instead of emails
- Working with others in real time on a document
- Instantly viewing likes, @mentions, or replies
- Adding files, notes, websites, and apps that are needed by the team

Let's now discuss integrating with Teams from within Outlook.

Sending an email message to Teams

Outlook's team integration has improved over the past years. It is now easier than ever to send an email message from within Outlook to Teams by using the built-in **Share to Teams** button:

1. Select the message or messages that you want to send to Teams. Currently, you can only send one message at a time. Click **Home | Share to Teams**.

Figure 13.22 – Share to Teams

2. Enter a name for the email you are sharing and a message to be included, as shown, and then click **Share**.

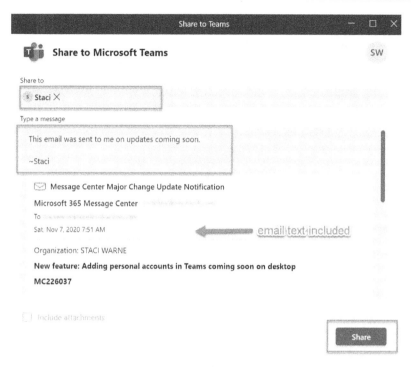

Figure 13.23 – Share to Teams

3. A message will appear indicating that your email is on its way to Teams! You can click either **Go to Teams** or **Close**.

Figure 13.24 – Email on its way

4. To view the email within Teams, click on **Chat** and the email will appear at the bottom of the **Chat** pane. Your team will be able to continue the conversation about this email using the controls at the bottom of the window.

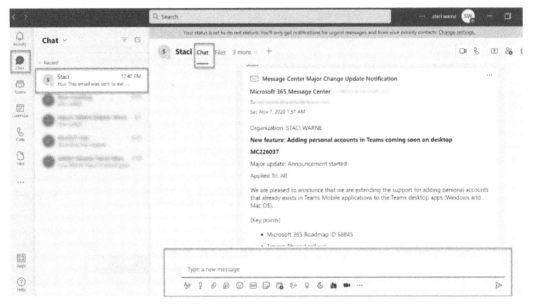

Figure 13.25 – Teams

Moving an email to Teams is a great way to start a conversation. Try this instead of writing an email. What I like is you don't need to wait for everyone to receive your email. The entire team will be able to see your message and collaborate. Once you use this feature, you will probably agree with me that it really can help you and your team save time.

Let's now show how you can create a Teams meeting through Outlook.

Creating a Teams meeting within Outlook

Keeping everyone informed is quite a difficult task, especially if your team is scattered around the world, working remotely. Video conferencing has become the norm for most corporations and that is here to stay. Outlook now integrates with Teams by creating meetings that you can hold within Teams and since Outlook's 2019 version and later, creating those meetings is made easier:

1. To create a Teams meeting, click **Home | New Items | Meeting**. The shortcut key for this is *Ctrl + Shift + Q*.

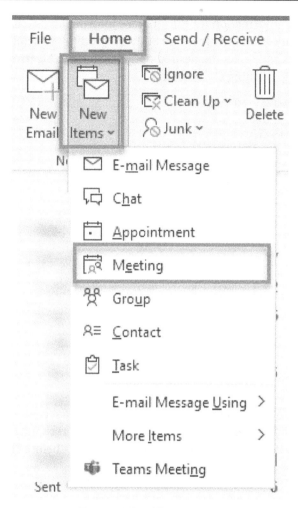

Figure 13.26 – New meeting

There are several alternative ways to create a Teams meeting from any window inside of Outlook. At the bottom of the preceding Teams meeting menu is an option that will give you the same results as selecting **Meeting**; however, this will not be available in every view for **New Items**, such as from the **People** icon.

2. Fill in the desired information for the attendee information, such as who is invited, the time, the location, and the message body. For additional details, click **Meeting | Meeting Options** and select the desired options from the **Meeting Options** dialog box that pertain to running the meeting.

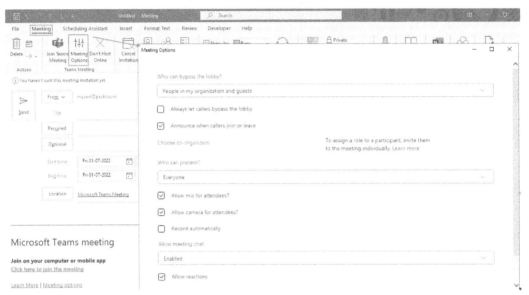

Figure 13.27 – Meeting Options

3. Click **Save** in the **Meeting Options** dialog box and the **Save** button will change to a **Close** button. Click **Close**. I would recommend taking a second look at the message of the meeting and ensuring that the details are accurate before clicking **Send**.

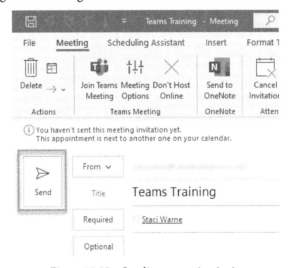

Figure 13.28 – Sending a meeting invite

4. The meeting will be sent to the recipient's email. The recipients should use the respond buttons in the email to let the sender know whether they will be attending or not.

Figure 13.29 – Teams meeting request email

5. Accepting the meeting will automatically create a calendar item for you and on the day of the meeting, you can open the calendar event and click **Join** or you can also click on **Click here to join the meeting** in the email sent to you.

I find it very convenient to have Teams meetings showing on my calendar. This of course works best if everyone is on Exchange Microsoft 365 and, if not, you may have some problems with people being able to interact with your email.

The Teams meeting add-in is automatically installed if you have Teams and Office 2013 or later installed on your system and the button will be found on the calendar ribbon. However, I like to start a Teams meeting with the **New Items** button on the **Home** ribbon. Either way is fine; just choose the best method for you.

This will lead us to our next item to discuss, which is the Outlook group tool. This tool is another option for you to consider using to collaborate with your teams.

Outlook groups

An Outlook group is a group that can be created in Microsoft 365 that brings together a group of people into a central group inbox for collaborating, such as sending and receiving emails. When you create the group, a shared workspace with SharePoint and other Microsoft 365 apps will also be created. Do not confuse an Outlook group, also referred to as a Microsoft 365 group, with a *contact group* or *distribution list*, which was explained in *Chapter 7, Contacts in Outlook*.

Creating an Outlook group

If you do not see the **New Group** button on the **Home** tab ribbon on the **Peoples** pane, then you will need to talk with your IT department and have them enable the group feature for your organization. Then, take the following steps:

1. Open the contacts or select the **People** button on the navigation pane.

2. Click **Home** | **New Group**, fill in the desired fields in the **Create Group** window, then click **Create**.

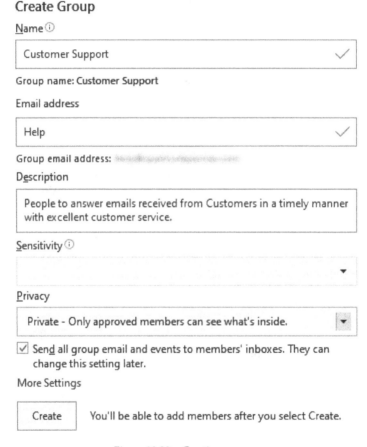

Figure 13.30 – Creating a group

A green checkmark will appear next to the name and email address if they are available. You must choose another name if the green checkmark does not appear and a message will appear letting you know that it is not available. The following lists each field in the **Create Group** dialog box:

- **Group name**: Create a memorable name for the group. This name can only be changed or edited by the group owner.

- **Description**: Enter a description that will help others to identify what the group's purpose is; keep in mind that this text will be included in a welcome email for the group participants.

- **Sensitivity**: These items will be set up by your administrator. An example would be confidential or public.

- **Privacy**: Select whether this should be a public or private group.

- **Send all group email and events to members' inboxes**: Select this box to enable members to see all of the group's conversations. Members can deselect this setting if they would like for their own mailboxes.

Now, let's add members to the group.

3. Add the members that you want to be included in this group by entering the email IDs and clicking *Enter*. Enter as many names as necessary and they will populate the members-to-be-added group.

4. Click **Add Members** once all the names are added. You may also enter the email IDs of people outside of the Exchange network.

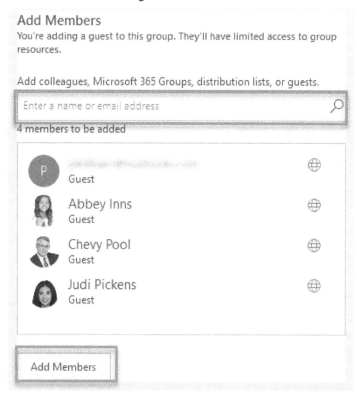

Figure 13.31 – Adding members to a group

5. The navigation pane for email will show the name of the new group in the **Groups** section. As mail is delivered into this group, you can view it here in the **Groups** section or in your email account. A welcome email will also be sent to the members of the group as they are added. (If you are not seeing any emails in the group after running a test email, you will need to close Outlook and open the application again for the mail to populate in the **Groups** section.)

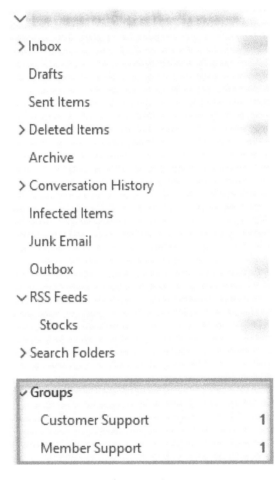

Figure 13.32 – Groups in the navigation pane

6. To make any changes to the group members or other settings, click on the group name in the navigation pane, then click **Home | Group Settings**. Make the desired changes.

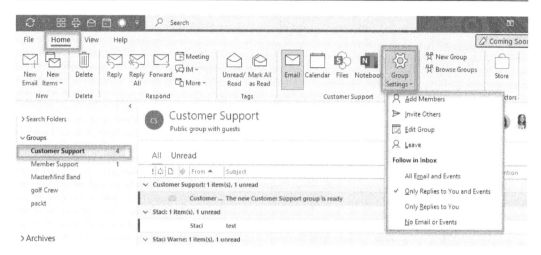

Figure 13.33 – Group Settings

You can still choose which method you want to use to collaborate with others on emails and other items. I like to use this **Groups** feature to be able to find my groups from one quick location when I want to collaborate with a group of people via email. I especially enjoy being able to devote 100% of my attention to the group when needed without having my other emails scattered throughout the list.

Mobile phones

Synchronizing your contacts with your smartphone will allow you to be connected on the go and is a great way to always have your data available as long as you have access to an internet connection. Mobile phones today use satellite communication to make calls and this technology can be converted into internet data signals, which allows us to check our email without a Wi-Fi connection. By installing the Outlook mobile app add-in on your mobile devices, you can sync your Outlook emails, contacts, calendars, and task items between your Outlook Microsoft 365 account and your mobile device.

To install the Outlook mobile app on your mobile phone, take the following steps:

1. From your phone's app store, install the Outlook app on your mobile device. Your phone should come with a preinstalled icon for the app store. For Apple, go to **apps. apple.com** and for Android go to **play.google.com**.

2. After installing the app, find the Outlook app on your mobile phone screen and open it. When the Outlook window opens, click **Get Started**.

3. When prompted by the app, enter the email ID associated with your Microsoft 365 account and click on **Add Account**.

4. When prompted, enter your Microsoft 365 password, then click **Sign In**.

5. You may be prompted to verify that it is you. This could be through a test message, a phone call, or an authenticator app, depending on your level of security. After entering the provided code, click on **Verify**. Once you enter the verify prompts, you will be able to click **Sign In**.

6. You will now be successfully signed in. Your emails will start to automatically sync to your mobile phone from your desktop Microsoft 365 account.

A tutorial should also be sent to you to learn how to use the Outlook app on your mobile device. The store will have several apps that you may want to consider using. I especially enjoy the OneNote app for my phone, which allows me to sync my OneNote with my Microsoft 365 account.

> **Note**
> You can only sync the calendar and contacts with accounts that use the Exchange network.

Add-ins

Add-ins are programs that help automate Outlook with more functionality. Microsoft has partnered with companies to build apps that function with Outlook and help you to be more productive. Some of these add-ins are built within Outlook and others can be downloaded for free or for a fee from the Office store:

1. To get add-ins in Outlook, click **Home | Get Add-ins**. This button will only be present in an Exchange account. If you have Exchange and this option is not available, you can activate it by clicking **File | Options | Customize Ribbon**. Select **All Commands** from the **Choose commands from** drop-down list. Scroll down through the list, select **Get Add-ins [Browse Add-ins]**, and add it to the ribbon menu on the right (click the **Add** button), as shown:

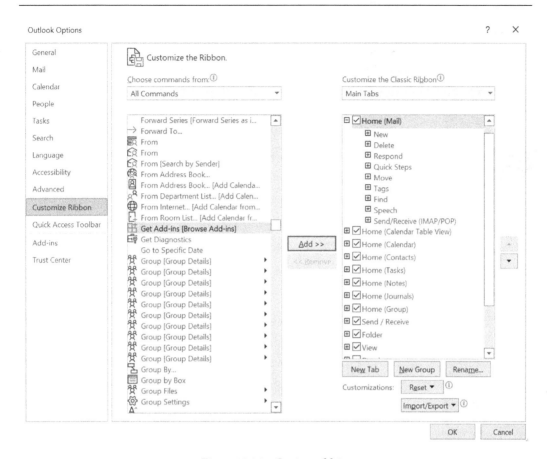

Figure 13.34 – Getting add-ins

2. Select the add-in that you would like to install and follow the prompts to
    download it.

Now, let's explore the problems with add-ins.

Problems with add-ins

Sometimes, add-ins become unstable and do not run properly. If you notice this happening, you can click on the **File | Info | Manage COM Add-ins** button.

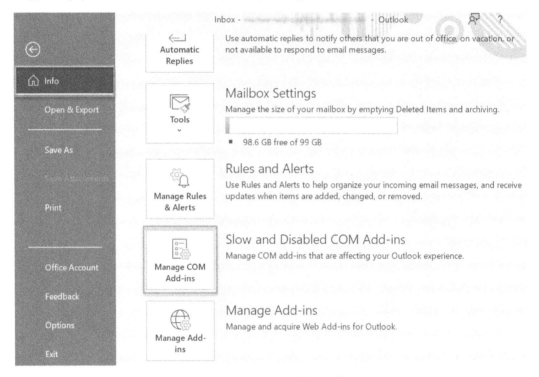

Figure 13.35 – Manage COM Add-ins

This will show you any add-ins that could be causing you problems and give possible solutions for the problem. If Outlook has identified decreased performance or has crashed, you would see a list of those problems in the **Slow and Disabled Add-ins** dialog box.

Managing add-ins

In this section, let's understand how to manage add-ins:

1. To manage and acquire web add-ins for Outlook, click on **File | Info | Manage Add-ins**.

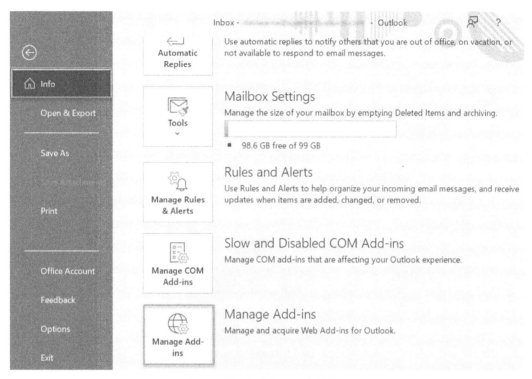

Figure 13.36 – Manage Add-ins

This will open your `outlook.office.com` online account with the store opened to **Add-Ins for Outlook**. You can search for specific items you may want to find in this window.

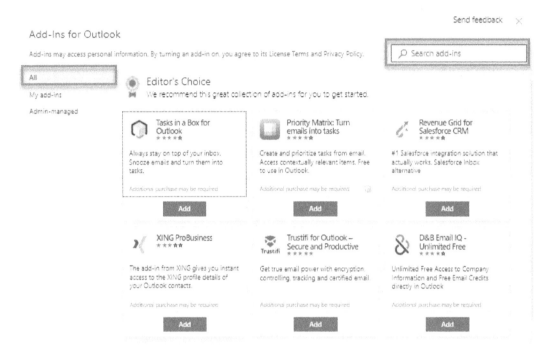

Figure 13.37 – All add-ins

2. On the left side of this **Add-Ins for Outlook** page, you can click **My add-ins** to view any add-ins for Outlook.

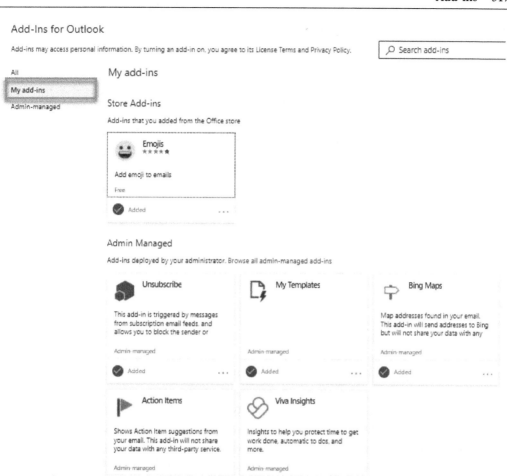

Figure 13.38 – My add-ins

3. Click on the **Admin-managed** tab to view any add-ins that are controlled by your administrators for your account.

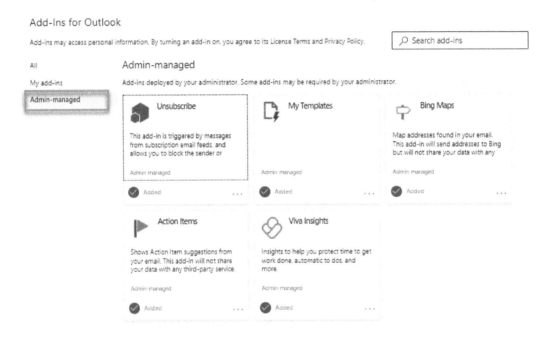

Figure 13.39 – Admin-managed add-ins

New add-ins are being added to Outlook quite often and others are being rebranded with another name, as we have seen with Insights being rebranded as Viva Insights, which now shows on the ribbon next to the **Get Add-ins** button.

Figure 13.40 – Viva Insights add-in

Once you open Viva Insights, you can easily set an out-of-office message and receive emails to inform you how you are doing with responding to people's emails, as well as several other insights.

This is like your personal built-in assistant.

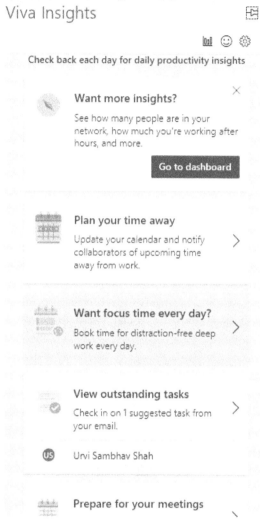

Figure 13.41 – Viva Insights pane

Add-ins are very easy to manage and use. They are intuitive and with artificial intelligence now being used in Outlook, these add-ins seem to know exactly what you need when you need it. I often find myself wondering how I ever got along without all these tools that are now available.

Let's now talk about an old technology that still exists today, called the RSS feed. However, I think this technology is slowly becoming extinct due to the increased use of mobile devices and having data from the internet and updates available to us in real time.

RSS feed

You can use Outlook as an RSS reader to read real-time updates from websites that publish updates in a program called an RSS feed. **RSS** stands for **Really Simple Syndication** and is a program that is provided to show updates to a website instantly. It is not as popular as it was in the past, which is due to the advancement of the web in the ability to report updates in real time instantly now through other means, such as social media, and our ability to always be online with our phones, tablets, and other media devices.

RSS feeds are created and maintained by a website publisher and include a list of articles or other types of data that are maintained within the feed, with the newest items appearing at the top of the list.

This has been a benefit for many news sites or podcast providers that are constantly updating their sites with new content. The advantage to linking Outlook to this is the distribution of new content will automatically feed into the RSS feed folder and you can view the new content of blogs, websites, social media, and podcasts within Outlook instantly.

Creating an RSS feed

To create an RSS feed within Outlook, take the following steps:

1. Select how you want to synchronize RSS feeds to the **Common Feed List (CFL)** in Windows. Click **File** | **Options** | **Advanced**. Click on the box to select **Synchronize RSS Feeds to the Common Feed List (CFL) in Windows**.

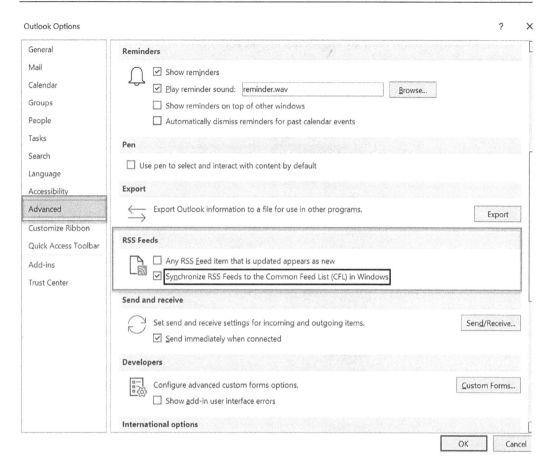

Figure 13.42 – Advanced options | Synchronize RSS Feeds

Once you make this selection, you can change it at any time later.

2. Access the web page desired and choose the RSS icon or button for the content you desire to receive. The RSS icon usually looks like a radio transmitter or a button with RSS or XML. Click on the RSS icon to access the page that has the code for the RSS feed.

3. Copy the address for the feed from *step 2* and subscribe to an RSS feed from within Outlook's navigation pane by right-clicking on **RSS Feeds** and selecting **Add a New RSS Feed…**.

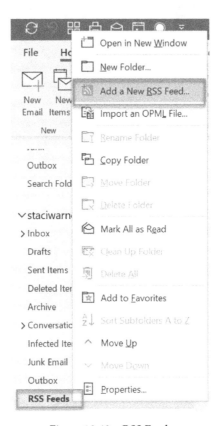

Figure 13.43 – RSS Feeds

4. Paste the copied address into the **Enter the location of the RSS Feed you want to add to Outlook** field. You will need to use the shortcut key to paste in the box, which is *Ctrl + V*.

5. Click **Add**.

Figure 13.44 – New RSS feed

6. Next, a dialog box will ask you to confirm that you want to add the RSS feed subscriptions and warn you that you should ensure you trust the source as viruses can be transmitted this way. Click **Advanced....**

Figure 13.45 – Confirmation for RSS feed addition

7. Enter a name in the **Feed Name** box. This is the name that will appear in the navigation pane when you select the RSS feed subscription. Click **OK** to return to the **Add this RSS Feed to Outlook?** confirmation and then click **Yes.**

Figure 13.46 – Advanced RSS Feed Options dialog box

The **Advanced RSS Feeds** dialog box has additional options you may want to explore.

Viewing an RSS feed

Let's see how to view an RSS feed:

1. Select the folder under **RSS Feeds** that you want to view.

2. The RSS feed downloaded messages will appear in the working window. An additional feature when this is selected is that the **Home** tab will have an **RSS** button, which will let you select additional buttons to download, share, or view the downloaded feed or articles on the web.

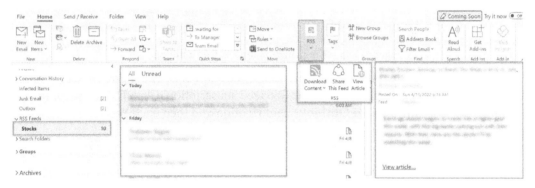

Figure 13.47 – Viewing the RSS feed folder

Feeds to the folder will be updated automatically as new content is created on the website. Any new feeds will appear at the top of the list automatically.

Deleting an RSS feed

When you no longer want to see an RSS feed, you can delete it from the navigation pane by right-clicking on the name of the RSS feed and selecting **Delete Folder**.

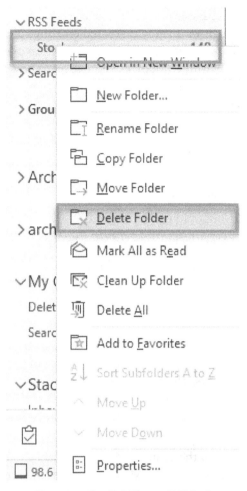

Figure 13.48 – Deleting an RSS feed

The RSS feed name and all the emails in the folder will be deleted. You also will not receive any messages to this feed any longer.

Summary

The cloud is here to stay, and in this chapter, we discussed several of the possibilities you have to collaborate with others by using cloud technology. By saving items to the cloud, it makes it convenient and easy to share files, pictures, OneNote workbooks, and groups and even integrate with Microsoft Teams. Teams has proven to be one of the finest ways to get your members together, either within your place of business or remotely. These tools can be used together or separately, with others or by you alone; the possibilities are endless, and you can decide which tools will or will not work for you.

In the next chapter, we will discuss several rules that you can create to enhance your Outlook environment. Although we already discussed creating rules in *Chapter 4, Organizing your Outlook Environment*, you will not want to skip over this next chapter if you truly want to work smartly with Outlook as you will learn how to create several rules that can save time within your workday. Or, after you apply these rules, you can grab a cup of coffee and sit back and feel confident that Outlook is at work, allowing you a few extra minutes or even hours.

Questions

1. Where can I find Translator for Outlook?

2. Why is the Teams add-in not in my Outlook?

3. I have a button on the **Home** ribbon called **Viva Insights**, what is this?

4. Where can I get more information about add-ins?

5. With groups, what collaboration tools are included in Microsoft 365 subscriptions?

Answers

1. Translator for Outlook is an app that you can purchase in the Microsoft Store and is used to translate documents. The translation will appear on the right of the reading pane when selected and will display the translated text in the language you have requested. The link for downloading the translator can be found in the *Further reading* section.

2. One possible answer is that the Teams add-in was disabled. To check this, click **File | Options | Add-ins**. Confirm that the Microsoft Teams meeting add-in for Microsoft Office is on the list. Select **Com Add-ins | Go** and then select **Microsoft Teams Meeting Add-in for Microsoft Office**.

3. *Insights* and *My Analytics* are add-ins that you may have seen on the ribbon in previous versions of Outlook. These two applications have now been rolled into one and rebranded as **Viva Insights**. Once you select **Viva Insights**, you will be able to control your time, meetings, and events and you will also start receiving emails on a regular basis from Viva Insights with analytic data, suggestions.

4. You can access the Office store to get more information about add-ins and purchase and download them. You can get information about add-ins there, such as ratings, prices, and reviews. To access the Office store, go to `appsource.microsoft.com`.

5. Upon creating a group inside of your Microsoft 365 account, you can begin collaborating with others with a set of tools that includes a shared Outlook inbox to share between group members and a SharePoint document library for sharing files. Groups will also have a shared calendar, OneNote notebook, and Planner. This is the best tool for those that prefer to collaborate through email.

Further readings

- Download OneDrive for Windows: `https://www.microsoft.com/en-us/microsoft-365/onedrive/download`

- OneDrive mobile app: `https://www.microsoft.com/en-us/microsoft-365/onedrive/mobile`

- Share OneDrive files and folders: `https://support.microsoft.com/en-us/office/share-onedrive-files-and-folders-9fcc2f7d-de0c-4cec-93b0-a82024800c07`

- Teams meeting add-in: `https://docs.microsoft.com/en-us/microsoftteams/teams-add-in-for-outlook`

- Translator for Outlook: `https://appsource.microsoft.com/en-us/product/office/WA104380627?src=office&corrid=f9fc2782-77f0-791a-42e3-2ebd685ad2b3&omexanonuid=&referralurl=`

- *Hands-On Microsoft Teams: A practical guide to enhancing enterprise collaboration with Microsoft Teams and Microsoft 365*, by Joao Ferreira, Packt Publishing: `https://www.amazon.com/s?k=Hands-On+Microsoft+Teams%3A+A+practical+guide+to+enhancing+enterprise+collaboration+with+Microsoft+Teams+and+Microsoft+365%2C+by+Joao+Ferreira+and+Packt+Publishing.&crid=24ATI7DVSMT7U&sprefix=hands-on+microsoft+teams+a+practical+guide+to+enhancing+enterprise+collaboration+with+microsoft+teams+and+microsoft+365%2C+by+joao+ferreira+and+packt+publishing.+%2Caps%2C125&ref=nb_sb_noss`

- Outlook for iOS and Android help: `https://support.microsoft.com/en-us/office/outlook-for-ios-and-android-help-cd84214e-a5ac-4e95-9ea3-e07f78d0cde6?ui=en-us&rs=en-us&ad=us`

Part 6: Powerful Ways to Automate Outlook

Using rules, macros, and a custom daily system will help you *Work Less*. You will learn how to choose rules that will benefit you, and at the same time, create your own rules and macros to enhance your working habits. By following these steps and being selective about which of these tips and tricks will make you more productive, you will soon gain control of your inbox once and for all and you will be able to focus on the work at hand.

This section contains the following chapters:

- *Chapter 14, Nine Useful Rules*
- *Chapter 15, Programming with Macros*
- *Chapter 16, Managing Your Day System*

14
Nine Useful Rules

Research shows that we spend 20–30% of our work week managing our emails. This means that in a 40 hour-a-week job, 12 hours will be spent reading and answering emails. This number does not include other emails you may be processing at home and other activities you are involved in.

To work more efficiently, we need to get our emails in order, and using rules as discussed in *Chapter 4, Organizing Your Outlook Environment*, is one way to do this. You can refer to the rules and alerts section in *Chapter 4*, before continuing with this chapter for a refresher on creating rules. This chapter is going to give you some useful suggestions to create rules for organizing your emails and work.

Let's look at some of the rules that we will create:

- Delaying sending after sending an email
- Receiving a text message
- To or Cc
- Automatic reply
- Processing emails that are delegated
- Purging emails with Newsletter in the subject line
- Applying a category as per the word in the subject line
- Redirecting email replies to another person
- Blocking out-of-office replies

Before we begin, I would like to make you aware that rules can slow your system down. Be selective about the rules you create and don't overload your system with too many. Now, let's identify some useful rules that you may want to use.

Rule 1 – delaying sending after sending an email

Rule 1: Delaying sending after sending an email
Description: Eliminate those "oh no!" moments when you forgot to add an attachment, include information in your email, or even add or delete an email ID and only realized it after you hit Send. This rule will give you a specified time before the email is sent by Outlook.
What conditions do you want to check? • Go to **Home | Rules | Manage Rules & Alerts | New Rule** • **Apply rule on messages I send** • Click **Next** • ☑ **on this computer only** • Click **Next** **What do you want to do with the message?** • **Defer delivery by a number of minutes**. • Click the **a number of** link and *enter the number of minutes* in the dialog box. • Click **OK | Next**. **Are there any exceptions?** • **Step 1: No exceptions**. • Click **OK | Next**. **Finish the rule setup** • **Step 1: Specify a name for this rule** . • **Step 2: ☑ Turn on this rule** . • **Step 3: Review the rule**. • Click **Finish**.
For a specified time, you will now find this email in the Outbox in the navigation pane; you can ignore it or retrieve it from this folder if needed. However, if you are working with someone in real time, you will have to remember that your email will not show up in their email immediately.

Table 14.1 – The delay sending rule

Rule 2 – receiving a text message

Rule 2: Receiving a text message
Description: When a message arrives in your inbox from a specified person, a text message will be sent to the mobile phone specified.
What conditions do you want to check? • **Step 1**: ☑ **From Recipient** (you can right-click on the email message). • **Step 2: If necessary, click on the link and enter the email ID**. • Click **Next**. **What do you want to do with the message?** • **Step 1: Forward it to people or a public group** **Are there any exceptions?** • **Step 2: Automatically fills in** **Apply this rule after the message arrives**: Click on the link for people or a public group. • Enter the 10-digit phone number with the *SNS gateway*, as shown in the **To field** *example*: `Staci(1234567890@tmomail.net)`. • Refer to the further reading section for a link to several of the carriers for their unique *SNS gateway*. Contact the carrier if they are not on the list. • Click **OK**	**Next** • Define any exceptions if desired in the **Step 1: select exception(s)**. • *Click* **Next**. **Finish the rule setup**: • **Step 1: Specify a name for this rule**. • **Step 2**: ☑ **Turn on this rule**. • **Step 3: Review the rule***. • Click **Finish** .
You can either respond to the message through Outlook or a text message.

Table 14.2 – The receiving a text message rule

Rule 3 – To or Cc

Rule 3: To or Cc
Description: This rule will look at your inbox and incoming emails and determine whether you are listed in the **To** or **Cc** fields. If you are not, it will send the message to the **Archive** folder or any folder you specify. This will ensure that mass mailings will not appear.
What conditions do you want to check? • **Step 1**: (No selection, as you want the rule to apply to every message in the inbox). • Click **Next**. **What do you want to do with the message?** • **Step 1**: ☑ **move to the specified folder** • Click on the link for the *specified* folder. In the **Rules** and **Alerts** *box, choose the folder to send message(s) to.* **Exp. Archive.** • Click **OK** | **Next**. **Are there any exceptions?** • **Step 1**: þ **except if my name is in the To or Cc box** • Click **Next** **Finish the rule setup.** • **Step 1**: **Specify a name for this rule** • **Step 2**: ☑ **Run this rule now on messages already in the inbox** • ☑ **Turn on this rule** • **Step 3**: **Review the rule** • Click **Finish**
After the rule runs and while emails arrive in the inbox, you will only see messages that are listed in the **To** or **Cc** fields. All other messages can be viewed in the folder specified, such as **Archive** in this example.

Table 14.3 – The To or Cc rule

Rule 4 – automatic reply

Rule 4: Automatic reply
Description: This rule will send a reply email to the sender if they have addressed the email to an address that you no longer want them to use. You first need to create the templates, as shown in *Chapter 16, Manage Your Day System*.
What conditions do you want to check? • **Step 1: þ With specific words in the recipient's address** • ☑ **sender is in specified Address Book** • **Step 2**: Apply this rule after the message arrives. • Click on the link for with **specific words in** the recipient's address. • In the search text dialog box, enter the words or the retired email ID. • Click on link for with **specified** from the recipient's address book and select **contacts**. • Click **Add | Next**. **What do you want to do with the message?** • **Step 1**: Select the second condition(s): **þ reply using a specific template**. • Click on the link for the **specific template**. In the **Select a Reply Template** dialog box, enter `User Templates in File System` and highlight your desired template. • Click **Open | Next | Next**. **Are there any exceptions?** • **Step 1**: No exceptions. • Click **Next**. **Finish the rule setup**: • **Step 1: Specify a name for this rule.** • **Step 2**: ☑ **Turn on this rule.** • **Step 3: Review Rule**. • Click **Finish**.

Table 14.4 – The automatic reply rule

Rule 5 – processing emails that are delegated

Rule 5: Processing emails that are delegated
Description: Use this rule to assist you in keeping track of emails that you have delegated to others. To have this work, you will need to Cc yourself to track the email, as well as set up a folder to send the delegated emails to.
What conditions do you want to check? • Go to **Home | Rules | Manage Rules & Alerts | New Rule** • **Step 1**: Select the **Apply rule on messages I receive** template. • **Step 2**: Apply this rule after the message arrives (automatically populated). • Click **Next** **What do you want to do with the message?** • **Step 1: þ from people or public group** • ☑ **where my name is in the Cc box** **Are there any exceptions?** • **Step 1: ☑ move it to the specified folder**. • Click the specified link and select the **delegated** folder that has been set up. • Click **OK | Next**. **Finish the rule setup**: • **Step 1: Specify a name for this rule** . • **Step 2: ☑ Turn on this rule** . • **Step 3: Review the rule** . • Click **Finish** .
When you copy yourself in the **Cc** line of a message, the email will automatically be moved to the **delegated** folder (or any other folder you specified). Click the **delegated** folder in the navigation pane to view emails moved to this folder through this rule.

Table 14.5 – Processing emails that are delegated

Rule 6 – purging emails with Newsletter in the subject line

Rule 6: Purging emails with `Newsletter` in the Subject line
Description: This rule will purge out and delete any newsletters that have the word `Newsletter` in the Subject line of the received emails.
What conditions do you want to check? • Go to **Home | Rules | Manage Rules & Alerts | New Rule**. • Ø **Apply rule on messages I receive**. • Click **Next**. **What do you want to do with the message?** • **Step 1**: ☑ **with specific words in the subject**. • Click the *specific words* link and enter `Newsletter` for the criteria. • ☑ **Delete it**. • Click **Next**. **Are there any exceptions?** • **Step 1**: ☑ **Except if my name is in the To or Cc box**. • **Step 2**: Edit the rule description (click an underlined value). • Click **Next**. **Finish the rule setup**: • **Step 1**: **Specify a name for this rule**. • **Step 2**: ☑ **Turn on this rule**. • **Step 3**: **Review the rule**. • Click **Finish**.
This rule is set up to delete newsletter. You may want to keep the newsletter and send them to another folder (instead of deleting) or send them to the **Archive** folder, with a category assigned to mark the email as a newsletter.

Table 14.6 – The purging the newsletter rule

Rule 7 – applying a category as per the word in the subject line

Rule 7: Applying a category as per the word in the subject line
Description: Applying a category to an incoming email if a specific word is in the header/ subject line of the email

What conditions do you want to check?
 	
  Click **Advanced Options….**
 	
What do you want to do?
 	
  • **Step 1**: ☑ **With specific words in the message header**.
  • **Step 2**: Apply this rule after the message arrives (filled in automatically).
  • Click the **specific words** link and enter the desired text that you want to apply this rule to.
  • Click **Add | OK**.
  • Click **Next**.
 	
Are there any exceptions?
 	
  • **Step 1**: ☑ **Assign it to the category link**.
  • **Step 2**: Click the **category** link and select the desired category.
  • Click **OK | Next**.
 	
Finish the rule setup:
 	
  • **Step 1: Specify a name for this rule** .
  • **Step 2**: ☑ **Turn on this rule** .
  • **Step 3**: **Review the rule** .
  • Click **Finish** .

A category will now be set as the messages arrive in the inbox, and if you prefer, you can use a view to show the categories at the top of the inbox.

Table 14.7 – The flag or pin emails rule

Rule 8 – redirecting email replies to another person

Rule 8: Redirecting email replies to another person
Description: Redirected messages sent to your account from a specified person will be automatically forwarded to another person's email ID. This is one way to delegate work to someone else without your client knowing, or you simply may need someone to complete some work that you don't have time to complete at a certain time. This is a great way to handle your email while on vacation.
What conditions do you want to check? • **Step 1**: ☑ **Sent only to me**. • ☑ **From (name of selected email to begin rule-change later)**. • **Step 2**: Apply this rule after the message arrives (automatically populated). • Click the **name** link and enter the email ID of the person who you will be forwarding to. • Click **OK | Next**. **What do you want to do with the message?** • **Step 1**: ☑ **forward it to people or public group**. • Click the **people or public group** link and enter the email ID to forward **To** box. • Click **OK | Next**. **Are there any exceptions?** • **Step 1**: None. • **Step 2**: Confirm the correct entries. • Click **Next**. **Finish the rule setup:** • **Step 1**: Specify a name for this rule. • **Step 2**: ☑ **Turn on this rule**. • **Step 3**: **Review the rule**. • Click **Finish**.
Your email will automatically be forwarded to the specified person, with a copy of the email remaining in your inbox.

Table 14.8 – The redirecting email replies rule

Rule 9 – blocking out-of-office replies

Rule 9: Blocking out-of-office replies.
Description: This rule will allow you to block any out-of-office reply emails that are sent to you by someone that has an out-of-office reply message automatically being sent to you from their computer. Many times, these emails are not necessary for your way of working.
What conditions do you want to check? • Click **Home | Manage Rules & Alerts | New Rule**. • **Step 1**: Select the **Apply rule on messages I receive** template. • **Step 2**: Apply this rule after the message arrives (automatically populated). • Click **Next**. • **Step 1**: ☑ With specific words in the subject. • **Step 2**: Click the **specific words** link and enter possible search words.   Click **Add** after each word entered: `Out of Office`, `Automatically reply`, `Auto reply`, or `out of Office AutoReply`. • Click **Next**. **What do you want to do with this message?** • **Step 1**: ☑ **delete it**. • Click **OK | Next**. **Finish the rule setup**: • **Step 1: Specify a name for this rule**. • **Step 2**: ☑ **Turn on this rule**. • **Step 3: Review the rule**. • Click **Finish**.
Now, when receiving emails with the out-of-office reply in the subject or any of the subject lists as shown previously, the message will be deleted from the inbox and you will never see it.

Table 14.9 – Blocking out-of-office replies

Hopefully, you have found a couple of these *rules* helpful for you becoming more efficient and automating the process for handling (or should I say *not* handling) your email.

Summary

In this chapter, you have learned nine rules that you can use to automate your email or the handling of email within Outlook. Having a system in place and monitoring it for a few weeks is key to making this work for you. Think of all the time you will be freeing up now that can be used on other projects or simply things in life that you enjoy.

In the next chapter, we will discuss another tool you can use within Outlook to further automate and increase your productivity skills while working in Outlook. We will learn the magic of creating macros and using them while programming Outlook. We will cover the basics of using VBA code and how to use it within Outlook macros.

Questions

1. What is the difference between server-based and client-only rules?
2. Can I set up a rule with server-based and client-only rules?
3. Can I use wildcard symbols, such as * and ?, within a *rule* in Outlook?
4. How do *rules* know when to run within Outlook?
5. How can I get my co-worker to stop sending me stupid jokes through email?

Answers

1. Server-based rules run on an Exchange server and apply to messages as they are delivered to your inbox. The rules cannot run until they have been completed on the server. If the rules can't run on the server, they are applied once Outlook starts. Client-only rules are only run on your computer through Outlook and do not get processed through the server. Client-only rules can only run when Outlook is open, whereas server-based rules run on the server only.
2. If your rule contains server-based and client-based rules, the server-based rule must process before the client-only rule.
3. No, rules do not support the use of wildcard characters.
4. When you see the rules listed in the **Manage Rules & Alerts** dialog box, they will run in the order listed from top to bottom. You can select a rule and move it up or down within the list to create your desired order of process.

5. Everybody has an email joker in their inbox. Use a rule that finds terms that go along with jokes, such as `funny`, `chain letter`, `pass this along`, or simply Fwd. The rule could automatically forward these emails to a **jokes** folder or archive, or delete them.

Further reading

- *List of SMS Gateways (rule 2)*:

  `https://www.liquisearch.com/list_of_sms_gateways`

15
Programming with Macros

Within Outlook, you can enhance its functionality by creating macros to automate tasks that you find yourself doing repeatedly. We will use the **Visual Basic for Application (VBA)** to learn how to apply programming features to Outlook to automate repetitive tasks and create macros.

Let's discuss the following topics:

- The Outlook object model
- The Visual Basic Application
- Macros

Through these topics, we will focus on the basics of programming within VBA to create macros within Outlook for beginners. This chapter will get you started with VBA and you will find several use cases, such as creating other code, for using VBA.

The Outlook object model

A data model is a blueprint that shows the hierarchical abstract model that organizes Outlook data in a particular order. Outlook, as well as other applications, has its own data model and it is called the **Outlook object model**. I have noticed in some documentation written on the Outlook object model that classes are referred to. Some of the classes/objects that Microsoft identifies as high-level or important objects are the following:

- **Application** – Represents the entire application
- **AppointmentItem** – A new appointment used with the `CreateItem` method
- **ContactItem** – A new contact object, used with the `CreateItem` method
- **Explorer** – Displays the contents of a folder and where displayed
- **Folder** – Represents a folder that contains email
- **Inspector** – Represents the Outlook item that displays when you double-click an item
- **MailItem** – Represents a new mail item in a folder
- **TaskItem** – Represents a task within a task folder

Microsoft defines a class/object as a description or template that is used to create or instantiate an object.

You can read more about the Outlook object model in the *Further reading* section of this chapter. The following table of terms will help further explain the object model and it will be useful for you to know these terms if writing VBA code:

Type	Description	Examples
Objects	A container, such as a form or a picture box, that can contain other controls	• **Application** object: represents the entire application • **Folder** object: represents folders that contain mail and other items • **MailItem** object: represents email messages • **Explorer** object: the contents of a folder that displays a window with items such as email, appointments, and tasks
Properties	Describes the objects	*Left, Top, Height, Width, Name, Enabled, Visible*
Methods	Causes an object to do something	*Move, Drag, SetFocus, ZOrder*
Events	This is something that happens when an object does something	*Change, Click, DblClick, DragDrop, GotFocus, LostFocus, MouseDown, MouseMove, MouseUp*

Table 15.1 – Objects and components

An example of using an object would be the **namespace** object. It is the root of the object model. The only item higher than the namespace would be the actual Outlook application. Within the namespace object, we can also have all kinds of folders, contacts, mail, people, tasks, and more. Depending on which folder you have selected will depend on what actions can be taken. For example, if I am in my mail folder (**Inbox**), I have access to my emails but not my **Calendar** information. Becoming familiar with the object model will help you be able to refer to names more easily. At first, you may find it confusing, but the more you use it and apply the features to coding within VBA, the easier and more robust you will find it to be. After some time, it won't seem as complicated as you once thought.

Visual Basic

Visual Basic (**VB**) was created by Microsoft and was released in 1991. Although many versions have been created since that release, it is still considered to be one of the easiest programs to learn and is especially one of the easiest programs to use to write programs for Windows. Most people find it is also fun to use.

There are three different types of VB:

- **Visual Basic (VB)** – Best for beginner programmers or novices to create their own Windows applications.

- **Visual Basic Script** (**VBScript**) – Used for Windows scripting and web page scripting for use in Internet Explorer or Edge.

- **Visual Basic for Applications** (**VBA**) – Used for all Microsoft Office applications, such as Outlook, Excel, Word, PowerPoint, and Access. It runs within the application rather than as a standalone product.

In 2002, Microsoft replaced VB with VB.NET as the successor to the VB language. There is talk of VB being retired as other programming options exist, such as C#, Java, and C##, which are more popular programs among serious developers.

Let's discuss creating code within Outlook by using the built-in VBA editor to create a macro. Within the editor, you can create code for a macro using VBA, which can include the use of objects, properties, methods, and events, as briefly described in this chapter.

Macros

Using VBA within Outlook, you will find, makes it easy to complete repetitive tasks and have the application behave according to your expectations. VBA code that is written to perform a task is called a macro. You can program macros to be as simple or complex as needed, as well as being able to program them to run automatically or with the click of a button, or simply to have something displayed.

You may be asking *what is the difference between a macro and VBA?* A macro is programming code, which happens to be written in VBA, that runs on application platforms such as Outlook, Excel, Word, and others to perform automatic routine tasks. VBA is the programming application built within Outlook (or other apps) that is used to create macros.

In Office applications such as Excel and Word, you can record macros using a simple tool, **Record Macro**. This tool will create the VBA code for you as you go through the steps on the screen while having the code generated and saved as a macro.

The record macro tool does not exist in Outlook as it does in Word and Excel. In Outlook, you must write the code in the VBA editor, which means it is necessary for you to know how to use the VBA editor, and then you'll need to know how to incorporate it into Outlook. Knowing how to write code in VB will help you to write code in VBA.

Let's start the steps necessary for writing code by turning on the **Developer** tab.

Activating the Developer tab

The **Developer** tab is hidden in Outlook and other Microsoft applications such as Excel and Word. It is most useful for writing VBA code within these applications. It does have other uses, such as running macros, using XML commands, using ActiveX controls, and creating applications to have fun with several applications. In my opinion, using the *Developer tab* is most useful for creating macros as well as using form controls.

Let's activate the **Developer** tab:

1. To activate the **Developer** tab, click **File | Options | Customize Ribbon**. Check the **Developer** box and click **OK**.

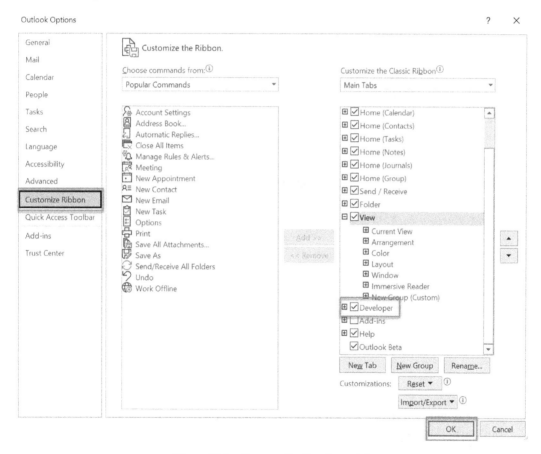

Figure 15.1 – Turn on the Developer tab

2. Locate the **Developer** tab, which will now be displayed in the menu.

Figure 15.2 – Developer tab

With the **Developer** tab activated, you can view, create, and run macros using the tools on the ribbon. Let's now use the Visual Basic Editor to create a macro.

Visual Basic Editor

Visual Basic Editor is used to create code in Outlook and other Microsoft applications. It is most useful for non-programmers. It is built into the applications and can be used by activating the **Developer** tab:

1. Click **Developer | Visual Basic** to open the Visual Basic Editor window:

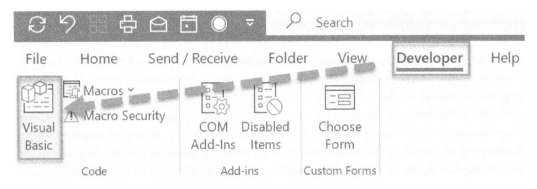

Figure 15.3 – Open Visual Basic Editor

2. The following **Microsoft Visual Basic for Applications** window will open, and you can start creating your macros in this window.

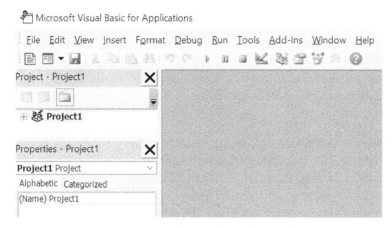

Figure 15.4 – Microsoft Visual Basic for Applications

Alternatively, you can press *Alt + F11* to open the Visual Basic Editor. This view may also be called the VBA developer **Integrated Development Environment** (IDE).

You will also want to be sure that you have activated the object model when writing the code from within Outlook or another application:

3. Click **Tools | References…** and check the box next to **Microsoft Office 16.0 Object Library**. You may have a different version number depending on your installed version of Outlook. Click **OK**.

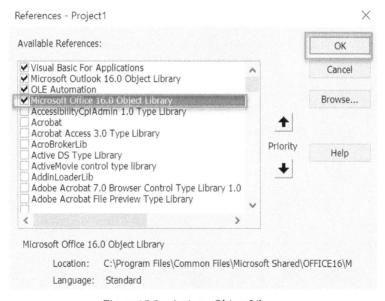

Figure 15.5 – Activate Object Library

Now you are ready to write code in the VBA editor window.

Macro scenario

For this example, we will create an Outlook macro to allow us to click on a button on the toolbar to have an email created from a template or created to reply with a template to an existing email that has been received. If you find yourself writing the same email repeatedly, you will benefit from this type of macro. Before we get started with this macro, we need to first create the email and save it as a template:

- **Create the email template** – Create an email as normal but *do not send*; save it as a template. Be sure to include any attachments, **To**, **Cc**, or **Bcc** headings, and messages in the body of the email. Do not include a signature if you have a signature automatically populate when you start a new email. Just delete the signature from this email before saving it as a template. The steps to create a template are detailed in *Chapter 16, Managing Your Day System, step 7.*

Creating a macro

Let's go through the process of creating a macro:

1. In the VBA editor, click **ThisOutlookSession**. Create Macro in a blank box or referred to as Module. The code for the two macros is as follows.

   The following is the code for the new email template:

   ```
   Sub NewEmailTemplate()


     Set msg = Application.CreateItemFromTemplate("<FILEPATH
         HERE>\<FILENAME HERE>.oft")
     msg.Display
   End Sub
   ```

2. The following is the code for the reply email template:

   ```
   Sub ReplyEmailTemplate()
       Dim origEmail As MailItem
       Dim replyEmail As MailItem

       Set origEmail = Application.ActiveWindow.Selection.
           Item(1)
       Set replyEmail = Application.
           CreateItemFromTemplate("<FILEPATH HERE>\
               <FILENAME HERE>.oft")
   ```

```
    replyEmail.To = origEmail.Sender
    replyEmail.CC = origEmail.CC
    replyEmail.Subject = origEmail.Subject

    replyEmail.HTMLBody = replyEmail.HTMLBody & origEmail.
        Reply.HTMLBody
    replyEmail.Display
End Sub
```

3. To copy your own template location to paste over the <FILEPATH HERE> and <FILENAME HERE> text within the code, click **Home | New Items | More Items | Choose Form…**:

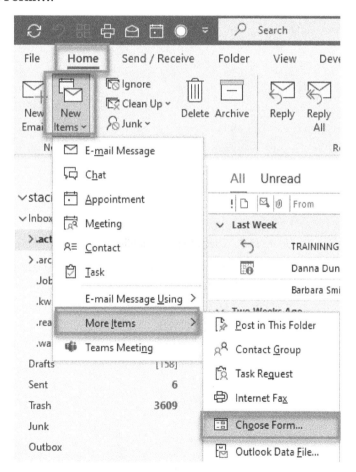

Figure 15.6 – Choose Form template

4.   From the **Choose Form** dialog box, choose the drop-down arrow for the **Look In** textbox and select **User Templates in File System | Open**.

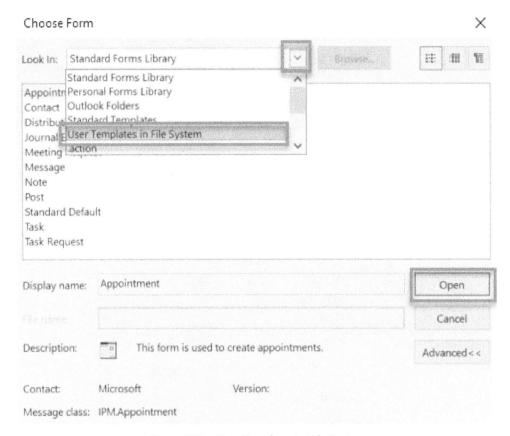

Figure 15.7 – User Templates in File System

5.   Select the template location from above the files listed in the **Choose Form** dialogue box, not including the \ * . oft filename.

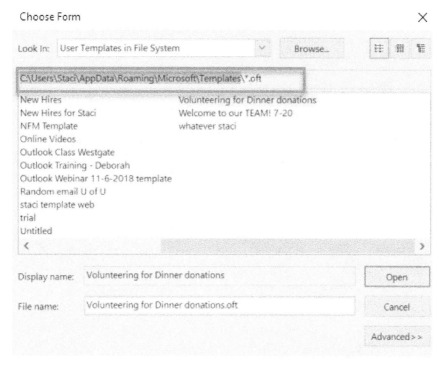

Figure 15.8 – File template location to copy

6. You have now created the two macros and they should look as follows, with your data in `<FILEPATH HERE>` and `<FILENAME HERE>` filled in with your file path and filename from your computer.

Figure 15.9 – Completed macros

> **Note**
>
> Comments are entered into the code with an ' (apostrophe) before the text, which will turn the text green. These comments are for explaining the code that is written below. This is a very useful coding technique to help describe what the code is written to do.

Running macros with the button on the ribbon

Now we need a way to run the macros. We could choose the **Macro** button from the **Developer** tab:

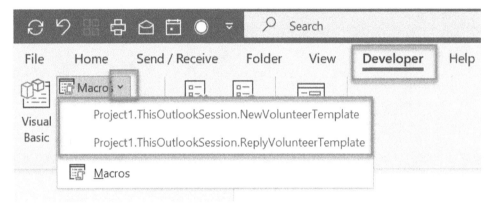

Figure 15.10 – New macros created

An easier way would be to create a button on the ribbon. I will place it as a new button on the **Home** tab in the **Respond** section.

Figure 15.11 – Respond section on the Home tab

1. Click **File | Options | Customize Ribbon | Expand Respond**. Under **Home** in the **Main Tabs** box on the right of the **Customize the Ribbon** window, select **Respond | New Group | Rename…**.

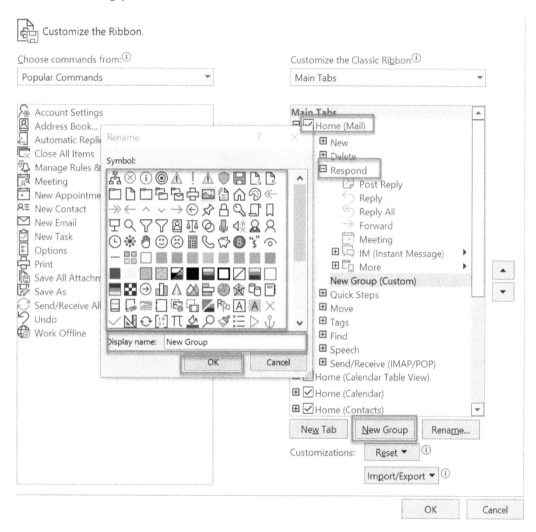

Figure 15.12 – New Group name

2. Enter a new name for the group in the **Display name** text field and click **OK** to confirm the renaming. In the box on the left below the **Customize the Ribbon** title, click the dropdown and select **Macros**, and drag each macro to the **New Group** item created, as shown in the following figure. Click **OK**:

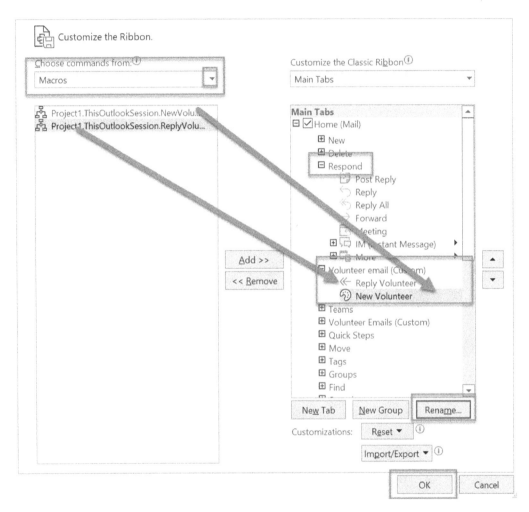

Figure 15.13 – Macros applied to the new group

3. Select each macro and rename the macro to the name to be displayed within a button on the ribbon. Click **OK**. Once this is done, you will find the buttons on the ribbon, as shown here:

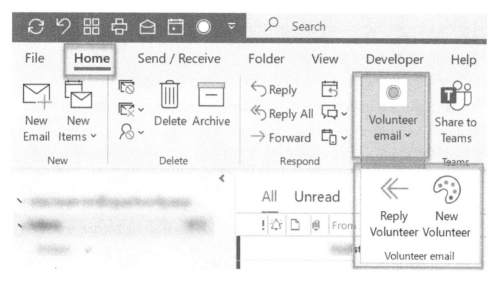

Figure 15.14 – New buttons for new emails from templates

When the **New Volunteer** button is clicked, a new email will generate the template with the header information filled in along with attached documents and the body of text. You can add the name of the person receiving the email in the header as well as the body of the email and click **Send**.

To use the **Reply** button, select but don't open an email that you wish to reply to with the template email created in the second macro that was created in the VBA editor. This will generate an email with the selected template and you will see the header information already filled in. Add the name of the person you are sending the message to in the body of the text, verify that you don't want or need to make any changes, and click **Send**.

These are two very useful templates that I have found save me a lot of time with new clients.

> **Note**
>
> Macros are one way for malicious code to access and run malware and ransomware. To help improve security, Microsoft has announced that beginning in April of 2022, the default for running macros will be to block macros in files from the internet. This means any emails with macros included will be blocked and a security risk message will indicate that it was blocked.

The following are some suggestions of what you could create macros for within Outlook:

- To export contacts to a database

- To save attachments from an email to a folder on your computer

- To update meeting information automatically for recurring appointments

- To download all attachments from a specific Outlook folder to a folder on your computer

- To send Outlook emails from Excel and Word

- To create automatic responses to meetings

These are only a few tasks that you could use macros for. I would suggest that you start watching the way you use Outlook and when you find yourself repeating steps over and over, creating a Macro for that repetition could save you time.

Summary

VBA is a very powerful programming solution for many problems, but keep in mind that it is not the only way. You may find other solutions. **Quick Steps**, for example, for many can replace the need for macros and there would be no coding necessary for these to run. Ask yourself as you choose a feature, is there an easier way? Take the time to evaluate all your options. Programming requires focus and can be very time-consuming and unpredictable. If you are a beginner, using the VBA editor is a great way to learn. Be sure you have the time to work it all through. If a deadline is approaching, it can make for a stressful situation, and you may want to do a repetitive action first and create the code after things settle down.

In the next chapter, we will discuss the **Manage Your Day** system. This is a system that I use with some of my favorite tools, tips, and tricks that can help you gain control of Outlook. If you would like to streamline your daily activities, which will have you working SMART with Outlook in no time at all, I highly recommend you keep reading.

Questions

1. Is VBA available in the current Microsoft 365 subscription?

2. How can I enable macros? I keep getting a message that my macros are disabled.

3. How can I back up my macros?

4. How do I open the VBA editor within Outlook?

5. Will macros be included in the MOS Outlook exam?

Answers

1. VBA is currently supported in the desktop version of Microsoft 365 and will be for some time in the future. However, keeping it working on all versions of Outlook will probably not happen. As of the writing of this book, there are no plans to retire VBA. Microsoft will continue to encourage users to learn JavaScript APIs as the VBA replacement.

2. Macros can pose a threat to your Outlook environment and Microsoft has now set the default to disable macros coming from the internet. To change this setting, click **File | Options | Trust Center | Trust Center Settings… | Macro Settings** and select the desired setting.

3. Back up or create a Word document with your Outlook macros. Open the VBA editor in Outlook and copy the code for the macros. Paste the copied code into a Word document and save it to your computer.

4. The shortcut key for opening the VBA editor within Outlook is *Alt + F11*.

5. The current MOS Outlook exam is exam MO-400. Macros are not included in the objective domains for this exam. See *Further reading* for the MO-400 exam objectives.

Further reading

- *Outlook data model*: https://docs.microsoft.com/en-us/office/vba/api/overview/outlook/object-model

- *VBA Objects – The Ultimate Guide*: https://excelmacromastery.com/vba-objects/

- *Macros from the internet will be blocked by default in Office*: https://docs.microsoft.com/en-us/deployoffice/security/internet-macros-blocked

- *Microsoft Outlook (Microsoft 365 Apps and Office 2019): Exam MO-400*: https://certiport.pearsonvue.com/Certifications/Microsoft/MOS/Certify/Outlook.aspx

16
Managing Your Day System

Email overload is a real thing and can be a real drain on your well-being, mental health, and productivity. Many people are being affected, especially now that so many people are working remotely, and email overload is also creating email anxiety.

Here are three signs that you may be in email overload:

- You are constantly checking your email, waiting to see whether anything came in even when you are not expecting anything.

- You are behind on reading and responding to new emails and your inbox is getting overfilled.

- You sort and search for emails more than reading new emails.

Not getting control of your emails can cause real headaches, especially if you are losing files and emails and spending too much time looking for specific emails. More emails in your inbox equal less productivity.

In this chapter, we're going to cover the following topics:

- Kanban
- Five SMART habits to be productive
- Power Hour

This chapter will give you some ideas for taking control of your emails to manage your day, at least within Outlook.

Kanban

A **Kanban board** is a model that was created and used in the 1940s by an engineer at Toyota named **Taiichi Ohno**. In the Japanese language, **kan** means sign and **ban** means board. In Japan at the time, as streets became overcrowded, shop owners would make signs called Kanbans to pull in people off the streets to gain business.

Mr. Ohno also noticed that store shelves were stocked with a specific amount of products to meet the demands of consumers. Once they saw empty space on the shelf, it would be restocked. Mr. Ohno wanted to create a similar system due to Toyota's decline. He needed a way to do the same thing within the factory while building cars. He developed a system that used Kanban cards to determine when a car was sold so another car could start production. This system helped to identify bottlenecks, reduce stockpiles, improve throughput, and maintain high visibility at the same time. This system also helped Toyota go from an operating loss to being a major competitor in the automotive industry.

In 2007, the software industry started using Kanban boards for the development of software programming. Microsoft developed its first Kanban system in 2010 and many others followed. Today, Kanban boards are not just for the corporate world; many utilize the concept in their personal lives as well. The Kanban concept has proven to be productive, made people and processes more effective, and in general lets people focus on doing more.

You will probably be asking right now, *what does Kanban have to do with Outlook*? By implementing the concept of Kanban boards within Outlook, you could be freeing up several hours within your day. The following figure shows a basic Kanban board with only a few columns:

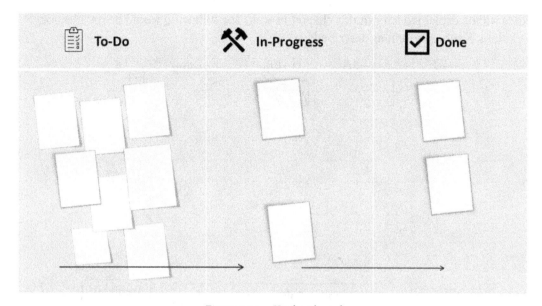

Figure 16.1 – Kanban board

Kanban was designed to help you visualize your work, as well as limiting what work you have in progress. Kanban starts with what you have in your inbox to do now. It is a pull system, which means you pull from one area on the left and follow the flow to the right. This is called a workflow, and eventually, the item ends up in the **done** column.

We could consider Outlook as a **Kanban board**. As an email comes into your inbox, you choose to leave it in there, bunching up, creating bottlenecks, and sometimes some of those emails may be forgotten altogether. You should instead try to minimize what is stored in your inbox and move emails into folders, create a system for working with those folders, and eventually move emails out of those folders into an `Archive` folder. These folders will be explained later in this chapter as well. The following would be my idea for an Outlook Kanban system as described:

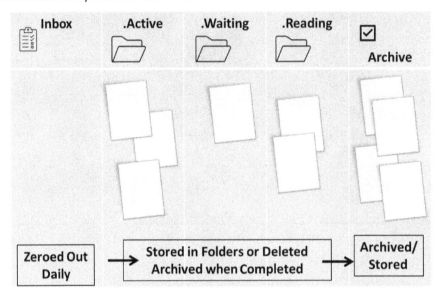

Figure 16.2 – Outlook Kanban board

Each of us has 1,440 minutes each day. I believe that being productive is becoming harder and harder to accomplish within those minutes. We need to keep focused on the task at hand yet stay engaged with our families and various social responsibilities as well, all while eliminating as many distractions as possible. Using a Kanban board may help with this, but using Outlook like a Kanban board could also help.

Outlook on the web, or OWA, has a Kanban concept built into the calendar. As of the time of writing this book, that feature is not part of the Outlook desktop version. If you consider your inbox as the **to-do** (backlog) items, the folder items as the **in-progress** items, and the **Archive** folder items as the **done** items, you can have a system that will have you running an efficient time management system just like a typical Kanban board.

Let us now talk about the five SMART habits to help you be productive and more efficient and streamline these SMART habits within your system for managing your day.

Five SMART habits to be productive

In this section let us understand the five smart habits to be productive.

SMART habit #1 – use search

In *Chapter 10, Save Time Searching*, we discussed several features you can use to search for multiple items within Outlook. Research shows that the average email user spends over 20% of their day searching for emails. The main reason for this is that most users browse through their inbox trying to find a specific email. This can be like finding a needle in a haystack, especially if you use the inbox as your main depository, or in the situation of a Kanban board, this would be your *To-Do* column that holds all your items/emails waiting to be processed.

Let us show you two methods for you to use to search for your items effectively:

1. Search with **FACT, F=From, A=Attachment, C=Contains, T=To**:

    A. Enter the search word or phrase in the **Search** field at the top of the Outlook window and click the drop-down arrow to the right:

Figure 16.3 – Search field

    B. Enter any known **FACT** information in the appropriate fields:

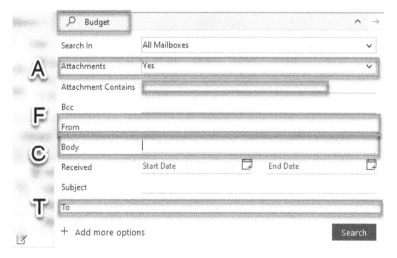

Figure 16.4 – Search expanded for FACT

Ask yourself where the **FACTs** are. Filling all these four search options the first time narrows down search results so you won't have as many items to wade through.

2.   Create search folders:

A. Click **Folder | New Search Folder**:

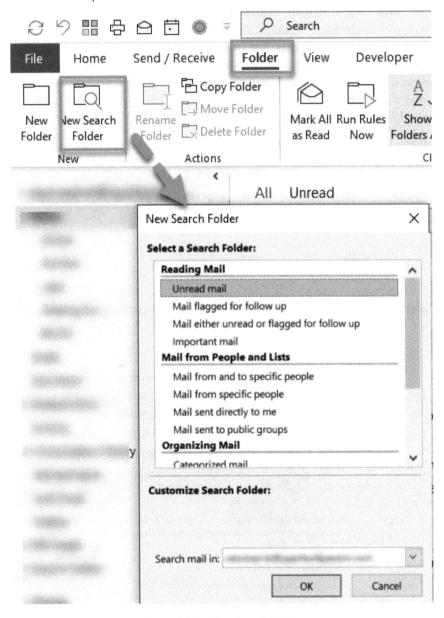

Figure 16.5 – New Search Folder

B. Select the type of search folder you want to create. I will scroll to the bottom of this list and select **Create a custom Search Folder | Choose...**, then name the folder and click **Criteria...**.

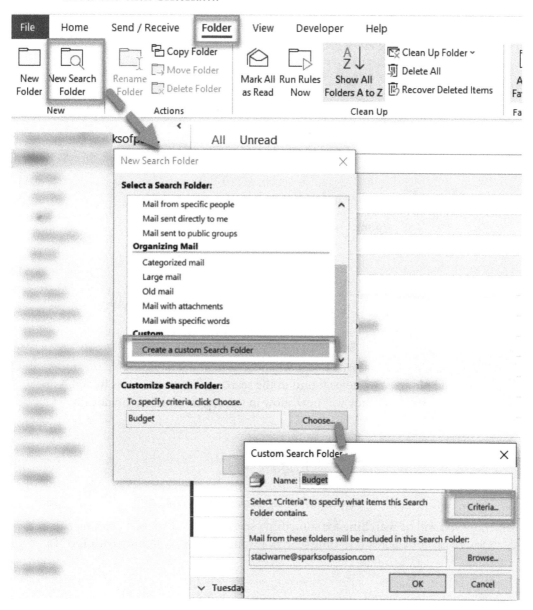

Figure 16.6 – New Search Folder

C. Enter the desired search criteria in the **Search Folder Criteria** dialog box using all three tabs if desired for **Messages**, **More Choices**, and **Advanced**.

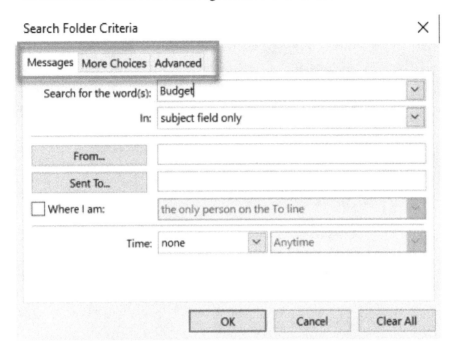

Figure 16.7 – Search Folder Criteria

D. Your newly created search folder will be shown in the navigation pane under **Search Folders**. Any items found in the search will appear in this folder. As new items are received, they will now show in the search folder automatically.

Figure 16.8 – Budget search folder

If you know you will be searching for something several times, I suggest creating a search folder. Otherwise, for a quick one-time search, I would suggest searching with **FACT**s.

SMART habit #2 – don't repeat steps

If you need to repeat a task more than three times (weekly or monthly), you need to put a system in place to be more efficient. These next three tips I have found to be helpful for applying to tasks I repeat several times while processing my emails:

1. **See the response in red below**: How many times have you had to respond to someone's email with the same text to answer a set of questions they have for you? Next time, follow these steps and Outlook will do that for you:

   A. Click **File | Options | Mail | Stationery and Fonts… | Personal Stationery**:

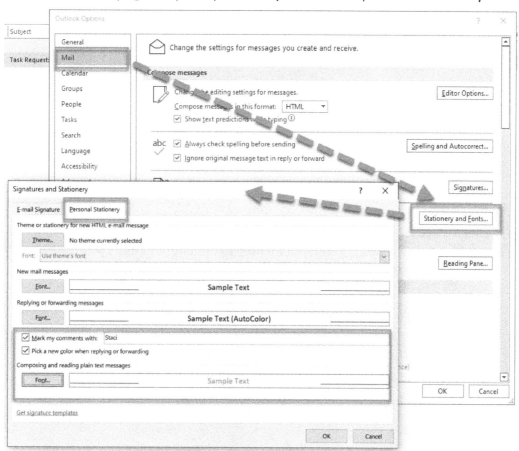

Figure 16.9 – Personal Stationery for replies

   B. Click **OK** and **OK** to close the dialog boxes. Now, when you reply to the message and scroll down through the document, your reply text will show your name, as well as changing the text color as you specified.

2. **Resend an email**: When you need to send an email a second time, usually due to the receiver claiming they never got it, follow these steps to resend it. These steps eliminate the need to copy the original email and paste it into a new mail message:

    A. Open the email that you need to resend (you must be the sender of the email).

    B. Click **Actions | Resend This Message…**.

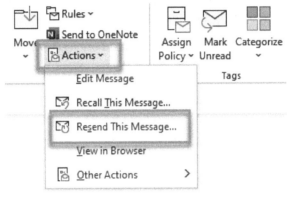

Figure 16.10 – Resend This Message…

This is what I call SMART as most users don't even realize this is available.
Now the email will look like a regular email to be sent out. Enter a **To** recipient and click **Send**.

3. **Create a quick step for replying with common text to an email recipient**: On social media, we are used to clicking a button to respond to or like a post. In Outlook, you can do this with a **quick step**.

    A. Click **Home | New Quick Step | Custom…**:

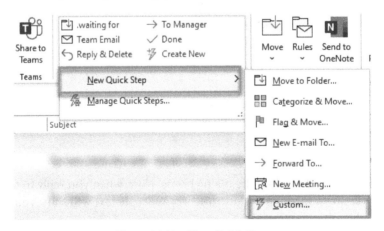

Figure 16.11 – New Quick Step

B. Enter a name for the quick step and choose **Reply** for the action step:

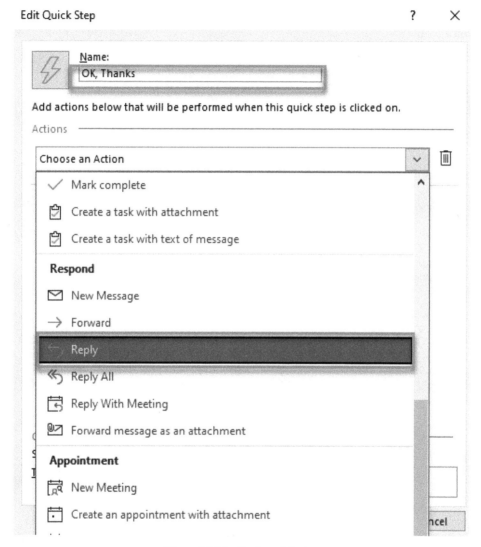

Figure 16.12 – Reply quick step

C. The drop-down list will close, showing the selection. Below this selected action item, click **Show Options**:

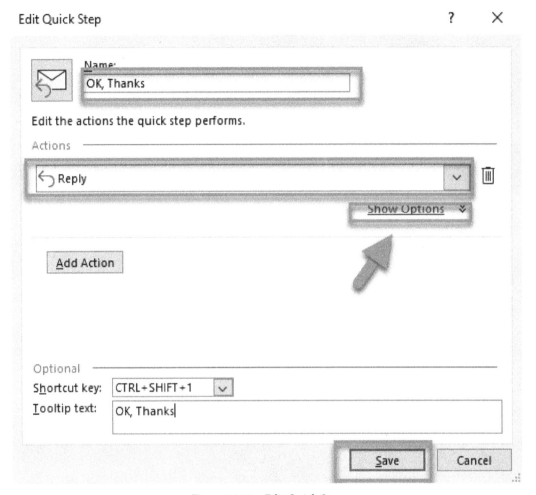

Figure 16.13 – Edit Quick Step

D. Within the new window that appears within this dialog box, enter the desired selections or text that you want to use when replying with the quick step. In the example, the words **OK, Thanks!** that are shown in the **Text** box will be applied to the email. Click **Save** to close **Edit Quick Step** and **OK** to close **Manage Quick** steps.

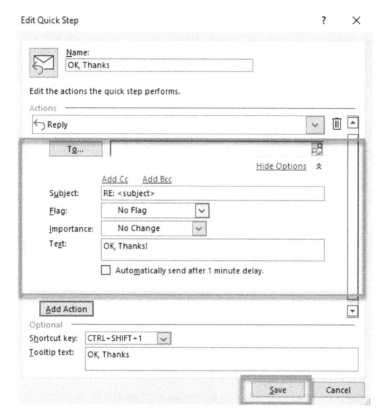

Figure 16.14 – Show Options for quick step

Now you can use this quick step to quickly reply to an email and this text will be applied.

SMART habit #3 – folders

Quickly process emails: I have three methods to help me process emails within my inbox and I also like to set up my computer so that when I open Outlook, the focus is not on my inbox but on an `Active` folder, which we will create.

- **Be selective about the folders that you set up**: Many people set up several folders to organize their emails and sometimes a duplicate of an email needs to be created to store it in multiple folders. This was necessary years ago but now that searching has been overhauled, you can be more selective about the number of folders you need. I like to set up these four folders:

  i. `.Action`: For emails you are actively working on, you may consider putting subfolders under this `.Active` folder to separate emails even further. I suggest you are selective, however.

ii.   `.Waiting for`: For emails where you are waiting on another person to finish something before it is complete.

iii.   `.Read`: Any items that you don't want to archive just yet and need to read first. This comes in handy when you are waiting on an event with nothing to do.

iv.   `.Archive`: Once processed, you will send an email to the folder to store for later use. You could also not create this folder and use the `.Archive` folder in the navigation pane.

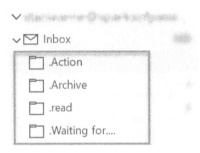

Figure 16.15 – New folders

> **Note**
>
> In the previous folders I have entered a **. (period)** before the name of the folder. The period will keep these folders at the top of the list directly underneath the inbox.

- **Process the four Ds**: This tip is to help you become more productive while processing your inbox. First, if you have thousands of emails in your inbox, you may want to create a separate folder just for those emails so you can start fresh on trying to keep your inbox clear of emails. When processing your emails, use the four Ds method:

  - **Delete it**: Send emails to the trash or delete them.

  - **Do it**: If it can be done in a couple of minutes, action/reply to and get rid of the email. Eliminate looking at an email twice.

  - **Delegate it**: Send it on to another person.

  - **Defer it**: If you're not done with an email, send it to one of your four folders created previously.

The final step is to take your attention away from your inbox. Some people find themselves working from their inbox, and this is not a way to be productive. Let's see how to have Outlook open in the `.Active` folder instead of the inbox now.

- **Open Outlook with the .Active folder open**: You can select any folder you want in this step. I find that I like working with the emails that I need to take action on and complete first, so I am choosing the `.Active` folder:

A. Click **File | Options | Advanced | Browse ...** by **Start Outlook in this folder** and select `.Active` or the folder you want to open when you first start Outlook.

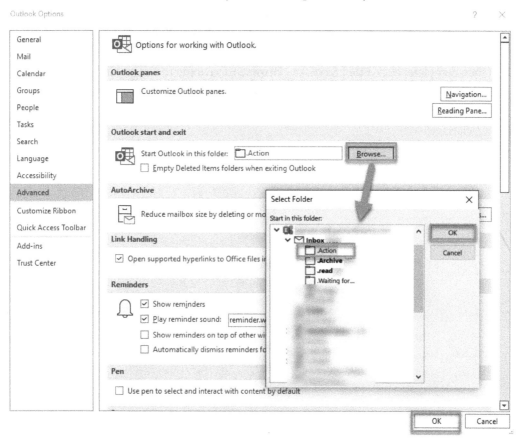

Figure 16.16 – Select folder to open Outlook in

B. Now close Outlook and open Outlook again. Upon opening, the focus will be on the `.Active` folder and not the inbox. It takes some time to get used to this step, but I have found it to be worth it to save time.

Now I check my emails or inbox three times a day: in the morning upon starting work, after lunch so that it does not stop me from taking lunch, and then before leaving the office for the day so I can do some cleanup and process as much as possible to get it out of the way for the next day.

SMART habit #4 – templates

An email **template** can be created for emails that you will be processing repeatedly. An example of this would be an email that you send to a new hire once they sign on with the company. You create this email with **To, Cc, Subject** text, attachments, and text in the body of the email. Include everything that you would normally include manually each time you need to send an email to a new hire:

1. **Create a template**: Create the email message as you would any message, including **To, Cc, Subject** text, and attachments.

2. Once complete, click **File | Save As | Browse** to save the message. Click the drop-down arrow by **Save as type** and select **Outlook Template (*.oft)**. Do not change the template location.

3. Click **Save**.

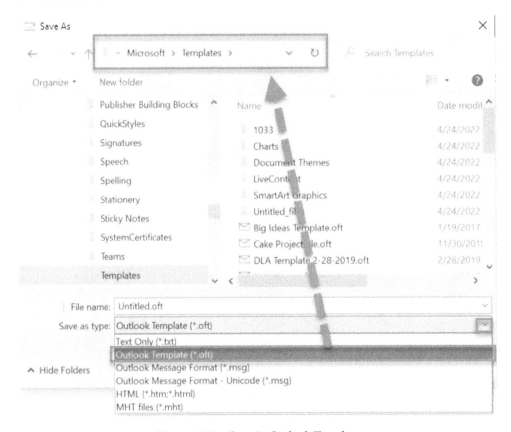

Figure 16.17 – Save As Outlook Template

Close the email that you created unless you want to address it to a recipient and send it. Now let us see how to open it.

4. To open the template when you are ready to use it to send to another recipient, click **Home | New Items | More Items | Choose Form…**:

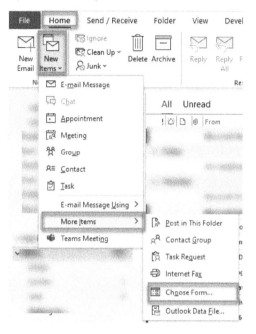

Figure 16.18 – Open template

5. To find the template, click the drop-down arrow by **Look In** and select **User Templates in File System**:

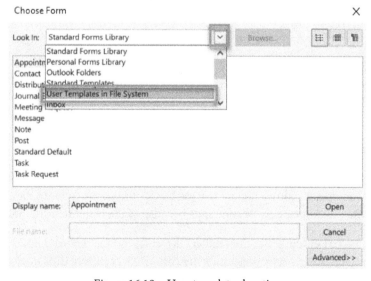

Figure 16.19 – User templates location

6. The templates that you have created will show in the window. Select the template that you wish to use and click **Open**.

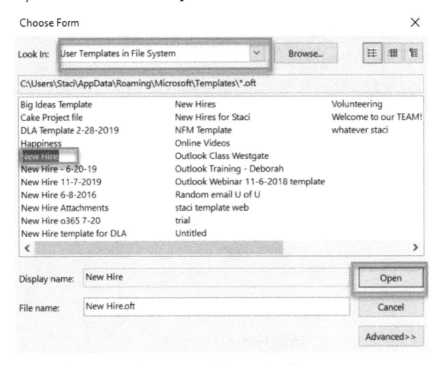

Figure 16.20 – Select template file

The email (with the template) will now be opened and you can customize it as needed before clicking **Send** to recipient(s).

> **Note**
>
> In *Chapter 15, Programming with Macros*, the file path that you see within the **Choose Form** dialog box is the path that you will copy to place within the macro VBA code example.

SMART habit #5 – journal entries

For service-based or client-based businesses where employees are on the phone a lot, this is a handy tip. You can create a journal entry to keep track of multiple types of data. I like to use this to keep track of phone calls or meetings because of the timer feature that is included:

1. **Create a journal entry**: This is useful to take quick notes, record data, or start a timer to track how long something is taking. Click the three dots at the bottom of the navigation pane, then click **Folders**:

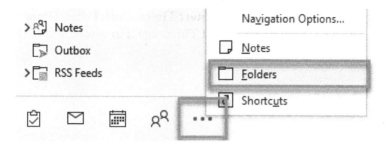

Figure 16.21 – Open Folders

2. Select the **Journal** folder that will now show in the navigation pane:

Figure 16.22 – Journal folder in navigation pane

3. Click **File | Journal Entry**:

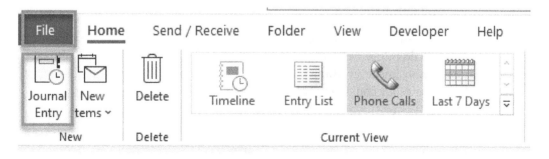

Figure 16.23 – New journal entry

4. To use the timer, click **Journal Entry | Start Timer**. Click **Pause Timer** to pause the timer, and if needed, you can click **Start Timer** again to continue after the pause:

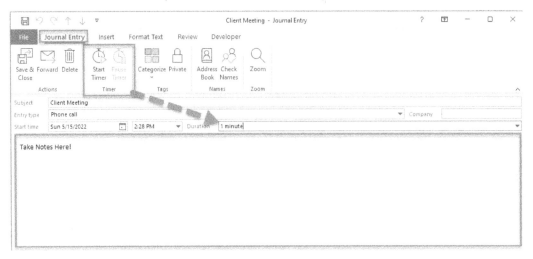

Figure 16.24 – Journal Entry timer

Once you are done timing the call, meeting, or event, you will see the duration shown in minutes. This is a terrific way to track the time of an event for billing purposes. When done, be sure to click **Save & Close** to save the journal entry.

Let us now talk about how you can implement these tools every day.

Power Hour

When you start to clean up and take control of your inbox, you must set aside time for a **Power Hour**. This is not the Power Hour that you might have had in college. Schedule this hour into your calendar. This is an hour that you set aside daily, weekly, or however often works for you, to open Outlook and do some cleaning up and organizing of your emails or use the Outlook productivity tool.

Consistency is the one thing that most people don't have in their lives. Is this a problem you have? We usually do things well for a while and then we fall into a rut. If you have ever seen a live assembly line, everything just flows until the product being created is completed. This Power Hour could help you keep the flow going in managing your day.

It should be on your schedule. I like to schedule this into my calendar every day. It is an hour, or however much time you need, to keep everything running and organized in Outlook. Check your calendars, empty your inbox, delegate items you can't complete, create tasks, and pass on communications with your team, clients, and so on. Do whatever you need to keep Outlook from getting overloaded.

Summary

I have a confession to make: I don't follow every one of these five SMART habits. I take the ones that work for me and keep the others for times when I may need them. The most important insight to gain from this chapter is that you structure Outlook to work in a SMART way for you and take notice of the bottlenecks that are slowing you down. Do what is comfortable and beneficial to the way you work.

I always say in my classes, *"You don't know what you don't know!"* What does this mean? To me, it means if you are going through life not learning, not trying to improve, and not moving forward, you will not know what you are missing.

If you have been using Outlook only to read and respond to the emails that you receive daily and nothing else, you are missing out on a great productivity tool. I hope you have learned and will implement many of the SMART techniques that have been demonstrated in this book, and that within a short period, you will be thriving and able to use the time you save from your 1,440 minutes a day doing something that will bring you joy.

Questions

1. What is Bookings in Outlook?

2. When I receive an email, I want to create a Teams meeting from that email. I would like to include the email in the Teams meeting. Is this possible without copying and pasting, which is what I do now?

3. Does it only take 21 days to create a habit?

4. Will using Outlook enhance my productivity?

5. Does Outlook have a Kanban board?

Answers

1. At the time of writing this book, the new **Bookings** feature was announced by Microsoft, to be released to selected subscriptions beginning in June 2022. Bookings is a web-based scheduling page that integrates information from your free/busy calendar. It will streamline the process of scheduling an appointment with others.

2. Great question. This is an example of what I call *You don't know what you don't know!* Open the email that you received and click **Message** | **Respond** | **Reply with Meeting**. *Ctrl + Alt + R* is the keyboard shortcut key for this button.

3. Research shows that it can take 18 to 254 days for a habit to form. The average number of days for a habit to form is 66 days. A simple way to create a habit is to use the 3 Rs technique: Reminders, Routines, Rewards.

4. Outlook cannot enhance your productivity – only you can make the changes necessary to enhance your productivity. Learning and creating habits with the tips and tricks that are offered in this book is one of several ways you can start to be a productivity ninja using Outlook.

5. In 2021, Outlook launched a Kanban-style board. The board can be viewed within the calendar on Outlook on the web app, or OWA. It is not available in the desktop version as of the time of writing this book.

Assessments

This section contains the answers to the questions from all the chapters.

Chapter 1 – Getting Started with Outlook

1. When you delete an email, it is moved to the **Deleted Items** folder. Once you delete the email, it will be available or recoverable for 14 days. Anything that has been deleted for 14 days can no longer be recovered. To empty the **Deleted Items** folder upon exiting Outlook, click on **Tools | Options | Other** and check the box that says **Empty the deleted items folder upon exiting**.

2. The default name on an account when it is set up is the email ID. To change this name, click **File | Info | Account Settings | Account Settings**. From the list of accounts, select the one that you want to change the name of and click on the **Change** button. In the **Account name** field, change the name to the one you prefer and click **Next**. You will be shown that your account was successfully updated, and you can then click **Done**.

3. If you are running Outlook 2007, you are running a 32-bit version, but since 2010, you could be running either version. You need to know what version Outlook is running when installing Outlook plugins and add-ons, as some of these are not compatible with the 64-bit version. To check what version your computer is running, select **File | Office Account | About Outlook**, and you will see a line of text indicating 64-bit (as shown in the following figure) or 32-bit:

About Microsoft® Outlook® for Microsoft 365

Microsoft® Outlook® for Microsoft 365 MSO (16.0.14326.20384) 64-bit

Figure 1.1 – 64-bit

There are so many Outlook apps and services that you can use to access Outlook. It's in your best interest to know which version of Outlook you have. To locate your version, select **File | Office Account**. The version will be listed under **Product Information**.

4. The **To Do** list is a collection of items that have been flagged for follow-up in Outlook. This is the list that will appear on the **To Do** bar (if it is displayed). This list also includes an Outlook task, which is a task that has been stored in the **Tasks** folder. Tasks are created and stored in the **Tasks** folder, and currently, the **To Do** list doesn't yet support Outlook **Task** fields, such as start and end dates, task status, task completion percentage, multiple priority levels, work hours, colors, or categories.

5. When you delete an email, it is moved to the deleted items folder. Once you delete the email it will be available or recoverable for 14 days. Anything that has been deleted for 14 days can no longer be recovered. To empty the deleted items folder upon exiting Outlook, click on Tools | Options | Other, check the box that says "Empty the deleted items folder upon exiting".

Chapter 2 – Sending and Receiving Emails

1. Create a new email message (you can also reply to or forward an email) and select **Insert** and the drop-down arrow next to **Link**. Choose a file from the most recently used items, or at the bottom of this list, choose **Insert Link...** and the file to attach, and click **OK**. To attach more than one file, hold *Ctrl* while selecting multiple files. The link for the file or picture, if selected, will appear in the message of your email.

2. This is most likely due to a temporary hiccup in the connectivity to the network/Virtual Private Network (VPN). Check to see whether you are still online by looking at the status bar, which will display **Connected to: Microsoft Exchange** or **Working offline**.

Figure 2.18 – Working offline

Outlook will automatically try to reconnect to the server, but if that does not work, you can click on the **Send/Receive** tab and then the **Work Offline** button. If this button is grayed out, you are offline, and no shading indicates that you are working online.

3. In a new email message window, select the **Message** tab and click on the **Signature** drop-down arrow. Any previously created signatures will appear in this selection. Select the signature that you want to swap the current signature for. You can also select the **signature...** option to create a new signature from this menu button.

4. **Outlook Web App (OWA)** allows you to access your email account from a web browser. Outlook on the web does not include all the features found in the Outlook desktop version. It is a slimmed-down version that allows you to access your email while away. You can access the web browser at outlook.office.com.

5. Microsoft has a 20 MB limit on attachments that you can send through email. It does not matter if this is a single file or several files attached to one email. The total size of all attachments cannot exceed 10 MB to 35 MB, depending on your plan. If you need to attach a file that is larger than what your plan allows, you should consider putting the file in a shared location and emailing a link to that location instead. See *Further reading* for the Exchange Online limits.

Chapter 3 – Managing Email Accounts

1. Outlook is a software application that can be installed on your computer, tablet, and mobile device. It is used to communicate and synchronize with Exchange. Exchange is the software that provides an integrated system for your email, calendar, messaging, and tasks. The two applications, Outlook and Exchange, must work together to run Outlook. With Exchange Server, you or your IT support company maintain the server and have full control of the infrastructure, whereas with Office 365, you do not have control of it, and it is maintained by Microsoft in the cloud.

2. The simple answer is no. Despite providing access to your email, they are not email marketers and do not allow you to use email contact lists and send campaigns to subscribers. An example of this type of provider would be Mailchimp or Constant Contact, and there are several others to choose from.

3. In one Outlook account, you can add up to 20 different email accounts. These accounts do not have to be Outlook accounts; they can be Gmail, Yahoo, and various others.

4. Outlook 365 does not exist. It was rebranded as Microsoft 365 on April 21, 2020, with the same productivity suite or services still being offered, including Outlook. The reason for the rebranding was the inclusion of additional software beyond the core Office software, such as cloud-based productivity tools and features with artificial intelligence.

5. Profiles in Outlook are created when you set up Outlook. Most people don't realize that you can have multiple profiles and so they only use one profile. It is convenient to set up separate profiles to help organize your emails – for example, you can have one profile for work and another for home. If you have several people using the same computer, you can set up a separate profile for each user. To set up profiles, go to **Control Panel | Mail | Show Profiles | Add…**.

Chapter 4 – Organizing Your Outlook Environment

1. **Quick Parts** (**New Email** | **Insert** | **Quick Parts**) are messages/text that can be inserted into a new email without retyping the text. **Quick Steps** are preformatted actions that are assigned to a **Quick Step** button to streamline a task, as was discussed in this chapter.

2. Turn the **Focused** Inbox on or off by going to **View** | **Show Focused Inbox**. Turning this on will show at the top of the inbox with tabs for **Focused** and **Other**. Bulk emails will be pushed to the **Other** folder so that you can use the **Focused** inbox for important emails. If an email gets through that you don't want in **Focused**, simply right-click on the message and choose **Move to Other**.

3. There are 25 color tiles available to apply a category to an email message. You can assign the same color to multiple emails.

4. For the email to switch to the next email, use *Ctrl* + the *.* key. To switch back to the previous email, use *Ctrl* + the *,* key.

5. Flagging an email message also adds a task to the **To-Do** list folder. If you delete the message, it also disappears from the **To-Do** list. Don't confuse the **To-Do** list with a task. A task is an Outlook item that is saved to the **Tasks** folder. However, the **To-Do** list contains all the flagged items and tasks, allowing users to see a list of all items that need to be done.

Chapter 5 – Outlook Mail Merge

1. Emails, letters, envelopes or labels, and directories.

2. Many people try to find the **Mail Merge** tool on the ribbon in the **Mail** object view, but it is not located there. You can find the **Mail Merge** tool in the **Contacts** object view under the **Actions** section.

3. Yes, you can send the emails through Outlook by selecting email as the output type for the merge.

4. You can set the date in **Mail Merge** to a future date using the **delayed delivery** feature. This, however, will only work if you are using Microsoft Exchange.

5. For Office 365 you can send a maximum of 10,000 emails per day. A single email can be addressed to a maximum of 500 recipients. In `Outlook.com` you can send up to 300 emails per day with a maximum of 100 recipients per message. These limits can be adjusted by your administrator, so it is best to check limits with that person. To see the Microsoft Exchange limits, go to `https://docs.microsoft.com/en-us/office365/servicedescriptions/exchange-online-service-description/exchange-online-limits`.

Chapter 6 – Managing the Calendars

1. The two calendars on the left side of the Navigation pane are a way to navigate and select days you want to view in the main **Calendar** window. You can use the arrows to navigate to other months. When you change the month of the calendar, the other calendar will change as well. You can also click on a date in these calendars to navigate to that date in your main **Calendar** window or even select two or more dates (by holding down the *Ctrl* key) to compare them side by side. This is a very useful tool that many users do not use because they don't know about its power.

2. Click **File | Options | Calendar | Calendar Options**, then *uncheck* the **Default reminders** box; you can change the reminder time here as well.

3. Yes, click **View | To-Do Bar | Check To-Do**. This will add the calendar to the To-Do Bar, which will appear on the right side of the calendar.

4. Yes, select the email that you want to convert to a meeting request and then click **Home | Reply with Meeting** (*Ctrl + Alt + R*). This creates a **New meeting** request, with the message sender on the **To** line and the email message included in the body of the meeting request.

5. As of now, the **Board** view is only available in the **Calendar** view for Outlook on the web. It is not yet on the desktop version. If you like Kanban boards, then you may want to sign in to Office 365 on the web and give this a try.

Chapter 7 – Contacts in Outlook

1. The social connector (which people also refer to as the **People** pane) is available in versions 2016 and earlier. Microsoft has retired that product now in Outlook 365 as of late July 2020

2. You can show people in the **Favorites** section of the **To-Do** pane; right-click on the sender's email address and select **Add to Favorites**. You will see the person's picture and email available for use in Outlook. The search box in **Favorites** will allow you to find people in your emails. Once you click on them in **Favorites**, you can email them from the open dialog box.

3.   Yes, this can be done with Mail Merge with limitations: refer to *Chapter 5, Outlook Mail Merge*.

4.   The easiest and fastest way to organize your contacts is in **Categories**, which allows you to apply color to the contact. Use red for family, blue for coworkers, or something that makes sense to you. Then, you can sort by color and focus on the group you want. Refer to *Chapter 4* for a detailed explanation of Categories.

5.   It can be assumed that you are using either a POP or IMAP account for email, as was discussed in *Chapter 3, Managing Email Accounts*. POP accounts will not sync anything, but IMAP will sync email and folders only. **Contacts** and **Calendar** items can only be synced with an Exchange account, which is included with an Microsoft 365 subscription as well as Gmail's Google Sync.

Chapter 8 – Outlook Notes

1.   *Ctrl + 5* is the shortcut key combination to open the **Notes** workspace.

2.   Sticky notes appear on Windows computers as well as inside OneNote and the OneNote app. When you add a note inside OneNote – a sticky note on your phone, for example – that note will automatically sync with the note in Outlook. If you turn on the sync feature and select your Microsoft 365 account on the Windows sticky notes, the notes created will also sync with OneDrive.

3.   In Outlook 2010 and 2007, you can change the fonts in the notes by clicking **File | Options | Notes and Journal**. This option was taken away in Outlook 2016 versions and later. The default font in these later versions is 11-point Calibri.

4.   You can retrieve a deleted note as long as it still resides in your **Deleted** folder in the Navigation pane. Click on the **Mail** button on the **Navigation** pane, then open the contents of the **Deleted Items** folder. You will find your deleted notes in this folder as well. To retrieve the note, move it to another folder.

5.   To open the Notes folder in a new window, click on the **Notes** button in the Navigation pane to display the notes in the workspace. Right-click on the Notes folder, which displays your email ID located on the **Navigation** pane for the notes, and click on **Open in New Window**.

Chapter 9 – Tasks and To-Dos

1. The shortcut keys for creating a task in Outlook are *Ctrl + Shift + K*. You can use this shortcut combination within any window inside Outlook.

2. To add a reminder to a task that is already created, you can either double-click on the task and add a time to the **Reminder** field, or in the **Tasks** view, you can right-click on the flag for the task and click **Add Reminder...**, and then set the time for the reminder in the **Custom** dialog box in the **Reminder** section.

3. To rename a task, right-click on the task name and click **Rename Task**. You can then change the name of the task as desired, as the **Name** field will be in edit mode. Click *Enter* when done.

4. You can make the To-Do bar display a combination of calendar items, people, and tasks. The items that show at the top will be the first items you select and will appear in the order selected. To have your tasks appear at the top, simply unselect all the current options and reselect the items again in the order that you want them to appear.

5. Yes, you can change the settings for how the icons appear in the Navigation pane. Click on the **...** button, then click **Navigation Options....** Select the desired object in the **Display in this order** box in the **Navigation Options** dialog box and then click the **Move Up** button as needed to move the selected object to the top of the list. Click **OK** and the selected icon will show as specified.

Chapter 10 – Save Time Searching

1. When you delete an email from the inbox it gets placed in the **Deleted Items** folder by default. This will reside in the **Sent items** for 30 days unless it is permanently deleted. To delete permanently, select the message, and click *Shift | Delete* on the keyboard.

2. **All Mailboxes** would include a search in all your emails within your mailboxes. **All Outlook items** will search your mailboxes, calendar, and task items.

3. You can change this in the options for the search. Click **File | Options | Search**. Under the **Results** section for the **include results only from**, select **All mailboxes | OK**.

4. Yes, the Outlook limit for search results is to display 200 items with Outlook default settings.

5. Yes, you can delete the entire contents of the **Deleted Items** folder at once or you can select each email and delete it individually. Emails will stay in **Deleted Items** for 30 days, but you can change this setting by going to **File | Options** for emails going forward. To delete all emails currently in the **Deleted Items** folder, right-click on the **Deleted Items** folder, and select **Empty Folder**.

Chapter 11 – Sharing Mail, Calendars, and Contacts

1. Unfortunately, giving too much authority to several people is not a great idea. Remember that with delegates, the last change wins. If an executive accepts a meeting invite and then the delegate declines the invite, the last change would win and, in this case, the delegate would overwrite the executive authority. You need to have one person who will be responsible for making any changes to appointments.

2. If the **Share your Calendar** button is grayed out and you can not click on it to activate the command, it's most likely because your administrator of the account or IT department has prevented you from sharing calendars.

3. If you don't want to assign a delegate for others to view your calendar, you can email the calendar:

   I. Click **Calendar | E-mail Calendar**, enter the calendar **Name** and **Date Range** that you want to email, then click **OK**.

   II. The new email will open the address of the recipient or the **To** field, then add any message, and click **Send**.

   III. The recipient of the email will see a snapshot image of your calendar.

4. Sign in to Office 365 on the web (`www.office.com`). Click **Admin | Settings | Org settings | Service Tab | Calendar**. From this page, select the settings you want to allow for the user to share the calendar.

5. Open Outlook and click **File | Office Account | Update Options | Update Now**.

Chapter 12 – Archiving and Backup

1. **AutoArchive** is on the **Advanced** tab underneath the Outlook Start and Exit title. If you do not see this, it is probably due to your IT department in your corporation not giving you the rights on the server to access this feature. Another reason for this is that you have an Exchange account, and the online archiving has been enabled for you with automatic settings.

2. If your Inbox is storing a lot of emails, usually because you never delete any messages, you will want to check the size of your folders. Click **File | Folder | properties | Storage**. If you have more than 2 GB of emails used, you need to archive some of your emails.

3. This message appears when your PST file reached its maximum storage limit. To fix this, you can manage the mailbox size by clicking **File | Info | Tools | Mailbox Cleanup…**.

4. Occasionally, your files may become corrupt in Outlook. To repair, click **File | Account Settings…**, select the account to repair, then click **Repair…**. If you don't have access to Outlook, you can run **Repair** in the **Programs and Features** object in the Windows Control Panel.

5. A `.pst` file is a file that is stored on your computer. This is typically the case for files created before Office 2016. If your file is a `.ost` file, you have a file that is maintained on an Exchange Server, and you will need to contact the administrator of your Microsoft 365 account to maintain this file.

Chapter 13 – Collaboration & Integration within Outlook

1. Translator for Outlook is an app that you can purchase in the Microsoft Store, and is used to translate documents. The translation will appear on the right of the Reading pane when selected and will display the translated text in the language you have requested. The link for downloading the translator can be found in the *Further reading* section.

2. One possible answer is that the Teams add-in was disabled. To check this, click **File | Options | Add-ins**. Confirm that the Microsoft Teams Meeting add-in for Microsoft Office is in the list. Select **Com Add-ins | Go |**Select **Microsoft Teams Meeting Add-in for Microsoft Office**.

3. **Insights** and **My Analytics** are add-ins that you may have seen on the ribbon in previous versions of Outlook. These two applications have now been rolled into or rebranded as **Viva Insights**. Once you select **Viva Insights**, you will be able to control your time, meetings, and events through this add-in and you will also start receiving emails on a regular basis from Viva Insights with analytic data, suggestions, and history of how Microsoft 365 tools can help you be more productive.

4. You can access the Office store to get more information about Add-ins and purchase and download Add-ins. You can get information about the Add-ins such as ratings, price, and reviews. To access the Office store, go to `appsource.microsoft.com`.

5. Upon creating a group inside of your Microsoft 365 account, you can begin collaborating with others with a set of tools that include a shared Outlook inbox to share between group members and a SharePoint document library for sharing files. Groups will also have a shared calendar, OneNote notebook, and Planner. This is the best tool for those that prefer to collaborate through email.

Chapter 14 – Nine Useful Rules

1. Server-based rules run on an Exchange Server and apply to messages as they are delivered to your inbox. The rules cannot run until they have been completed on the Server. If the rule can't run on the server, it is applied once Outlook starts. Client-only rules are only run on your computer through Outlook and do not get processed through the server. Client-only rules can only run when Outlook is open, whereas server-based rules run on the server only.

2. If your rule contains server-based and client-based rules, the server-based rule must process before the client-only rule.

3. No, the rules do not support the use of wildcard characters.

4. When you see the rules listed in the **Manage Rules & Alerts** dialog box, they will run in the order listed from top to bottom. You can select a rule and move it up or down within the list to create your desired order to process.

5. Everybody has an email joker in their inbox. Use a rule that finds terms that go along with jokes, such as *funny*, *chain letter*, *pass this along*, or simply *Fwd*. The rule could automatically forward these to a Jokes folder, archive them, or delete these emails.

Chapter 15 – Programming with Macros

1. VBA is currently supported in the desktop version for Microsoft 365 and will be for some time in the future. However, keeping it working on all versions of Outlook will probably not happen. As of the writing of this book, there are no plans to retire VBA. Microsoft will continue to encourage users to learn JavaScript APIs as the VBA replacement.

2. Macros can pose a threat to your Outlook environment and Microsoft has now set the default to disable macros coming from the internet. To change this setting, click **File | Options | Trust Center | Trust Center Settings… | Macro Settings** and select the desired setting.

3. Back up or create a Word document with your Outlook macros. Open the VBA Editor in Outlook and copy the code for the macros. Paste the copied code into a Word document and save it to your computer.

4. The shortcut key for opening the VBA editor within Outlook is *Alt + F11*.

5. The current available MOS Outlook exam is Exam MO-400. Macros are not included in the objective domains for this exam. See the *Further reading* section for the MO-400 exam objectives.

Chapter 16 – Managing Your Day System

1. At the time of the writing of this book, the new **Bookings** feature was announced by Microsoft to be released to selected subscriptions beginning in June 2022. **Bookings** is a web-based scheduling page that integrates information from your free/busy calendar. It will streamline the process of scheduling an appointment with others.

2. Great questions. This is an example of what I call *You don't know what you don't know*! Open the email that you received and click **Message | Respond | Reply with Meeting**. *Ctrl + Alt + R* is the keyboard shortcut for this button.

3. Research shows that it can take 18 to 254 days for a habit to form. The average time for a habit to form is 66 days. A simple way to create a habit is to use the three Rs technique: reminders, routines, and rewards.

4. Outlook can not enhance your productivity. Only you can make the changes necessary to enhance your productivity. Learning and creating habits for the tips and tricks that are offered in this book is one of several ways you can start to be a productivity ninja using Outlook.

5. In 2021, Outlook launched a Kanban-style board. The board can be viewed within the calendar in the **Outlook web app** (**OWA**). It is not available in the Desktop version as of the writing of this book.

Index

`Packt.com`

Subscribe to our online digital library for full access to over 7,000 books and videos, as well as industry leading tools to help you plan your personal development and advance your career. For more information, please visit our website.

Why subscribe?

- Spend less time learning and more time coding with practical eBooks and Videos from over 4,000 industry professionals

- Improve your learning with Skill Plans built especially for you

- Get a free eBook or video every month

- Fully searchable for easy access to vital information

- Copy and paste, print, and bookmark content

Did you know that Packt offers eBook versions of every book published, with PDF and ePub files available? You can upgrade to the eBook version at `packt.com` and as a print book customer, you are entitled to a discount on the eBook copy. Get in touch with us at `customercare@packtpub.com` for more details.

At `www.packt.com`, you can also read a collection of free technical articles, sign up for a range of free newsletters, and receive exclusive discounts and offers on Packt books and eBooks.

Other Books You May Enjoy

If you enjoyed this book, you may be interested in these other books by Packt:

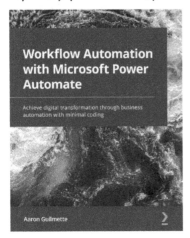

Workflow Automation with Microsoft Power Automate

Aaron Guilmette

ISBN: 9781839213793

- Get to grips with the building blocks of Power Automate, its services, and core capabilities
- Explore connectors in Power Automate to automate email workflows
- Discover how to create a flow for copying files between two cloud services
- Understand the business process, connectors, and actions for creating approval flows
- Use flows to save responses submitted to a database through Microsoft Forms
- Find out how to integrate Power Automate with Microsoft Teams

Work Smarter with Microsoft OneNote

Connie Clark

ISBN: 9781801075664

- Understand how to create and organize notes in your notebooks
- Discover how to turn handwritten notes into typed text
- Explore how to access your content from anywhere even if offline
- Uncover ways to collaborate with your team or family and stay in sync
- Understand how to insert your emails, documents, or articles from the web
- Find out how to integrate with other Microsoft products such as Outlook or Teams

Packt is searching for authors like you

If you're interested in becoming an author for Packt, please visit authors. packtpub.com and apply today. We have worked with thousands of developers and tech professionals, just like you, to help them share their insight with the global tech community. You can make a general application, apply for a specific hot topic that we are recruiting an author for, or submit your own idea.

Share Your Thoughts

Now you've finished *Working Smarter with Microsoft Outlook*, we'd love to hear your thoughts! Scan the QR code below to go straight to the Amazon review page for this book and share your feedback or leave a review on the site that you purchased it from.

https://packt.link/r/1-800-56070-2

Your review is important to us and the tech community and will help us make sure we're delivering excellent quality content.

www.ingramcontent.com/pod-product-compliance
Lightning Source LLC
Chambersburg PA
CBHW081501050326
40690CB00015B/2885

* 9 7 8 1 8 0 0 5 6 0 7 0 3 *